The Responsibility of Mind in a Civilization of Machines

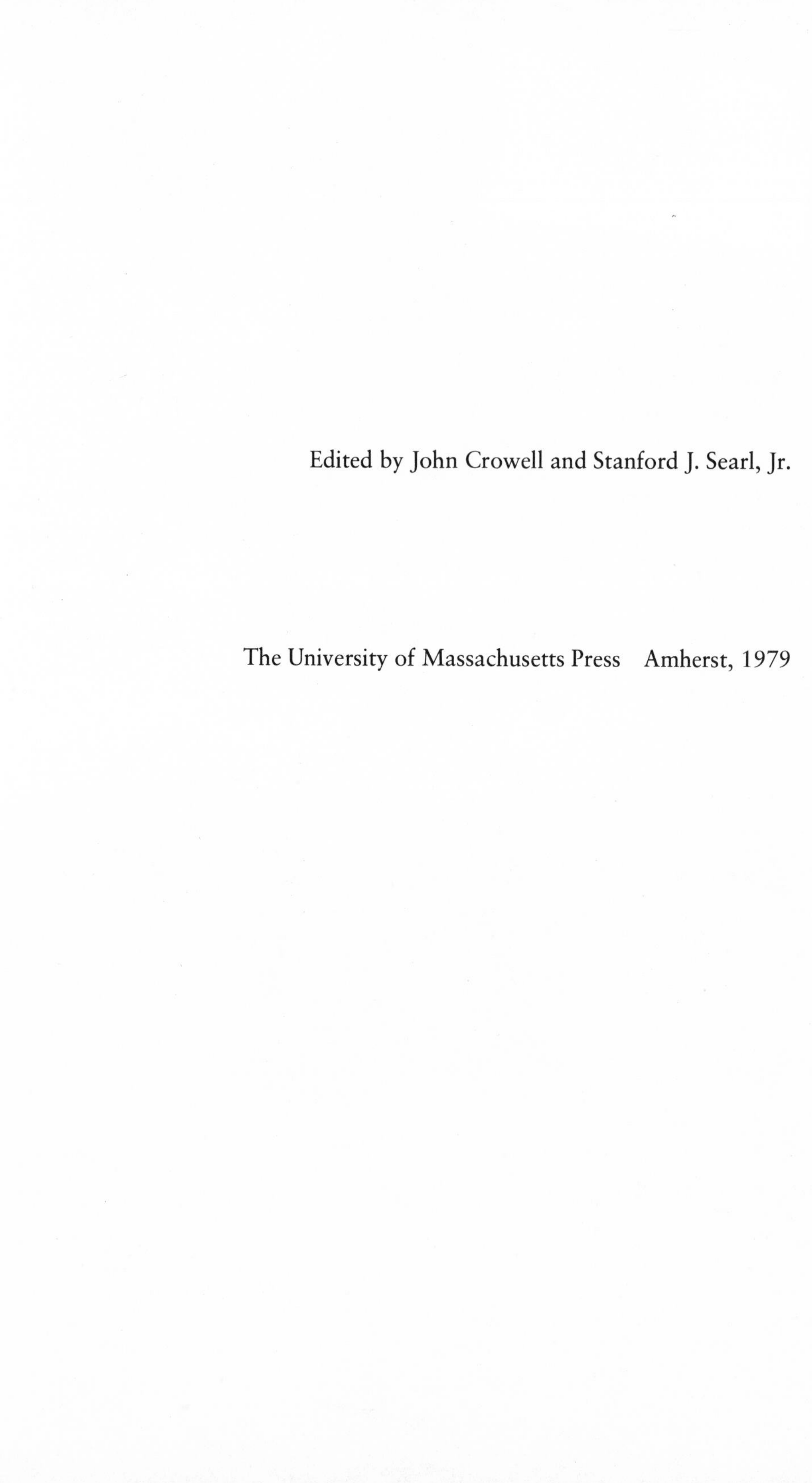

Edited by John Crowell and Stanford J. Searl, Jr.

The University of Massachusetts Press Amherst, 1979

The Responsibility of Mind

in a Civilization of Machines

Essays by Perry Miller, 1905-1963

Library of Congress Catalog Card Number 79-4699
ISBN 0-87023-281-9
Printed in the United States of America
Permission to reprint copyrighted material appears
at the end of this book.
Library of Congress Cataloging in Publication Data
appear on the last printed page.

Contents

Introduction

WHEN PERRY MILLER left the University of Chicago in 1923 after his freshman year, at the age of eighteen, it was for the inspiriting life of the road. Over the next three years his quest for adventure took him to Colorado, where he lived briefly in an isolated mountain cabin, to Greenwich Village, where he performed as an actor, and on to the Belgian Congo, as a seaman on an oil tanker.[1] World War I had offered his older contemporaries the "boon" of adventure, as he put it.[2] But the war had also caused the "disintegration of the social fabric" of Western culture, the destruction of "a whole way of life that had been the heritage of classical Christianity." Those of his generation felt betrayed, adrift, belonging nowhere. "How could they have a place in space, whose roots, whether deliberately or through the uncontrolled accident of war, had been destroyed in time?" So "from Land's End to the Golden Horn they scattered."[3]

If indeed a sense of uncertainty provided the informing impulse of Miller's sojourn, it soon dissipated. From the banks of the Congo in the mid-1920s Miller looked back at what was still the "inexhaustible wilderness of America." It was at this time, he later recounted, that he conceived his life's mission—that of "expounding my America to the twentieth century." It was via an "epiphany" (his term) that he had thrust upon him "the mission of expounding what I took to be the innermost propulsion of the United States."[4]

Miller's account of his calling has become accepted lore in the historical profession. What is of significance is not how it came about —whether it was indeed *vouchsafed* or not. As Walter J. Ong, S.J., remembers: "Perry was given to epiphanies, or at least interested in them. He had enough of the Protestant search for conversion in him to look for things that would suddenly change his life. It was the kind of thing he liked to remember."[5] What is important is the transformation of Miller's quest, for it is apparent that in significant ways the sense of drama, the energy and even mystery inherent in his outward pursuit of adventure, were to turn decisively inward—to an intellectual adventure. Throughout his career Miller was to remain a man of action, appropriating the roles of actor and adventurer to the world of ideas.

Perry Miller returned to the University of Chicago in 1926 and graduated two years later. He remained at Chicago as a graduate student, and in 1930 went to Harvard to complete research on his dissertation. His doctorate was from Chicago, but he stayed on at Harvard, where he taught until his death in December 1963.

Miller's scholarly reputation rests upon his studies in Puritanism, particularly on his two volumes of *The New England Mind*.[6] But as Alan Heimert points out, he did not think of himself as solely "a historian of a portion of America"; as with Brooks Adams, his New England studies were "metaphysical and philosophical inquir[ies] as to the action of the human mind in the progress of civilization."[7] In terms of range and variety this volume, as do the two previous collections of Miller's essays, *Errand into the Wilderness* (1956) and *Nature's Nation* (1967), demonstrates that his domain comprised a good portion of American culture. Herein, as scholar and historian of America, Miller attempts to embrace the truth of the past *and* to make thoughtful connections to the present: he explores the contemporary importance of the Puritan tradition; he probes the historical and cultural tensions between individual freedom and social responsibility; and he rejects the power of the state and the pressures of social and political conformity. Above all, he warns against the looming surrender of "mind" to its own mechanical creation. In a word, herein is reflected Perry Miller's practice as American *scholar*, defined in Emersonian terms as "man thinking," from 1940 to the early 1960s.

The title essay, "The Responsibility of Mind in a Civilization of

Machines," is a self-portrait of the scholar at work. Originally delivered as a lecture, it attacks, with all the immediacy and vigor of that mode, democracy's "mental fog of perpetual neutralism" and irresponsibility. At least since 1949, with the publication of *Jonathan Edwards*, Miller had been struggling with the question of the fragmentation of culture and the dilemma of mind in Western culture. In "The Responsibility of Mind" he declares that the split between the sciences and the humanities implies a deeper reality: "The mind, as our Western culture has conceived it since the antiquity of Thales, is cut adrift." With the "looming nihilism" engendered by the possibility of nuclear destruction, these concerns have taken on a particular urgency. Yet despite the apparent triumph of technology, Miller closes with a statement of faith in the paradoxical powers of the human mind: "Like the precious, beautiful, insupportable and wholly irrational blessing of individuality, with all the myriad quandaries of responsibilities therein involved, the responsibility for the human mind to preserve its own integrity amid the terrifying operations of the machine is both an exasperation and an ecstasy."

The self-portrait of the scholar that emerges from these essays reflects that "beautiful, insupportable and wholly irrational blessing of individuality." Indeed, Miller considered himself a scholarly lone wolf, an inwardly competitive, combative dissenter. In "The Plight of the Lone Wolf" he identifies himself as an anachronism: he is an adherent of the nineteenth-century conception of the scholar as solitary thinker, "a kingdom unto himself, sole ruler and only citizen." But the academic community which once supported the scholar in such dignified isolation is now distracted by the "allurements of foundation programs and the temptations of group ventures." In such a world, Miller asks, does the solitary scholar "dare appear as a single being, full of crotchets, utterly unassociated and forever unassociable with some comprehensive scheme?"

Throughout the collection Miller's answer is yes: the essays are a sustained expression of scholarly individualism, variously brash, paradoxical, cantankerous, witty, hyperbolic, ironic, dramatic. For example, in "Liberty and Conformity," a commencement address, Miller develops the theme of scholarly nonconformity, assuming the posture of the polemicist who punctures the banalities of conformity. Much of the address hovers on the edge of hyperbole, as he outlines the essential dilemma of the scholar's position. With ironic delight, he describes the scholarly career as a "perverse dedication to failure." He argues that if the assembled graduate students remain dedicated to a life of investigation and discovery, they will have taken the vow "not only of poverty but of failure." Throughout, he echoes Emerson and Thoreau: "We refuse to conform. We are not to be bought. We wear no price tag." The portrait is of the scholar as polemicist—tough-minded, combative, wittily self-assertive, delighting in the play of language and in the quality of the performance.

Such versatility reaches a climax in the concluding paragraphs of the essay. Remarking on the paradox of the "exciting insecurity and inspiriting inconclusiveness" of the modern intellect, he asserts that the scholar must "face the labor of learning for its own sake—bare, stark, tedious though it may be. How otherwise dare he look out from these ivy-cloaked walls upon the panorama of manufacturing and huckstering, and still keep in his eye the glint of disapproval?" This portrait of the scholar at work dramatizes nonconformity as an act of intellectual courage; defiant, Miller asserts that "he who hunts outside the pack, hunts alone."

Miller's concern about nonconformity is neither a quirk of personality nor a rhetorical posture. Rather, it is an expression of his belief in the primacy of the human intellect. Central to an understanding of his work are his statements that "the human mind is the most unsettling force, and the most uncontrollable, that afflicts humanity" (in "Liberty and Conformity") and "I have been compelled to insist that the mind of man is the basic factor in human history" (preface to *Errand into the Wilderness*). This vision about the primacy of mind in history is apparent also in both volumes of *The New England Mind* as well as in *Jonathan Edwards* and *Consciousness in Concord*. Furthermore, as David Hollinger suggests, Miller never fully resolved the tension within consciousness itself between "Understanding" and "Mystery"; in part, Miller valued such figures as Edwards and Thoreau because they faced a version of this paradoxical tension.[8]

Miller's approach is always original and eclectic, based on independent investigation, and "intensely purposive and creative."[9] With a sense of imaginative adventure about the consequences of ideas, he searches for underlying tensions and conflicts beneath the surface of apparent meanings. As Donald Fleming describes this search, "The unmistakable impulse at work in all of Perry Miller's writing is his determination to get beneath the surface of his materials and reveal an esoteric pattern. Things are never as they seem, and the habituated reader learns to wait for the moment of truth when the master impatiently thrusts aside all concealments and triumphantly turns the key in the lock." In a similar vein, Alan Heimert suggests that Miller's approach reflects an "historical imagination" and "a quest for a sublime that both stretches the mind to the utmost and arouses the power and passion of the soul."[10]

Throughout this collection Miller probes for latent ironies and contradictions, demonstrating a sensitive and critical imagination which challenges traditional assumptions and conventional wisdom. Because so many of the essays were delivered as lectures or addresses to particular audiences, he also can challenge his listeners directly, with dramatic immediacy. He can engage the audience in difficult, ironic confrontations and recognitions. "Individualism and the New England Tradition" is one example of this approach. A prolonged, elaborate recognition scene, it ends when the orator "triumphantly turns the key in the lock." The address is Miller's version of the election-day sermon, and he makes the most of it, urging the gathered ministers to recognize the ironic discrepancies between the Puritan's sense of higher purpose and moral responsibility and the "exalted pretensions" of contemporary individualism. His thesis unfolds dramatically, as he cites Henry Adams and Henry James on the feeling of dislocation—what James termed a "strange stranded feeling"—that originates from the recognition of the discrepancy between past purpose and present uncertainty. At the end it is apparent that Miller has thoroughly enjoyed the investigation—his careful historical analysis is preparation for the final debunking, a dismissal of foolish "exalted pretensions" about individualism.

In yet another essay on the need to recognize a deeper truth within our heritage—"Nineteenth-Century New England and Its Descendants"—Miller emphasizes the significance of Thoreau. He sketches the historical background of the "ascendancy" of New England over the American mind, dramatizing his perception by setting the conservative Barrett Wendell against the liberal Vernon

L. Parrington. This involves more than a mere intellectual perspective on the "multifold rejection in American culture of the hegemony of New England." Himself a product of the cultural revolt of the 1920s, Miller notes: "anyone alive in 1926 who was responding to the fresh interest in things American which blew like a gale across the country will remember the excitement of Parrington." With this historical perspective, Miller uses the metaphor of a "quadrilateral" to elucidate the meaning of New England's heritage, arguing that there is a distinct unity among what he terms the three congruent sides of his quadrilateral—the Household Poets, moral idealism, and economic development. In a recognition scene characteristic of his approach to history and ideas, Miller reveals an "esoteric pattern" that satisfies his quest for a deeper coherence:

> Finally abandoning historical causality altogether, you permit yourself the purely intuitive divination that here, at the beginning of the dramatic century was a culture with a highly developed personality, amazingly homogeneous despite its many divisions and its inner animosities. We may then hazard a guess that we get some sense of what was really the configuration of this culture when we see that it was, at one and the same time, expressed in the genteel elegance of the Brahmins, in the fiery energies of the reformers, and in Nathan Appleton's ecstatic encounter with beauty in a power loom.

This exploration of underlying coherence within a complex pattern of contradiction typifies Miller's genius. He has formulated a persuasive metaphor—a holistic vision of the New England legacy—that allows us to think and feel differently about the principal heritage of New England. For, Miller asserts that Transcendentalism—particularly as embodied in Thoreau—represents the contradictory fourth side of the heritage. Thus, Transcendentalism can be understood as "a protest against the internal linkage of our other three actors. The fourth side of our parallelogram does not join at the corners, it breaks away. And yet it is as authentically of New England as the others." Thoreau connects past and present; his challenge is the twentieth century's principal legacy from nineteenth-century New England.

The vitality of mind at work throughout this collection commands our attention. With demanding intellect and passionate conviction Miller takes genuine delight in his exploration of America's ironic heritage. The volume as a whole reflects his enduring presence as an American scholar. Perry Miller's scholarship demonstrates that it may be possible to combine the imagination of the artist, the discipline of the scholar, and the dedication of the thinker into a coherent vision about America. His achievement, as Edmund Morgan summed it up, was "a series of books the like of which had not been seen before and will not be seen again."[11]

Notes

1. Kenneth Lynn et al., "Perry Miller," *Harvard University Gazette* 60, no. 17 (16 Jan. 1965): n.p.
2. Perry Miller, *Errand into the Wilderness* (1956; rpt. ed., New York: Harper & Row, 1964), p. vii.
3. John Peale Bishop, "Homage to Hemingway," in *After the Genteel Tradition: American Writers Since 1910*, ed. Malcolm Cowley (1937), rpt. in *The Collected Essays of John Peale Bishop*, ed. Edmund Wilson (New York: Scribners, 1948), p. 37; Irving Howe, "American Moderns," in *Paths of American Thought*, ed. Arthur M. Schlesinger, Jr., and Morton White (Boston: Houghton Mifflin Co., 1963), p. 313; Bishop, "The Missing All," *Virginia Quarterly Review* (1937), rpt. in Wilson, *Collected Essays*, p. 72.
4. Miller, *Errand*, pp. vii, viii.
5. Ong in an interview with John Crowell, 12 June 1974, Center for Advanced Study in the Behavioral Sciences, Stanford, California.
6. *The New England Mind: The Seventeenth Century* (1939; rpt. ed., Cambridge: Harvard University Press, 1954); *The New England Mind: From Colony to Province* (Cambridge: Harvard University Press, 1953).
7. Alan Heimert, "Perry Miller: An Appreciation," *Harvard Review* 2 (1964): 30.
8. David A. Hollinger, "Perry Miller and Philosophical History," *History and Theory* 7 (1968): 193–96.
9. See ibid, pp. 190, 196. Hollinger demonstrates how the tension between "the Conscious" and "the Mechanical" was the central philosophical assumption in Miller's work. For a similar analysis, see Robert Middlekauff, "Perry Miller," in *Pastmasters: Some Essays on American Historians*, ed. Marcus Cunliffe and Robin W. Winks (New York: Harper & Row, 1969), esp. pp. 173–75.
10. Donald Fleming, "Perry Miller and Esoteric History," *Harvard Review* 2 (1964): 25; Alan Heimert, "Perry Miller: An Appreciation," in ibid., pp. 41, 47.
11. Edmund S. Morgan, "Perry Miller and the Historians," *Harvard Review* 2 (1964): 59. For a checklist of Miller's published writings see Keneth Kinnamon, "A Bibliography of Perry Miller," *Bulletin of Bibliography and Magazine Notes*, 26 (Apr.–June 1969), 45–51.

The Plight of the Lone Wolf

HENRY ADAMS, as readers of his *Education* are rather weary of being reminded, insisted that although physically he was born in the Boston of 1838, intellectually he came out of the eighteenth century. I was born in 1905 on the West Side of Chicago. As I look back upon my boyhood or compare the effects upon me of that experience with those left upon friends and colleagues of a youth spent amid more suburban or (even then) exurbanite circumstances, I realize that I was peculiarly fortunate in thus having had borne in upon me the full impact of the twentieth century, in which I was to live. But alas, I never quite got the good of my advantage: I went as a moderately young freshman to the University of Chicago, and so came of age in the nineteenth century after all.

This was pre-Hutchins. It was a great university then, and embodied a serene assumption—at least, to my adolescent sense of things it did—that it would automatically continue to be great in precisely the same terms as those in which it then so beautifully flourished. The essence of this beauty was the nineteenth-century conception of the dignified isolation of each member of the faculty. The atmosphere so deliberately contrived at the university may have been only a pale American imitation of Berlin and Göttingen,

Written for the 25th anniversary of *American Scholar*, which had as its theme "New Departures and Directions, 1932–1956."

but in the city of Chicago it was so impressive as almost to stifle one's breathing. A professor was a kingdom unto himself, sole ruler and the only citizen. These august figures bowed to each other when passing on the campus—I imagined that they even ate lunch together at the Quadrangle Club in the same aloofness—with the self-possession of two battleships belonging to separate sovereigns with nothing in common, neither hostility nor friendship, saluting in mid-ocean. They all seemed so magnificently a law unto themselves that I could conceive of no greater measure of earthly felicity than to grow up, learn enough, and become as like them as possible.

I have had my share of misfortune in the twenty-five years since *The American Scholar* was founded, but I have been supremely lucky in one respect: I have been able to examine the idols of my youth with a cold, objective eye, and to find that upon the most critical study they stand up. True, their work often appears less world-shaking today than their students supposed: only specialists in the Elizabethan period with fairly antiquarian interests spend much time, for instance, upon Charles Read Baskervill's *The Elizabethan Jig*. Many failed to realize their promise in publication; those who knew John Matthews Manly and Philip Schuyler Allen must lament that so little survives from their teeming brains. But even so, I am not indulging, not in the slightest, a middle-aged nostalgia for a vanished past when I assert that they were giants—these three—along with others such as Lovett, Paul Shorey, Breasted, Goodspeed, William Dodd, George Herbert Mead. They were gigantic not so much because they were surpassing geniuses, but because the academic ethos cast them in the part.

The same ethos, I hasten to admit, prevailed over other academic communities. I came to Harvard in 1930, and the legend of the magnificent individual, at least in the humanities, was still alive. There was a vivid memory of William James, and in the Yard could be seen Kittredge, Lowes, Whitehead, Grandgent, Irving Babbitt, while in a curtained room on Francis Avenue there lingered the shattered body of Charles Haskins. I need not call the list of other polymaths of that era: Dewey at Columbia, Jastrow at Pennsylvania, Parrington at Washington (though for so long he labored in obscurity). Suffice to say, all of them worked as individuals, alone in their studies, at the head of their own excavations. They spoke for themselves out of their own researches, their own notes (transcribed, not photostated), or their own violent prejudices. The point is, not one of them can be imagined as ever forming part of a "team."

There have been, over the last two or three decades, "developments" in technology, transportation, advertising, communication, which have much more altered our manners than has this dwindling in the universities of the ideal of the lonely scholar. I point to this phenomenon as the one that has most interested, not to say appalled, me because it is the one I am closest to, because I am so much the academician I can barely look beyond the college gates. Even so, I argue that it is a transformation of immense importance, not only because it intimates a change in the way our (presumably) better young minds are to be instructed, but even more because it makes a dramatic index to what has been steadily at work in our culture. It is entirely plausible that the perfection of the assembly line should turn workers into digits in an organized operation, that radio and television should require battalions of script writers and producers, that "colossal" films need disciplined regiments for their production, that modern weapons make so anarchic a soldier as Jeb Stuart as remote from our comprehension as Richard the Lion-Hearted. But that one who wishes to analyze the structure of *Paradise Lost*, to rethink the problem of reality, or to translate the Bible should go about it any other way than by shutting the door of his study—well, even to suppose otherwise is indeed a revolution in the modern mentality!

Assuredly, the mounting enrollment in our colleges will force us to employ mass methods in the classrooms. There is no point in deploring these inevitable "developments." But I am not thinking about lecturing through a microphone or over television: what worries me is the research, the evaluation of sources, the writing, the publication. Surely, even in the days I recall, the scientists had already gone far toward transforming the laboratory into a corporate enterprise. That is in the nature of the material: I gather that even in nuclear physics the figure of an Einstein sitting by himself armed only with a pencil and a pad belongs with that of Jeb Stuart. I will further concede that distinguished professors of the humanities put their seminars to work on material of use to themselves—Edward Channing certainly did—and that they employed research assistants, sometimes not giving these the credit due. But such practices are not the same thing as getting up a committee to survey American literature, to write the cultural history of New York, to classify the marriage dances of the Hopi, or to formulate a group definition of the nature of social action. I am the last to grieve because advertisers bring standardized procedures into the kitchen or even into the bedroom, but I tremble for the future of our civilization when the methods of Madison Avenue penetrate the scholar's sanctuary.

It has become the fashion to blame the foundations. Yes, the largess they have distributed, especially in the last decade, has accelerated the tendency of humanists to devise ways for getting aboard the gravy train. I am not the only one who has found himself dismayed at gatherings of academics (I mean those in areas with which I am concerned) when proposal after proposal is advanced with the suffix, "We might try to interest the Ford or the Rockefeller." Obviously, anybody can see how a comprehensive experiment in physics or chemistry should present itself to a foundation; also, an oligarchy of sociologists can, apparently, just as easily outline a large operation, and can promise startling disclosures. Propositions of either sort fall in with what the foundations call "programs." But can any self-respecting scholar in the humanities so comport himself? If not, how can he fit in? Dare he appear as a single being, full of crotchets, utterly unassociated and forever unassociable with some comprehensive scheme?

I have, I am proud to say, friends who are executives of foundations, and they protest that all I am saying is a canard of the humanists. They do support individual scholars. I have no statistics, and I suspect that in some measure they are justified. We have always to be grateful to the Guggenheim Foundation, even though the concrete awards are such that few of the chosen can live through the designated year without some further visible means of support. Nevertheless, the impression does march through the faculties that unless the humanists can somehow band together and devise some majestic undertaking, involving numbers, secretaries, equipment, the foundations have no time to consider them. It costs money in order to give money away; executives at high salaries can hardly fritter away their responsibilities in appraising this or that forlorn request of a lone-wolf historian. I know that the foundations work conscientiously over the problem, and their record is amazingly honorable. Be that as it may, the effect is to propel humanists into dreaming up team projects. And the dreadful reality is that the humanities just don't work that way—or, at least, so far they haven't. Whereupon you face the question, which I have not time to discuss, of what in the last ten years or more have the humanists in America accomplished anyway?

It has become a gnawing question in modern education: just where are the humanities? They may be lost, and possibly that is where they should be, for they were always a lost cause. When I recall the luminous names of three or four decades ago, I am reminded of one forgotten fact: generally these scholars had some sort of income; either they inherited money or they married it. The young man who elected in, say 1880 or 1890, to become a scholar rather than follow his father into business, had something to go upon. According to report, President Lowell could never bring himself to give thought to the salary scale at Harvard because he assumed that nobody would try to teach there unless already possessed of an independent income.

Even at Harvard, times changed. Ultimately, the humanists also learned to plead with foundations. They began to argue that in union there is strength. I am the last to excoriate the foundations. Advocates of humanistic studies seldom have the humanistic imagination to conceive how the thing looks from the other side of the table. But then, what has happened to that arrogant scholar of the generation long since gone? His successor, distracted with course reports, committees, faculty meetings, letters of recommendation, finds himself endowed less and less—even to the vanishing point—with those moments of solitude that permitted a William James or a John Lowes to pursue the phantom of making a contribution to knowledge.

In 1922, as I have noted, the University of Chicago beguiled a boy out from under the tracks of the Oak Park Elevated to the Midway, out of the twentieth century into the bosom of the nineteenth. The onus can be put upon President William Rainey Harper: he died a year after I was born, but he wore himself out to make the university I attended. I am not unfair in saying that more than any other in the country, his university enshrined the dream of nineteenth-century scholarship. Harper thought not in terms of fields or areas or of departments—he sought *the* professor and, therefore, collected personalities. Some of his selections proved more than even eccentric Chicago could tolerate—notably Thorstein Veblen. But Harper bet on individuals, and long after, although he did not live to see all the outcome, his gambles paid off. But in this game of hazard, he never played fast and loose with the grim disciplines of the basic humanities. He was spared the agony —and we can exult that he was spared—of ever being tempted to subvert the teaching of English composition into "communication skills." Likewise, he had never to argue against the citizens of Illinois the right of a professor to criticize the orthodox working of the American economy.

Thus I got my glimpse of the golden age, and golden it still seems to me. But at the time I did not comprehend that the sun was setting. I do not mean that I or my present colleagues, dedicated to research, annotation, questioning, have lost faith in what we are doing. And as long as I and they are permitted, we shall do just these things. But there is, of course, that other worry: whether liberality itself has not bred so wide a license that the humanists have nobody else but themselves to blame for the incoherence of the picture they offer to the pragmatic world. That is another story, and a long one, which I shall not now try to tell; in this context, the moral is that the free and easy posture of the self-sufficient scholar, within these areas, becomes for this reason all the more difficult to maintain. He is never quite sure—although he dresses atrociously—that he doesn't really belong with the bankrupt dandy, and that he, like his fellow wastrel, isn't concerned with nothing more than keeping up appearances.

There really is no point in arraigning the foundations and not much in accusing Madison Avenue. The issue is out in the open. We still endeavor to train those we hope to be the scholars of the future by compelling them to write a dissertation which, in theory, is their own creation. Those instructors who rely on the approved methods of promotion still publish monographs to impress the heads of their departments. Each remains commendably jealous of his own findings.

Yet, what seems to me most tragically to have happened is that the ideal of scholarship on the grand scale is never held up to the aspiring youngster. Let us thank our lucky stars that we won our liberation from the Germanic disciplines that held us in thralldom at the turn of the century, and that the sway of the philologists is past. But with all their shortcomings, the dictators of that era conveyed to the democracy of our students something of what it means to be a scholar. They labored in the image of Ranke, Macaulay, Harnack, Masson—and, we might add, Francis Parkman.

With many, alas too many, of the young scholars, the issue of their success has become a behavior pattern. To the seductive pattern of achievement in the natural sciences has now been added the overpowering model of the social. In a recent estimate of the "behavioral sciences" at Harvard there appears a list of misguided "lone wolves," and there I find myself at last catalogued.

There are, I need not say, innumerable exceptions. I do not seriously suppose that the scholar who walks by himself can be entirely ruled out of our universities. But what has most factually happened is that the young students are little instructed in what scholarship signifies: instead, they are urged by all the pressures of the times to find for themselves a place in the program. Some of the best are allured into taking up "communication skills."

Yet, it is clear that I misname this response to *The American Scholar*'s inquiry by orating about my "plight." I am in no more serious plight than what amounts to a nerve-wracking explanation of why I am so antisocial. Despite the allurements of foundation programs and the temptations of group ventures, the historic defense remains. The scholar can always close the door of his lonely chamber, and nobody can lure him out if he elects to stay there. Pascal said that humanity's inability to remain at ease in such seclusion was a proof positive of the universality of human depravity. But here and there the refutation has been made. What has formerly been done may, *mutatis mutandis*, still be done, even in the era of television.

Religious Background of the Bay Psalm Book

ACCORDING to the instructions of a seventeenth-century manual, with which I should like to open this discussion, the captains of a frontier post in the American wilderness were to lead their companies or their squads to prayer both in the mornings and in the evenings, and when the troops had been commanded to fall upon their knees, the captains were thus to lift up their voices to Heaven: We have sinned against God, they were to say,

> through our blindnesse of mind, prophanesse of spirit, hardnesse of heart, selfe love, worldlinesse, carnall lusts, hypocrisie, pride, vanitie, unthenkfulnesse, infidelitie, and other our native corruptions, which, being bred in us, and with us, have defiled us even from the wombe and unto this day, and have broken out as plague sores into innumberable transgressions of all thy holy lawes, (the good waies whereof we haue wilfully declined) & have many times displeased thee, and our own consciences in chusing those things which thou hast most iustly and seuerely forbidden us.

After several paragraphs in much the same vein—to a greater length than most congregations would contentedly sit through, and

An Address Delivered at the First Meeting House in Roxbury, Massachusetts, May 12, 1940.

certainly much longer than the Blitzkrieg would allow to modern soldiers—the prayer concludes with a request that the God of Israel, Jehovah Himself, will cast down the idols of Dagon—by which is meant the red Indians—and begs Him to "let such swine still wallow in their mire."

I should be willing to engage with you, that if I read this prayer to you as coming from a frontier outpost in New England during the hard days of King Philip's War you would accept it for an accurate transcription, and would have little difficulty in recognizing an utterance of the ancient Calvinism of New England. Perhaps if you are wise in the ways of the founders of the First Church in Roxbury, you might be slightly distressed about the fact that the prayer exists in written form, since it was one of the definite intentions of the Puritans that in their societies prayers should *not* be read out of a book—they had come three thousand miles that they might pray as the Spirit directed and that faith should not be shackled to formulae. But otherwise the spirit of the prayer, its insistence upon the depravity of man, its long catalogue of the plague sores of sin, followed by so exultant a declaration that these very sinners were nevertheless the chosen of the Lord, a peculiar people like unto Israel of old in the presence of the heathen Philistines, otherwise, I say, the prayer would sound very familiar to those who have read anything of the written records of Eliot and Welde and Richard Mather.

But it happens that this particular prayer was not penned for a New England encampment; it is the prayer which captains of forts in Virginia in 1613 were to read to their soldiers every morning and every night. The traditional picture of Virginia in colonial times—the great tidewater mansions, the easy-going, horse-racing, cockfighting aristocracy, the splendor of the now restored Williamsburg, and the spacious rationalism of Washington and Jefferson—does not seem to have much in common with a prayer that proclaims Virginians to be sinks of vanity and hypocrisy, even while asking the Lord of Hosts to grind their enemies into the mire. It may be a long and cumbersome way to approach the Bay Psalm Book through Jamestown, Virginia, but my reason for taking this circuitous road is, I think, very simple. When we speak of the Puritans today, if we ever take time to speak of them at all, we think of them primarily as men of a gloomy piety, laboring heroically under a crushing and unnecessary conviction of sin, and bucking up their courage with the persuasion that they were a peculiar and chosen people, holier than their neighbors and predestined by God to triumph over the unregenerate. I merely wish to point out, to begin with, however true such a description of the Puritan religious psychology may be—and in great part it is true—that it was a pervading assumption of much European thought in the seventeenth century and was not particularly limited to the New England Puritans. The worldly Virginians of the eighteenth century are a much later development; and how the piety which was enforced upon the first settlers evolved into the genial hedonism of the Revolutionary times is a long story that need not detain us now. The important fact is this: though the settlers of Virginia were in the main Anglicans, if they were anything at all, though they were not motivated by the explicit religious ambitions of the New England pioneers, though from the beginning their interest in the new land was much more avowedly economic, yet when they thought of themselves in relation to their creator they thought in terms which were essentially at one with those of New England.

I might illustrate the point a moment longer, if you will bear with me in this digression, by considering the case of John Rolfe and his love for the beautiful Pocahontas. The story of Pocahontas's timely rescue of Captain John Smith is a piece of American mythology as dear to all New Englanders as is the legend of Miles Standish's courtship to Americans from south of the Mason-Dixon Line. Whether because she had saved the old sea dog or merely because she was a friendly sort of person, she became a welcome visitor in the settlement at Jamestown, and in 1612 or 1613 John Rolfe, one of the leading settlers and a widower, took an interest in her. We have in his own words the story of what I hesitate to call his courtship, but of what were in any event the preliminaries of his marriage to Pocahontas. I am sure that if we could change the names, and put the scene on the banks of the Charles or of the Connecticut, we would experience no difficulty in recognizing that here is unmistakable evidence of the Puritan mind at work, and at work at its very worst. For Rolfe writes to the governor, Sir Thomas Dale, protesting that his wish to marry the Indian girl has been nothing less than a call from God, asserting that he is not motivated "with the unbridled desire of carnall affection: but for the good of this plantation, for the honour of our countrie, for the glory of God, for my owne salvation, and for the converting to the true knowledge of God and Iesus Christ, an unbeleeving creature." He says that when the idea of marrying her first occurred to him, he was horrified and by dint of prayer and meditation upon those texts of the Bible which forbid Israelites to marry strange wives, he overcame the temptation; but upon second thought it occurred to him that if by marrying her he could become the means of converting her, not only would he win one soul to Christ, but he would become the means also of establishing friendly relations with her father, the powerful chief Powhatan, that he would further the cause of the colony, aid the British colonial empire, prepare the way for the conversion of all Indians, and incidentally assure his own salvation. Only when he had seen the business in this light, he declares, could he imagine that this marriage might be justified; only thus could he be assured that he was not seeking merely his own interest, but was doing the Lord's work. And here is the spirit in which the Virginian conceived of doing the Lord's work: "Why was I created?" he asks, and replies without hesitation, "If not for transitory pleasures and worldly vanities, but to labour in the Lords vineyard, there to sow and plant, to nourish and increase the fruites thereof, daily adding with the good husband in the Gospell, somewhat to the tallent, that in the end the fruites may be reaped." If this is to be the task assigned him, Rolfe concludes, achieving the heights of Christian resignation, let the Lord do with his own as the Lord chooses, "and I will never cease, (God assisting me) untill I have accomplished & brought to perfection so holy a worke, in which I will daily pray God to blesse me, to mine, and her eternall happiness." Sir Thomas Dale was convinced by this reasoning and gave his consent. We know that Pocahontas did marry John Rolfe; probably she had her reasons as John had his, but we may doubt if they were of the same sort. It may be that she, poor unbelieving creature that she was, had simply fallen in love with him.

Pocahontas, you will remember, died in England, where Rolfe took her and put her on exhibition as a native princess, until the fog and the damp overcame her forest-born lungs. Rolfe, his Christian duty thus fulfilled, returned to Virginia, married once more, and was killed in the terrible Indian massacre of 1622. It is not recorded just what Indian swung the tomahawk that ended his life; sentimental romancers have imagined that it might have been a disappointed lover of Pocahontas who thus revenged his broken heart upon the successful rival. I like to think, on the contrary, that it was simply some especially intelligent young man of Powhatan's tribe who learned of the process by which John Rolfe had persuaded himself to take the Indian maiden to his bosom, not for love or affection, but for the conversion of her people, the advancement of the British empire, and the glory of the church; I like to think that the analytical young savage, bewildered by this strange method of courtship, sat down to think it over and came at last to the matured conclusion that Rolfe had offered an unpardonable insult to Indian womanhood. I like to believe that this admirable youth went out to avenge, not his own broken heart, but the indignity suffered by his race when the loveliest of its girls had been wooed and married for any other reason than for herself alone.

The forthright and untutored savage, who in the simplicity of innocence would have thought that a spade was a spade and a girl somebody you fell in love with, could never be expected to understand that in the most intimate affairs of life the Christian acted for what would seem to pagan eyes ulterior motives. But no Puritan in New England would have had the slightest difficulty in understanding and approving John Rolfe's conduct. Obviously he had confronted what they would have known at once was a "case of conscience," and a very nice one indeed! The Providence of God, the Puritan would have said, appoints us certain tasks in life: we must marry, have children, support our families, work hard and, if Providence permits, make money. Sometimes it happens that the tasks are pleasant, sometimes they are dull chores; but whether they seem to us agreeable or disagreeable is incidental to the reason for their existence. These things must be done first and foremost because they are required in the economy of a divine plan, because the end which God has had in mind from before the beginning of time, the ultimate intention of the cosmos, must be accomplished in these particular events. Therefore be thankful if you can carry out your assignment and like it, if you can marry for love and work at a trade you enjoy, whether as a parson or as a pig-reeve. But to the seventeenth-century mind it was almost unthinkable that any, except perhaps some contemptible vagabond players and poets, should so far forget themselves as to entertain the blasphemous notion that a man ought to marry a maid merely because he had fallen in love with her, that he should not first make sure that there was a call from God in it and that his primary motive was to obey the ancient commandment of Jehovah to mankind, who are his creatures and his subjects.

In short, John Rolfe's attitude toward his Indian bride was not very far removed from the Puritan's attitude toward the Psalms which they had published in the volume of which we today celebrate the three-hundredth anniversary. They did not attempt to offer smooth verses, because God's Altar, they declared, does not need polishing; they had attended conscience rather than elegance, fidelity rather than poetry, so that they in Sion might sing the Lord's song of praise according to the Lord's will, "untill hee take us from hence, and wipe away all our teares, & bid us enter into our masters ioye to sing eternall Halleluiahs." The character of Protestant piety has changed so much in the intervening centuries, the long history of new ideas and differing insights which could be represented by the successive teachings of the pastors of this very church, has so altered our conceptions of the Christian life, that we can only with great difficulty bring back to our imagination how the world appeared to believing souls of the seventeenth century when the Bay Psalm Book was compiled. So difficult is the task that we are very apt, once we have gone back to the documents and texts of the period, to such a statement as the preface of the Psalm Book, to assume that everything we find there is uniquely Puritan. We forget that it was a religious age; even a tough old soldier like Sir Thomas Dale assumed that all men were children of wrath, that men sinned when they sought their own ends apart from God's ends, that the God of Hosts intervened actively and decisively on the side of his saints. He and the Puritan parson would have started from the same assumptions. The Bay Psalm Book was the work of Puritans, but the Puritans themselves were the work of an age in which religion was not something apart from ordinary life, the life of work and marriage, in which religion was the end-all and the be-all of that life. Literary critics have had great sport with the crudity of the Bay Psalm Book's meters and the clumsiness of its rhymes; no doubt they could be improved, but the important thing to remember is exactly what the translators declared in their preface, that for them religion came first and literary elegance, a poor second. It was extremely important that the words of God be translated accurately and precisely; it was important to put into print the exact meaning, but it was not important to attain the purely human delight of stylistic polish. The glory of God, as it might be thus understood, came before all mere human concerns. And as we can perceive in John Rolfe's attitude toward his marriage, such a frame of mind was not limited to Puritans alone.

And so I say that to read the Bay Psalm Book as it appeared to those who wrote it and published it, we must look at it first of all as the work of an age of intense and all-pervading piety. But this book was after all made by Puritans and not by Virginians, no matter how pious. John Rolfe may have married Pocahontas for the glory of God and as a means to convert the poor creature, but he married her in an Anglican church and if he taught her to sing the Psalms, he taught her out of the authorized version. In Roxbury and in all New England they sang the Psalms as we have been trying to sing them today. The question then remains, just what difference does this really make, or rather what does it signify? Because John Rolfe and John Eliot could conceive of man and God in terms so very similar, are we to conclude that there was in truth no divergence between them? Why then should there exist this book which is so obviously a Puritan work, which took learning and time and industry to compose, and which John Rolfe would never have thought was worth a day's work in the tobacco fields of Virginia?

The answer, I believe, can be found succinctly stated in the preface to our volume. John Rolfe was obviously a man of piety, and he probably had no very great love for that party in the Church of England, led by William Laud, which was then attempting to make the church more Catholic in tone, to restore the medieval ritual which the first English reformers had cast out; at least, most Virginian settlers seem to have been of the so-called "Low" Church party. But Rolfe was content to use the Book of Common Prayer because it was the form prescribed by authority, by the king and the national church. He had come to Virginia to further the glory of God, to extend the English dominions, and to make money out of tobacco; it would never have occurred to him, however, that he should have ventured across the sea merely in order to be free to sing the Psalms in a literal version.

But the Puritans thought they should. We can see what lay behind their thinking in the first paragraph of this preface, where the reverend pastors are not at all content merely to publish the book, but must first of all explain the religious reasoning that has produced it. It was not enough for them to sing the Lord's praises; they must first of all prove by the word of the Lord that his praises are to be sung, that they are to be sung by the singing of David's Psalms, that they are to be sung as nearly as possible in the original meters, and finally that they are to be sung by the whole congregation together, not "by one man singing alone and the rest joyning in silence, & in the close saying amen." You have the essence of Puritan piety in that passage, the motive which directed the composition of this book and also the migration to New England—in so far, at least, as that migration was religiously inspired. The Puritan argued not merely that he should do whatever he did, whether in choosing a wife, or a profession, or a habitation, for the glory of God, but that he should prove by infallible deduction from the written word of God the grounds for his choosing. He had to give Scriptural warrant for worshiping in this way and not in that, and furthermore, once he had discovered what was right and what was wrong, he had to do the right in despite of Satan, the pope, or the king of England. The Bay Psalm Book was more than a book of verses; it was the living symbol of a cause, the banner of a victory. It proclaimed that the Puritans had come to New England, not merely for some general and vaguely defined pious purpose, but for the specific purpose of doing exactly as God had commanded, and that in Roxbury, when they sang these very Psalms, they had succeeded.

Of course, we can recognize that here is one more instance of the root-principle of the Reformation, the Protestant appeal to biblical authority in the face of the traditions of men, the conventions of society, and the edicts of princes. John Rolfe and the Virginia settlers were Protestants, but the New England Puritans were more rigorous, more consistent, more extreme Protestants. They carried the essential contention of Protestantism to its ultimate lengths, and one result of their radicalism was the Bay Psalm Book. If the Bible was the written word of God, then upon the Bible the Puritan would take his stand, and so help him God, he would do no other. And he intended that it should be the Bible as God had phrased it, not as crusted over with men's embellishments or as twisted to suit the convenience of vested interests, of bishops or of politicians.

Yet, as we all know, time has proved that even the Puritans did not escape the problems of interpretation. When they argued from the Bible that God himself had commanded these Psalms to be sung, and only these Psalms, and in the most literal translation possible, we now perceive that they were reading the Bible in their own fashion, and we do not feel compelled to agree with them. When Protestantism appealed to the authority of the Bible, we now universally declare, it was in fact appealing to the right of private judgment. It proclaimed the priesthood of all believers, and that declaration has come to mean liberty, freedom, toleration of religious opinions, the right of every man to read the word of God by his own light and to interpret it as he sees it. It has come to mean that no state, no college, no synod can dictate what any conscientious student of God's word or of his works takes to be the meaning of God. We find in Protestantism the sources for democracy, individualism, laissez-faire, freedom of the press and the little red school house, and especially in the aggressive Protestantism of New England. We can see the origins of the tradition in the care and the solicitude with which John Eliot sought for biblical warrant, in his fidelity to the words of the Bible as he saw them, in his refusal to be turned aside by any merely human considerations of elegance or decorum or convention.

This part of the Puritan tradition has been celebrated over and over again, especially in the last hundred years of New England and American history. The great pastors of this church in the nineteenth century looked back upon the seventeenth, and felt that they were being faithful to the spirit of their forefathers when they cast off the letter of the original theology. Just as the authors of the Bay Psalm Book went fearlessly to the text, disregarding traditions and venerable orthodoxies, so they too refused to be bound by the inherited orthodoxy of New England once they had seen the further light of liberal Christianity. We are all familiar with this version of New England history, and I can hardly do more than repeat what has been said a thousand times on this particular score.

But I should like to point out that the Bay Psalm Book, both by its very existence and by the words of its preface, can be taken to indicate another element in the Puritan tradition which the subsequent development of liberalism, of freedom, of the right of private judgment, has often managed to hide from sight. On the basis of the word of God, the translators of the Psalms concluded that the verses were to be sung by the whole congregation, not by one man singing alone, while the rest joined in silence and in the close merely said amen. The New England Puritans searched the Bible for a rule of life and a platform of church government, but they came out with a rule not merely of private life, of the individual conscience and the soul's walk with God, but with a rule of society, of the state, of the corporate body. The Psalms were translated, they were sung, as the symbol of the unity of the saints in a covenanted church; the churches were autonomous congregational groups, but all were united in agreement and in their obedience to orthodox magistrates. I think nothing would more horrify the compilers of the Bay Psalm Book, could they be brought back to earth today, than to learn the terms in which they have been so fulsomely celebrated during the recent decades; even if they could be persuaded that out of their own tenets had grown by legitimate descent the principles of private judgment and freedom, they would still, I feel very sure, remain greatly distressed that religious freedom had meant the disappearance of the concept of a close-knit society—of a church which, resting upon the covenanted consent of the membership, prescribed rules for every department of life—of a state which, originating in a compact of the citizens, enforced the moral law upon businessmen and merchants, laborers, and college professors. That these Psalms were translated for the whole congregation to sing in unison was a symbol to the Puritans of the social bond, a sign that they still thought of society in what we now call medieval terms. They were firmly assured that man has duties not merely to God but to other men, and that his performance of such obligations was not a matter apart from his religious life or the church's supervision. When the Great Migration was on the high seas approaching these then desolate shores, the great leader John Winthrop delivered a lay sermon on the deck of the *Arabella*, and in it he declared emphatically that element in the Puritan creed which it seems to me the heirs of the Puritans have been ready to forget: in the land whither we go, he said,

> wee must uphold a familiar Commerce together in all meekenes, gentlenes, patience and liberallity, wee must delight in eache other, make others Condicions our owne, reioyce together, mourne together, labour, and suffer together, allwayes haveing before our eyes our Commission and Community in the worke, our Community as members of the same body, soe shall wee keepe the unitie of the spirit in the bond of peace.

I am not here, of course, to deliver a sermon or to supply an exhortation; I would not have one to supply were it expected of me. But I think, in view not merely of the event we celebrate today but of what has happened in the three hundred years, it is well to go back once more to our beginnings and see whence we have come; it may be well to ask ourselves, since we are here to testify to the vitality of a tradition, whether there might be in it a vitality which we do not often recognize. I leave that suggestion merely as a suggestion, intending at the last to make but this one observation. The Bay Psalm Book was the work of men who were inspired in their every thought and action by a deep and intense piety, by a religious conviction which we describe as Calvinism, which to them was no mere "ism" but rather the law of life. As a result of their religious convictions they translated the Psalms of David, literally out of the word of God, thus testifying to the rule of conscience in their individual bosoms. But at the same time they provided these texts not simply to satisfy their personal conviction, not merely to work out their individual salvations, but to furnish an occasion for the coming together of a society, to give a form and a bond to the group, to symbolize the membership of each particular person in the community. If the Bay Psalm Book tells us of the Puritan emphasis upon freedom, it tells us no less that Puritanism sought freedom only within the unity of the spirit and the fellowship of man.

Individualism and the New England Tradition

IN THE YEAR 1641 the Colony of Massachusetts Bay, which for ten years had been enjoying a prosperity hitherto unprecedented in the annals of colonization, suddenly fell from the heights of economic well-being into the depths of depression. You and I encounter no difficulty in explaining the collapse of this colonial boom. No matter what religion we profess, we have all so partaken of the rationalism of the eighteenth century, the mechanism of the nineteenth and the materialism of the twentieth, that we unhesitatingly expound this economic crisis as a simple cause and effect. For ten years, we tell our students, the colony lived upon its immigrants; the immense flow of newcomers (relative to those already on the ground) provided a market for the stuffs raised or prepared by the previous settlers, and since the immigrants brought money with them, they supplied the indispensable specie. But in 1641 the Long Parliament had assembled and the Puritan cause at home seemed miraculously revived; whereupon the immigration to Massachusetts abruptly ceased. Immediately the settlers perceived that they no longer had a market for the few items they could wring from the New England soil, and without customers they could not procure the money which they must have if they were to

An address delivered at the annual meeting of the Unitarian Ministerial Union, held at King's Chapel, Boston, May 18, 1942.

import tools and clothes from London. What happened then is a commonplace of American economic history. Driven to finding a cash crop, the Puritans explored the deep and discovered the sacred cod; they carried fish to the West Indies and to the Papist countries of southern Europe, to exchange their haul for the solid bullion with which they could purchase the necessary manufactures of England. This was a more complicated, not to say dangerous, way of making a living than they had foreseen during the first decade, but it was full of possibilities. By the eighteenth century the compulsion that had driven New Englanders to the sea was no longer regarded as a misfortune; it had become the foundation of a commercial prosperity little short of fabulous.

Thus modern historians, who write for people like you and me, explain what happened in terms you and I think constitute explanation. If they belong to the school that holds the sum of economic wisdom to consist in the principles of rugged individualism and free competition, that contends that government interference in "business" is immoral, and that has been distressed by the policy of the national government in recent years, they often close their account with a hymn of praise to the solid virtues of the old Yankee stock, to its ingenuity and self-reliance, with the obvious implication that we should do well to forget the academic nonsense lately emanating from Washington and fight our way out of our economic troubles by imitating our ancestors. Now I come before you as one who also reveres his ancestors, and especially the founders of New England; up to a point at any rate, I am an admirer of the Puritans as well as their historian, and I should certainly feel chagrined, on this occasion, this anniversary week, which keeps alive the memory of the spring election and the annual election sermon, were I obliged to stand in this venerable pulpit and to confess that we are less than our forefathers. Before I will admit that we have so degenerated, I should like to examine for a moment the question of just how much the ancient Yankee individualism, just how much the economic and self-seeking man who made his own way without a security number, with no unemployment assurance, and assuredly with no reliance on the WPA, can be held the true explanation of the commercial triumph that so marvellously enriched Boston and Salem and made the name of the pious New Englander synonymous in many parts of the world with the skinflint, the horse-trader, and the peddler of wooden nutmegs. Let me assure you at once that I do not intend herein to attempt a discourse on economic history, for it is not the business cycle in which I am really interested. I am concerned about religious history, and above all, in this year of grace, about the state of religion, especially among the children of the Puritans. It was customary in the ordination sermons of the seventeenth and eighteenth centuries for the preacher who delivered the charge to the newly consecrated youth to call upon him to maintain the pure doctrine in matters of Faith, Practice, and Worship, but to close always with the supreme injunction, that he keep alive the "power" of religion.

> Tho' these things are needful, and useful, and helpful, yea and honourable to Men, . . . yet the bare attending of these is too often made by men their Righteousness, and so becomes an abomination to God. Much less can that pass for Religion that spends itself about *Forms* and *Opinions* and *Parties*: These however strict and Orthodox they be, may be separable from the *Power of Godliness*; but Religion lies in Mens being Good, and doing Good.

I am venturing to suggest that certain connotations which for us have come to cluster about the word "individualism" are in fact part of the reason why our religion is, as many confess it is, liable to the accusation of lacking somewhat of the ancient power of Godliness.

To return, then, to the depression of 1641. This is the way we expound it: cessation of the flow of immigrants produced a crisis; the crisis stimulated men to find a new crop; the sea supplied the crop, and Catholic countries, the market; the Puritans harvested the crop, sold it in the markets, and waxed rich. Then they built fine houses, had their portraits painted, sent their sons to Harvard College, and became Unitarians. It is as simple as that.

Simple though it be, I should like to put in a slight demurrer, that when we resort to such an explanation we make, generally without noticing their enormity, several staggering assumptions, which I am sure our ancestors themselves would hardly understand, or could they be made to understand, would angrily condemn. We assume that one physical fact causes another—cessation of immigrants a crisis, a crisis a new expenditure of energy; furthermore we assume that this particular chain of causes and effects is a segment of the continuous, unending sequence that has been operating forever and will operate forever, that one event will always produce something else, and it in turn a further something, and so on *ad infinitum*; finally, we take for granted that the whole business was haphazard and accidental. Had the Long Parliament not been called, immigrants would still have come; had the fish not happened to be there, the colony would have failed; had the Reformation crossed the Alps there would have been no fish-consuming Catholics to take the surplus cod. We praise the colonial Yankee for making the best of his opportunities—and in the very act we confess by implication that the universe in which he throve and we live is mechanical, pointless, and contingent. Things are arranged in no logical or meaningful patterns, and men may treat the world as their oyster, since oysters are to be eaten by those who can find them and have the wit to open them.

There is some evidence in the Puritan writings—perhaps not as much as I might wish, but still I speak confidently out of my certainty of how the Puritan mind worked—that the men who actually fished the cod and first found their way in Yankee sloops to the West Indies, to Spain and Italy, did not think of what they were doing in precisely the terms we use in celebrating their achievement. To them, the sequence of cause and effect was quite opposite from what it is to us; they started not from the premise that they were to make the most of their opportunities, but that God had predetermined the prosperity of His people, for New England must prosper in order that the true form of church polity, the Congregational, might have a place in which to live; therefore, in order to provide the material basis necessary to the accomplishment of that end, God contrived in the infinitude of His providence that the superstitious Papists would continue to eat fish on Fridays; then he created the cod and put them in the banks of Newfoundland to await the appointed time; then He planned the depression of 1641 so that the saints should be led by the stern hand of providential necessity to the fish; and that the necessity might come upon them only after they had survived the first hazards of settlement, He kept Charles I from calling the Long Parliament until ten years after Winthrop had brought settlers into the Bay. It was indeed part of God's plan that when the day came for His saints to go to work, they should work with a will, work hard and for long hours, that they should go down to the sea in small ships and encounter there the leviathan, the storm, and other evidence of His wrath. It was also part of His plan that most of the faithful laborers—a few, of course, would be cast away in order to show that He could do as He wished with His own—should receive the reward of pious labor in the form of gold and silver, and that they should then wear better garments than in the days of their poor beginnings and should give their children advantages they had not themselves possessed. But what I think we must endeavor thoroughly to understand is that for the prospering fisherman and merchant, this process was no mere exploitation of natural resources. It was part of a divine plan; it was the fulfilling of a design; it was the submission of the private self to the interests of the public. They fished and trafficked not for the increase of estates but for the glory of God and His churches.

I should perhaps confess that I dwell upon this episode because I have already found it a convenient way to bring home to Harvard students how differently they might look upon certain matters could they conceive the universe, not as free, open and indifferent, not as blind and inhuman, but as having some meaning. You will forgive me if I impose upon you an illustration I have frequently used in the classrooms, for I take it you are aware that one of the chief joys of exchanging pulpits is the chance you obtain of employing your pet devices on an audience not yet surfeited with them. The point, therefore, is that the Puritan universe was ruled, not by mechanical efficient causes, but by *the* final cause; it had significance, and a man in such a universe, by the very fact of his existence, had what I should like to call a moral responsibility. That was not something he might or might not take upon himself; it was inescapable, inherent. In this universe there was distress, anguish, loss of life, danger, torment, and in it every man had a job to do. But not for what he might get out of it—rather for what the job had to contribute to the pattern of the whole.

If the founders of Massachusetts thus conceived the universe itself, if for them the very structure of the cosmos was so contrived that men, by doing what they had to do, by exerting their wills and energies in their callings, simply performed their appointed rounds in the intelligent and intelligible purpose of God, then they naturally and inevitably conceived their churches in analogous terms. We can, of course, perceive the workings of the seventeenth-century mind more closely in the realm of ecclesiastical doctrine than in the economic, and especially in the theory of the Congregationalists, who, since they founded the vast majority of New England churches, really formulated the peculiar religious tradition of New England, into which King's Chapel, although founded by persons of a hostile persuasion, became gradually assimilated by a kind of obscure osmosis which visiting Anglicans from other regions still try vainly to comprehend. Both the founders of King's Chapel and the Puritan founders of the First Church of Boston were Protestants, but the Puritans were the more vigorous protestors. They protested not only against popes but against bishops, not only against superstition but against sacerdotalism, not only against Rome but against Lambeth and Whitehall. Now, we have all been told, time after time, that Protestantism enthroned the right of private judgment, that it required the individual to walk with God alone, though the encounter slay him; it said that in the Bible is the Word of God, which a man must read in the seclusion of his closet. It said he could not be saved by good works or by endowing masses, by offering flowers to the Virgin Mary or purchasing indulgences in the market place; it put a man on his own, it made him a solitary, and it required him to find his own salvation within himself—or else to go to Hell. On the awful day of judgment each man will stand by himself, and the real judge of his fate will be not God or Christ, but his own single conscience:

> Now it comes in, and every sin unto Mens charge doth lay:
> It judgeth them, and doth condemn, though all the world say nay.
> It so stingeth and tortureth, it worketh such distress,
> That each Man's self against himself, is forced to confess.

Puritan individualism was in fact so drastic that Michael Wigglesworth—who appears in life to have been a gentle and kindly soul—had no scruple at proclaiming in the one literary work that all New Englanders read and re-read, that on the ultimate day the ties of even the most intimate affections would dissolve into callous indifference; the Day of Doom, as he portrayed it, became in effect rugged individualism run riot, what might be called an orgy of social irresponsibility. The regenerate brother sorrows not a jot over the condemnation of his reprobate twin, the godly wife sheds no tear over the fate of her erstwhile dear mate, and the adoring husband suddenly ceases to care about the wife who has become "a damn'd forsaken wight"; and even

> The tender Mother will own no other of all her numerous brood,
> But such as stand at Christ's right hand acquitted through His Blood.

One wonders, at times, why we should assume that only in the nineteenth century, with the emergence of liberal Christianity and humanitarianism, of capitalism and laissez-faire, the idea of the disparate individual could come into being; the isolation of the self, the utter severance of both the saint and the sinner from his fellows, was so devastatingly set forth in the Puritan theology that by contrast a Channing, an Emerson, or a John D. Rockefeller seem downright socialists.

Hence the Protestant sense of the individual, of the single entity which is one entire person, who must do everything of himself, who is not to be cosseted or carried through life, who in the final analysis has no other responsibility but his own welfare, this ruthless individualism was indelibly stamped upon the tradition of New England. I think it does not require great ingenuity to trace the persistence of this concept through the many subsequent revolutions and modifications of theology, to see that it is indeed one of the unbroken threads of development from the days of Wigglesworth to this very anniversary, to prove even that it is the principal ingredient in what I have ventured to call the New England tradition. In fact, the existence of this continuing idea justifies us in speaking of the New England tradition as something that has objective existence, and we can trace its effects both in the various theologies and in the equally various banks and counting-houses. Group by group the children of the Puritans ceased to believe in the phantasmagoric flares of *The Day of Doom*, but few of them ever doubted that nothing can force a man to confess but himself; in the Mathers, in Edwards, in Channing, in Emerson or in Henry Adams we can follow the workings of this principle, that in the supreme and crucial moments a man will be ruled only by his own conscience, "though all the world say nay."

That this Protestant individualism should have been kept so particularly alive in New England must in great part be attributed to the fact that from the beginning it was institutionalized in the Congregational polity. No matter how much the subsequent generations declined in zeal, or took their faith for granted, or came to doubt the infallibility of John Calvin, they had to live with churches to which no man could belong unless he voluntarily consented. There were attempts to infringe or to hedge the great idea; children who could not evoke enough will power to make a good profession might be kept within the easier confines of the Half-Way Covenant—on the assumption that they were able to give half a consent! Sometimes the criteria of consent were so whittled down that the slightest stirring of an inclination would be treated as a full-fledged resolution, but still, in every crisis, the idea of the founders revived, and the New England churches could not, even when they tried, escape their inheritance. These churches were built, every one of them, upon a covenant, and the great point about a covenant is that nobody can sign one until he first makes up his mind to it. The Puritans of New England were consistent Protestants with a vengeance; men were not to be saved in batches and crowds, but one by one, through a special, inward reception of grace that enabled each particular individual to stand on his own feet and say, "I believe." Only such individuals could become members of a New England church, only those who actively wanted to be, and the very church itself had no corporate existence but as the sum total of the consents of particular members. The state could exile a heretic, imprison an Antinomian and hang a Quaker, but the mightiest theocrat in Massachusetts would never admit that the state could force an individual to become a church member. The churches could use their influence upon public morals, but no church could actually censure or excommunicate a sinner who had not previously submitted himself to the rule of the church. He who would eat of the cod had to go out and fish for it, and he who would feast in the fellowship of the saints had to knock upon the door. He had to take the initiative. That in order to muster such an initiative a man had first to receive the grace of God did not alter the fact that the responsibility was his, and the Puritan never saw any contradiction between his doctrine of predestination and the voluntarism of his church covenant. The important fact was that both in economics and in salvation, the individual had to do everything of himself. On earth there was no dole and in heaven there was no largess.

If during the last century, especially in the last ten years, there have been reasons why certain economists have sought a blessing from the founders of New England upon their particular opinions, there have for over a century been still greater incentives for many theologians. All the voluminous and bitter controversies of Protestant New England, even those that began before all the founders were dead, generated repeated though often conflicting appeals to the example of the founders. But during the nineteenth and early twentieth centuries, all the groups that had descended from the New England Way were pretty much at one, whatever their other disagreements, in assuming that freedom was the supreme desideratum in this life and that the rights of the individual were sacred above all other claims. They were part of an expanding, capitalist, exploiting America, and we should not wonder that they identified the ethics of that America with Christianity, and that one and all they celebrated the founders of New England for being the pioneers of liberty—political, economic, and religious. How many times, in how many pulpits and on how many bedraped platforms, on how many centenaries, anniversary weeks, and Fourths of July, have Winthrop and Cotton and their colleagues been hailed as the progenitors of those virtues which have made Yankees the best, or at least the smartest, businessmen in America and the freest churchmen in all Christendom. True, Winthrop and Cotton misguidedly exiled Roger Williams, but they also left us the precious principle, enshrined in the very constitution of our churches, that no man need belong to anything unless he is willing—that he has the right, as Robert Frost likes to put it, to go to Hell in his own way. If they did unfortunately resort to compulsion when they confronted an occasional and especially obstreperous Quaker, or if they did quickly learn to scalp more Indians than could scalp them, nevertheless they dowered us with the principle of consent. Out of that principle has grown the whole American code: freedom, private judgment, liberalism, democracy, the due process of law—above all that individualism which both in the religious and economic life came in the nineteenth century to be the cardinal tenet.

My reason for beginning with economics rather than theology may at this point become a little clearer than I fear it has been so far. I think that an analogous misunderstanding of the original theory of Congregationalism has, over the centuries, insensibly grown up among the churches that divided the inheritance of the Puritan. This misunderstanding was perfectly natural under the circumstances, and it was eminently plausible, because in fact it was not so much a misunderstanding as an emphasis upon one part of the original theory to the neglect of what had been, at the beginning, an equally important other part. Yet all these considerations do not wholly excuse the New England churches, or their leaders, for having let something go which was once a source of strength to New Englanders and which, were it with us today, might enable us to meet our problems head-on with the resolution that so distinguished both the Puritan saint and sailor. That something which it seems to me we have so nearly and so tragically lost was in religion the same something that in economics made the life of the Puritan merchant such a different business from the life of the twentieth-century capitalist. At the grave risk of oversimplifying my point, let me put it bluntly: for the founders of New England there was a purpose in the world; they called it the purpose of God, but we need not be put off by hackneyed terminology, for in the actual, everyday life of ordinary men, the great idea that this universe was no accident and that it was constantly directed by providence to intelligible ends was an ever present reality, though the language in which we attempt to expound it to modern ears is apt to sound archaic. Consequently, for the founders of New England, the free man was he who could bring himself heart and soul to accept and submit to that which God had decreed would come to pass whether he submitted or not. When the regenerated man consented to the church covenant, the important point was not that he had consented, but what he had consented *to*. Liberal historians have praised the New England churches because they did not require men to subscribe a particular creed; in the seventeenth century it did not occur to Puritans that saints should subscribe a creed, because there was only one truth that a saint could possibly entertain anyway. The liberty of the Christian man, like the liberty of the economic man, was to be exercised, as John Winthrop succinctly put it, "in a way of subjection to authority." We chose, and if we chose rightly, we were saved, but if we chose wrongly, we went to eternal torment. In Protestantism there was indeed the right of private judgment, but only one judgment was right; if the private individual missed it, the exercise of his freedom, the sovereign prerogative of his individuality, led him to destruction. There was freedom—but the freedom, to quote Winthrop once more, to do only that which was good, just, and honest. God led the Puritans through His providence down to the sea and to prosperity, but in His revealed word He also taught them, as John Cotton was obliged to explain to the profiteering merchants of Boston, that it is impious and wrong to maintain "that a man might sell as dear as he can, and buy as cheap as he can." In the mart of trade there existed a just price, to which bargainers must come, will-they nill-they, and in the temple there was a truth, a core of belief, authoritative and single, to which Christians must consent, no matter what their individual tastes or preferences.

It is worth remarking again, though many have remarked it before, that this one authoritative truth was a grim doctrine that cannot be accused of palliating or concealing the harsher realities of life. Of course in many quarters, especially in this particular quarter, the doctrine has for over a century been copiously accused of being altogether too harsh, and the "moral argument against Calvinism" has proved so cogent that Calvinists themselves have for a century been steadily yielding to it. Obviously it would be the height of folly for me to come at this late date before the Unitarian Ministerial Union with the intention of reconverting it to Calvinism, for nobody, least of all I, can any longer take seriously the comic, the grotesque eschatology of *The Day of Doom*. But this much I think we must be prepared to recognize, though the recognition be unpleasant and difficult: within the forms of this theology the more terrible moments of human life—the ravages of disease, the pains of childbirth, the tomahawk, and the foundering vessel—could be presented to ordinary men as belonging in the scheme of things, as having a reason for being. Say if you will that this theology was naive and unscientific, but whatever its many shortcomings, it did not leave individuals unequipped, with no other resources but themselves, to meet the onslaught of war, of death, of tyrants. When the free man took his place in the ranks of the Christians, when he took up his calling, he went forth to do battle with evil; he did not content himself with expatiating on the beauties of a world in which men were indulged with the freedom of choice, nor did he stop short with the act of choosing as though it were the end-all and be-all of creation.

To survey the history of theology in New England, from the middle of the seventeenth century down to our time, is to behold one of the most fascinating spectacles in the whole panorama of history. It is to watch the unfolding of a game in which the luxury of choosing ceased to be a condition of the play and became the reward itself. The history of the New England tradition is a series of splinterings, of divisions and subdivisions and the subdivision of subdivisions, until you are left breathless as you try to keep pace with the accelerating pace of Yankee individualism. No sooner had Calvinists and Arminians split than the Calvinists separated into New Lights and Old Lights, and the New Lights had no sooner come into being than they were dispersed into the schools of exercise and taste, into Hopkinsians and Bellamyites, ino the camps of Taylor and Tyler and Bushnell, and at last one is ready to perceive that, as far as the "orthodox" side is concerned, the constitution of Andover Seminary was the perfect symbol of their state of mind, wherein the faculty was obliged to swear to so many quirks and eccentricities of doctrine that nobody could tell what anybody was supposed to believe or what after all was orthodoxy. But the story on the "liberal" side is no more reassuring: the so-called Arminians divided into Universalists and Unitarians, and the Unitarians were so fearful of dividing among themselves that for a long time they refused to say what, if anything, they stood for. But even such circumspection was not enough to inhibit the splintering of Unitarians, and individual Unitarians, exercising still further the right of private judgment, had to be denounced by Andrews Norton for propagating "the latest form of infidelity," though it might well seem to a Calvinist like Lyman Beecher, who also had a sense of humor, that Norton was piqued merely because his own doctrine had so soon ceased to be the last word in heresy. Where beyond Emerson and Theodore Parker could the tradition of New England individualism go? Where indeed, but either to Walden Pond or into Big Business. Was it not a straight line, was it not the *great* line, that led from Wigglesworth's *Day of Doom*, wherein each man's conscience proved at last his final judge, to the Babel of sects that became the religous life of nineteenth-century New England? Was it not a proper fulfillment of the New England tradition, that having commenced with the assertion that a man's own conscience was his guide, "though all the world say nay," its greatest literary prophet should deliver as its ultimate injunction, "Whosoever would be a man, must be a nonconformist"; and its finest stylist should declare, "Wherever I go, men pursue me and paw me with their dirty institutions," intending to include among the dirty institutions even the freely covenanted church of Concord? Yes, this persistent, this invigorating individualism is the heart and soul of the New England tradition. This is what we are and what we have been. But how did it happen, the timid historian has all this while been wanting to put it—and only in the present serious juncture has he found the courage to speak up—that while the right of private judgment thus flourished like the green-bay tree, John Cotton's admonition to Robert Keayne, that he should not sell as dear as the traffic would bear or buy as cheap as he could force men's necessities to yield, got transformed into the maxim, "The public be damned"?

I have often wondered if perhaps the major tragedy in New England history was not the peculiar circumstances under which the liberal movement was obliged, in the middle of the eighteenth century, to get under way, the extreme caution and diffidence with which it only reluctantly merged into the open as the Unitarian Association of 1825. Of course, when one remembers the temper of New England in those years, one can hardly blame the liberal leaders for seeking to avoid controversy, for working behind the scenes, for not giving their opponents a chance to get at them. By that time all New Englanders had become proficients at the game of cat and mouse; I say "game" advisedly, because it is all too obvious that they enjoyed it immensely. Every parson was perpetually crouched to jump upon his brethren, even his closest friends or classmates, at the first sign of heresy, and the sport of denunciation, hair-splitting, and mutual recrimination had come so to absorb the energies of New England thinkers that they had few left over for the thinking itself. The Unitarians, to tell the truth, were getting bored with this provincial pastime; as they discovered larger and more genial views, became men of a more worldly breeding, travelled in Europe and learned to read poetry, they longed to cultivate other graces than the *odium theologicum*. So they worked as quietly as possible, and preferred to ignore the disagreeable rather than to flatter it by admitting its existence. I believe it was Chandler Robbins—was it not?—who modestly boasted in 1866 that in his church throughout the Civil War he had never, in sermon, prayer or hymn, permitted to appear the slightest overt suggestion that the nation was at war. It was natural that the opponents of Unitarianism, who in the first decades of the century were having a wonderful time lambasting each other, were thrown into paroxysms of rage over this refusal to abide by the traditional rules, at this supercilious disdain of joining the free-for-all and contributing to the common delectation. Not merely Calvinists in New England were exasperated by what seemed the excessive prudence of the Unitarians; William Hazlitt, whose father was a fighting champion of English Unitarianism and had spent two rather unhappy years in Boston, fulminated over a volume of Channing's sermons that he had never seen anything more guarded, more suspended between heaven and earth. Channing, he said, "keeps an eye on both worlds; kisses hands to the reading public all around; and does his best to stand well with different sects and parties. He is always in advance of the line, in an amiable and imposing attitude, but never far from succor." Lyman Beecher had more reason to be enraged at what he was bound to call the hypocrisy and deceit of the Unitarians. From the time their blasphemy began to show itself, he declared, "it was as fire in my bones," but these damnably subtle heretics would not come out and fight like men. "Their power of corrupting the youth of the commonwealth by means of Cambridge is silently putting sentinels in all the churches, legislators in the hall, and judges on the bench, and scattering every where physicians, lawyers, and merchants." Like a species of fifth-columnists, as Beecher would have called them had he known the phrase, they wait until the good old minister dies, and then they install a bright young sophisticate from Harvard "and take house, funds, and all." "It is time," he thundered in 1821, "high time to awake out of sleep, and to call things by their right names."

However, by that time it was clear even to the most prudent that silence was no longer in order. In 1815 Channing had appeared in print, in the letter to Thacher and the two letters to Dr. Worcester, to defend the Unitarians publicly against the charge of concealing their real opinions. We know that he was not the kind of man to stoop to such a melodramatic and absurd "plot" as the lurid imagination of Beecher envisaged, and Hazlitt's strictures cannot in any sense be considered a just comment upon the Baltimore sermon, one of the most forthright, clean-cut utterances in all American history, which ought to have convinced even Lyman Beecher that a Unitarian could call things by their right names. And eleven years afterwards he delivered the election sermon—the old Puritan custom was still observed in 1830—and there pronounced certain words which it is a pleasure to repeat after him on this anniversary above all others:

> I call that mind free, which jealously guards its intellectual rights and power, which calls no man master, which does not content itself with a passive or hereditary faith, which opens itself to light whencesoever it may come, which receives new truth as an angel from heaven, which, whilst consulting with others, inquires still more of the oracle within itself, and uses construction from abroad, not to supersede but to exalt and quicken its own energies.

One would think that Lyman Beecher might have perceived that Channing was not so great a traitor to Puritanism, that his being a Socinian was of less import than that he, in his own fashion, was saying with *The Day of Doom* that the private man's inward oracle must be his only judge and condemner, though all the world say nay.

But why, you may well ask, do I then characterize the long period of incubation, of the fastidious reticence which enabled Unitarianism to take shape, why do I call it "tragic" if at last, however surreptitious the methods, if finally produced such stirring statements in 1819 and 1830—statements which I obviously admire? I should prefer, lest you think I am merely riding some private hobby-horse—for I too am an heir of the Yankee tradition and idolize my own eccentricities—to let speak for me certain persons who knew at first hand the state of mind that followed in Unitarian circles hard upon Channing's magnificent work of liberation. No doubt my witnesses are prejudiced, since they are as cranky a pair as may well be adduced in a long history of oddities. Nevertheless, a few years after Channing had told the General Court that that mind is free which jealously guards its intellectual rights and powers, Emerson brought down upon his head the wrath of many Unitarians—they reserved their unperturbed serenity in the presence of a rustic boor like Beecher, but they betrayed that they had their share of the Yankee irascibility when they confronted this heretic grown up in their own ranks—by telling young men at Harvard: "I have heard it said that the clergy—who are always more universally than any other class, the scholars of their day—are addressed as women; that the rough spontaneous conversation of men they do not hear, but only a mincing and diluted speech." And then there is the well-known passage from Henry Adams, describing a boyhood passed in circles where the principles of Channing, the freedom which consists in jealously guarding one's own rights and powers and in consulting the inward oracle before all others, had come entirely to prevail:

> The religious instinct had vanished, and could not be revived, although one made in later life many efforts to recover it. That the most powerful emotion of man, next to the sexual, should disappear, might be a personal defect of his own; but that the most intelligent society, led by the most intelligent clergy, in the most moral conditions he ever knew, should have solved all the problems of the universe so thoroughly as to have quite ceased making itself anxious about past or future, and should have persuaded itself that all the problems which had convulsed human thought from earliest recorded time, were not worth discussing, seemed to him the most curious social phenomenon he had to account for in a long life.

Allow what you will for Emerson's hyperbole and Adams's dyspepsia, still Channing himself in 1815 had made, along with his vigorous assertion, an admission that goes far to bear out both Emerson and Adams. He objected to Dr. Worcester that the method sometimes employed by the Calvinists for driving Unitarians out of the churches, the trial for heresy, was actually inconsistent with the principles of Congregational polity, because in order to condemn a member for heresy in a Congregational church the whole body must pass judgment; but, said Channing, if the whole church is to judge an intricate point of theology, then the people must be so skilled as to know what is right and what is wrong; yet nowadays, as is obvious, the people are so engaged in active business that they have no time to devote to these curiosities.

Hence, Channing argued, they easily become the tool of a domineering minister, and so it would be better, all things considered, that nobody ever be tried for heresy. In other words, out of the long period of stealthy preparation and cautious growth came the liberal Christianity in whose name we assemble today; but under the circumstances of its emergence, compelled as it was to walk softly and forego doctrinal discussion, it came in the end to take its stand firmly within the sacred preserves of the private judgment, to emphasize as its primary teaching the right of the individual to go his own gait, to guard his powers, to be jealous above all of the inward oracle. It vindicated man's right to choose, as Puritanism had vindicated man's right to choose or reject the covenant; but the question is, after it had so placed its emphasis and had parted company with "orthodoxy," when it had become a church with no set creed, with no doctrinal stereotypes to intrude upon the individual jealousy, after it had made men free to choose, what did it leave for them to choose?

Mr. Mark Anthony DeWolfe Howe tells in his delightful *Venture in Remembrance* of standing with Henry James at the head of Marlborough Street and of James's saying, in his slow, elephantine hesitations, "Do you feel that Marlborough Street . . . is precisely . . . *passionate?*" Henry James was not, at that time, being unduly disparaging; he was a mild critic of Boston, but his love for the city flowed into the affectionate cadences of *The American Scene*, and no one better understood than he that if Marlborough Street was not precisely passionate, it was spacious, civilized, and jealous of its own integrity. But I have recently had occasion to re-read a letter he wrote some time after this observation to Mr. Howe, in August of 1914. The letter makes, to me, even more poignant reading than ever before, if only because what he perceived in 1914 is really much more patent today, and if only because what he did see in 1914 so many of us contrived to blind ourselves to for another twenty-seven years. He who had been, no one more so, very much at home in a world of liberal elegance and civilization, suddenly recognized in August 1914, that he had been all his life deceived by appearances. "That above all," he wrote,

> is the strange stranded feeling—the disconnection in everything *by* which we have during all the period of my long life, and long before that still, supposed ourselves to be living. I

> say supposed ourselves, because the most dreadful effect of it all is to make the past which we believed in as a growth of civilization and a storing-up, despite everything, of some substantial treasure, take on the semblance of a most awful fraud, a plausible villainy that all the while was meaning and intending and leading to this horror—had it all the while, so to speak, up its sleeve.

My mood today is, I believe, somewhat like James's in 1914. Again let me say, I am not intending to preach Unitarians back into Calvinism, but I think I am not alone in feeling that however legitimately and rightly our culture has developed over the last three centuries, certain elements in our tradition, those which have gone for freedom, for private judgment, for doing what one will, all those which we may lump together under the rubric of "individualism," have been developed at the expense of certain other elements that once were equally a part of our tradition. There was, as we have remarked, a powerful sense of the individual and of his spiritual freedom in Puritanism, and it has correctly been praised as supplying the New England peoples with the vitality, the drive, that made them what they have become; but that freedom, that individualism which for many generations we have celebrated as though it were the whole story, once had sanctions which we have almost forgotten, and they were, by our more sensitive standards, harsh, grim, and rigorous. The individual had to work out his destiny, not in a world of comfort or of margin, not of security, but in a world where sin and death and strife were always upon him. If a man would be a Christian, he had not only to choose the church covenant, but to take up arms against the Devil, who was no mere figure of speech. The individual could be free only *for* ends, not *from* ends, and his liberty was achieved only upon terms. I do not need to dwell upon the plight of the world or the nation today. Certainly the creed of Channing is being, to say the least, challenged; the position of the liberal Christian, to call him still by his nineteenth-century title, is becoming uncomfortable. Is it, we must ask, tenable? That it is quite enough to be free, that it is enough to guard one's intellectual rights and powers and to consult the inward oracle, is not so clear as it once was, and there is, furthermore, the ugly suspicion growing and growing, that all the time we were preaching the freedom that would call no man master, something else was at work which we did not suspect, some plausible villainy that all the while was meaning and intending this present horror. The optimistic assumptions, which have for generations supported the growing liberalization of the Puritan tradition, have in the last two decades been subjected to a devastating analysis by the most sensitive of our poets and the most profound of our novelists; our philosophers have been challenged by psychologists, physicists, and biologists to make good the claims they have been so long advancing for the inherent dignity of man, and now two or three dictators and several thousand bombardiers have brought the challenge directly home to us, where face it we must.

But I have sadly mismanaged my statement if I leave you with the impression that I am preaching despair. I am trying, haltingly and with some embarrassment, to say that we do have resources, though not perhaps of the sort which Channing had in mind, not so much in ourselves as in our past, in Protestantism and above all in *our* Protestantism. If it is no longer enough merely to be free, but if we must say for *what* we intend to be free, then like the Puritans we shall devote ourselves to formulating anew the ends of existence. If in order to make those ends prevail we may be required to curtail our freedom, to surrender some of the more exalted pretensions which we have ignorantly and foolishly adopted, then again like the Puritans, who after a conviction of sin looked with scorn upon their formerly untroubled arrogance, we too shall put our chastened wills to the service of something that all along has been, and still is, greater than we are.

The Cambridge Platform in 1648

IT IS FITTING and suitable that we should signalize the three-hundredth anniversary of the Cambridge Platform. This is beyond all doubt a basic document in the American tradition. It is the pioneer formulation of the principle that a corporate body is created by the consent of constituent members. "This Form," the text has it, "is the Visible Covenant, Agreement, or Consent whereby they give up themselves unto the Lord." And it adds, "For wee see not otherwise how members can have Churchpower one over another mutually." Since this doctrine, or something very like it, is central in both the Declaration of Independence and in the Constitution, its first enunciation on American shores is a date to be remembered.

In these terms, as a charter of liberalism, the platform has been widely celebrated, especially during the last century. Indeed, eulogy has so often presented the framers as though already foreseeing 1776 and 1787 that there is required an insistent belaboring of the obvious to remind ourselves that Puritans in the Cambridge of 1648 had no such aims in mind. Had they at that moment been presented with either the Declaration or the Constitution, they would emphatically have repudiated both philosophies, and would

An address delivered at the Tercentenary commemoration of the Cambridge Platform, held October 27, 1948, in Cambridge, Massachusetts.

have denied that anything in their undertaking could ever possibly contribute to such a pagan result.

This is to say, the authors of the platform had no interest in political democracy or in religious liberty, and to them separation of church and state—as we understand the phrase—was a shocking notion. If the Congregational idea later became an ingredient in these ideals, that is because of the accidents of subsequent historical developments, for none of which can the Puritans of 1648 be held responsible. It is not an honest or an accurate celebration of the platform which speaks of it as though the seventeenth chapter, that on the civil magistrate, is not an integral part of the document, or as though when the platform says that the civil authority is to put forth his coercive power to castigate schismatical churches, it does not mean exactly what it says.

Furthermore, celebration of this anniversary, if it is to be anything more than pious oratory, must recognize that almost from the beginning the platform did not work. If this were 1748, and if we were noting the first centennial, we should be forced to acknowledge, however reluctantly, that the plan was a failure. First of all, it proved most tragically deficient, not to say evasive, concerning the status of children and of the children of baptized but unprofessing children. Within a decade the need for amendment became pressing, and the "Half-Way Covenant" was devised as a clarification of the platform, though many argued, with a fair show of logic, that this was a makeshift device to prop up a shaky vessel. By the 1670s, Solomon Stoddard at Northampton concluded that the whole structure was hopelessly rickety because it was founded upon a false hypothesis, namely, the church covenant. "There is no Syllable in the Word of God, intimating any such thing," Stoddard declared, "neither is there any need of it." By the time of his death, in 1729, Stoddard had detached western Massachusetts from allegiance to the Cambridge Platform; in 1708 Connecticut had followed his lead by adopting the Saybrook Platform, which was in fact a rejection, not to say a refutation, of the Cambridge. Then came the terrible explosion of 1740; whatever else the crisis of the Great Awakening proved, it assuredly demonstrated the impotence of the Congregational system to cope with internal disorder. Without a civil government prepared to assist the churches by such peremptory measures as the government under the old charter had not hesitated to employ, without such hard and resolute statesmen as Winthrop or Dudley to wield the sword, the churches could not discipline their people, keep enthusiasts under control, or protect themselves from the intrusion of countless "itinerants." In 1750, when Jonathan Edwards meditated migration to Scotland, he declared that he would have no qualms about accepting Presbyterianism because he was utterly disgusted with the confused, disorderly, independent system of New England. Of course, he spoke out of the special bitterness engendered by his ordeal at Northampton, but the way in which that expulsion was managed by his enemies, their prostitution of the church—in the name of old Congregational principles—to a family feud and to the community's lust for vengeance, left him, as well as many others, completely disillusioned with the Cambridge Platform.

We ought to become wary of the many incautious claims which a modern and unhistorical reading of the platform is apt to produce when we reflect that it was not until well into the eighteenth century—not until the rivalry between the commercial interests of the colonies and those of the Mother Country began to take shape—that the platform was interpreted as though containing those ideals of liberty and of the Bill of Rights which were later proclaimed in the Declaration of Independence and in the first ten amendments. That is, the platform was made over in men's minds in conformity with their changing political aspirations; it was interpreted in the light of the new social theory. But this does not mean that the platform itself was the source or the supplier of these conceptions. It is to say that certain features in the seventeenth-century polity proved compatible with an altered state of affairs, and that therefore these particular features, judiciously interpreted, could be enhanced by eighteenth-century patriots as being an expression in the realm of polity of what they were contending for in politics. This does not infallibly mean that the founders themselves designed to further what the eighteenth century came to feel—for reasons that are historically accountable—was liberality and freedom.

For example, in 1738, the Rev. John Barnard of Marblehead declared in a convention sermon that the civil power has no right to form churches, to ascertain who shall and who shall not belong to this or that particular church; he said that men have "a natural and religious right" to choose their membership, that they have "an unalienable Right to make the best of their Bibles." So, he concluded, if authoritarian principles ever come to prevail among us,

> I must have leave to lament over our Churches, . . . and to write upon them *Ichabod*, the Glory of New England is departed. For whatever Cry any may make of the Platform, and Congregational Principles, it is very certain that by such Means, the very Essence of Congregational Churches will be utterly overthrown.

Barnard's words are, no doubt, stirring, but on an occasion like this we should consider the circumstances. First of all, "Johnny" Barnard was one of those early rationalizing divines whom Edwards called "Arminian"; he really no longer believed in the Westminister Confession, but was one of the proto-Unitarians of the type of Chauncy and Mayhew. Second, while he was proclaiming the inalienable right of congregations, he was thinking not only of defending the immunities of churches against the threat of an American episcopate, but more particularly about protecting his prerogatives and those of his particular wing of the clergy against the accusation of heresy which the majority of the New England churches were ready to level against him. Thus the principle—which is indeed in the platform—of the independence of particular churches became for Barnard a weapon to be used in defense of what he already had. For him it was a negative principle of resistance, and what the concept meant in 1648 had conveniently slipped from his view. He no longer thought of the independence of the particular consociation of visible saints as a positive engine of regeneration or as a means of achieving a holy society. He was concealing—by a tactic which Edwards said was characteristic of the liberals and which he openly denounced as dishonest—the fact that the platform of 1648 declared emphatically that the civil authority must restrain and punish idolatry, blasphemy, heresy (of which he was then suspect), or that the magistrate is to put forth his coercive power "if any church one or more shall grow schismaticall."

We should further be wary in our use of terms during public eulogy—again, if we acknowledge a responsibility to historical accuracy—because the full-blown idealization of the platform as a pioneer prophecy of democracy and the Bill of Rights, veneration of it as the seed-bed of civil liberties, became the fashion only in the early nineteenth century. It was mainly—not entirely, but mainly—a creation of the Unitarians. The analytical historian can hardly avoid sensing a connection between their patriotic version of the platform and the fact that according to the principles of democracy—that is, as at Dedham, by the vote of a majority of the tax-paying parish rather than of the professing membership alone—they were getting their hands on a considerable amount of church property. It would, in other words, be a shallow, not to say a smug, manner of observing this anniversary were we to hail the platform as a landmark in the history of human freedom, but fail to show ourselves at least aware that liberalism in its eighteenth- and nineteenth-century character has recently been subjected to a manifold analysis which emphasizes its connection with certain limited social interests. I would agree that we have every right to be proud of the succession of great spirits who progressively made the platform over, until it has indeed become a symbol of freedom. On this occasion, they should be saluted no less than the first framers. But let us be free and scientific enough to recognize the process for what it was. Let us not betray ourselves by reading our own terms into the minds of Mather, Cotton, and Hooker.

Because, if that is all we are doing, we are praising only ourselves and not the platform as it was written or understood in 1648. I think my whole point can be epitomized by a small episode in the conventional interpretation of the early days of Massachusetts, an episode which would be too minute to discuss here except that the legendary approach has blown it into gigantic proportions. Hence profound issues of self-knowledge hang upon it. After the advance guard of what soon was to become the Massachusetts Bay Company arrived at Salem, in the winter of 1628–1629, the settlers suffered from scurvy; Deacon Samuel Fuller of Plymouth, who had studied medicine at Leyden, came up to help them. The following summer the church at Salem was organized, indubitably the first covenanted, Congregational church in Massachusetts Bay. Now, it is entirely a nineteenth-century version that has concluded, from these simple facts, that the Massachusetts settlers arrived with no notion at all of what they intended in the way of church polity, that they were confused and muddled and blundering, and that Fuller rescued them by telling them, out of the void, just how to set up a Congregational church. About the time this myth was taking form, in 1848 the Massachusetts Historical Society published a manuscript history written by William Hubbard in 1680, which does declare that these men were not beforehand molded into any order, that they were "like rasa tabula, fit to receive any impression that could be delineated out of the World of God." Since Bradford's *History* contained the letter Endecott wrote in 1629 from Salem, thanking Bradford for Fuller's help and saying that he had been satisfied by Fuller "touching your judgments of the outward forme of Gods worship," the story seemed wonderfully simple to commentators of the mid-nineteenth century: in 1629 Endecott obviously had not the least idea of what to do next until Fuller told him about the covenant. The doughty Puritan captain thereupon snapped it up, as though it were the panacea he had been hunting for all his life without being able to name it, learned the lesson overnight, and thus New England became a Congregational community.

This version has been refuted by modern scholarship, and it would be tedious to rehearse the detailed argument. Hubbard's *History* was composed under peculiar circumstances, and he so misrepresented certain matters that the General Court, which had commissioned the job, refused to publish it in the 1680s. There is every reason to suspect that Hubbard belonged to the party of appeasement in the struggle to retain the charter, and that he wanted to make out that the founders had not been too profoundly opposed to the Church of England. Indeed, the whole story of Deacon Fuller's influence reveals more about the mental world of the legend-makers than about that of the men who composed the platform. For one thing, the belief that the minds of the leaders were ecclesiastical *rasa tabula* until Fuller came up and wrote Congregationalism upon them leaves out of account the highly sophisticated metaphysical premises upon which the platform is constructed. When, for instance, the framers speak of visible saints as the matter, and of the covenant as the form, of a particular church, they are using the terminology of scholastic physics and logic; this technical vocabulary had for them profound meanings, and was not something improvised to suit a thesis so haphazardly acquired as the Fuller legend would suppose. It could not have been worked out to such theoretical precision even in the twenty years between Fuller's visit and the final drafting; the underlying philosophy of the platform lies deeper in the tradition and thought of the age than this, and only an epoch that has become obtuse to the immense implications of such terms as matter, form, essence and existence could so misjudge what must have happened.

Of course, when the actual composition of the platform was undertaken, there were political urgencies that compelled Richard Mather to seek for simplicity of statement. He tried as far as possible to play down the technical vocabulary; hence, in order that we may understand the implications of many passages in their context of 1648, we must read behind them the intricate metaphysical elaboration of Mather's own treatise on church government, or the even more subtle arguments by which Thomas Hooker, in *The Survey of the Summe of Church Discipline*, demonstrated the Congregational system to be at one with the system of the physical cosmos. If we really want to understand our origins—and if we do not, why should we hold this memorial observance?—we must take not the platform alone but the apparatus of scholarship which Hooker's great (and too much neglected) book supplies. It is shamefully to cheapen the dignity and majesty of his mind to suppose that he had not come to such a comprehensive "survey" out of a long and sustained intellectual effort that was well under way before he ever set foot in New England.

There is, furthermore, abundant evidence that Hooker, Mather, Peter, Davenport, and most of the leaders were fully possessed of the Congregational theory before their migration. In Holland they had acquired practical experience in administering the polity; they needed no advice from Plymouth, and had little to learn therefrom, except possibly to be surprised that Plymouth had translated the theory into such sane practice. (That is just what Endecott meant in his letter when he said to Bradford that the polity was "the same which I have professed and maintained ever since the Lord in mercie revealed him selfe unto me"; rumor had led him to doubt that the Separatists had actually grasped the idea, and so he was happy to assure Bradford that Fuller's account of Plymouth church was far from "the commone reporte that hath been spread of you touching that perticuler.") The Fuller legend disregards the biographies of the authors of the platform in the years before they set sail from Europe.

Furthermore, it errs unforgivably by leaving out of all accounts the great pioneers of the doctrine that finally was crystallized in the platform. These were not Separatists like Browne, Barrowe, and Greenwood, but learned and cautious scholars like Jacob, Bradshaw, Parker, Baynes, and above all the profound William Ames. In fact, the real begetter of the Cambridge Platform was this William Ames, who died in Rotterdam in 1633, just as he was about to migrate to Boston; had he lived another ten years, there is no question but that he would have stepped at once into the ecclesiastical hegemony of Massachusetts (in which case, it might have been Cotton instead of Hooker who would have found it advisable to go to Connecticut—though this is sheer speculation!). For the moment it is enough to remark that Ames's textbooks were the foundations of education at Harvard and Yale until the middle of the eighteenth century, that they were written well before Dr. Fuller visited Salem, and that there was nothing Fuller could tell such readers of Ames as Endecott, Skelton, or Higginson that they did not already know more clearly and distinctly than he could ever phrase it.

My point in all this pedantry is that the platform was not the whimsical or capricious result of a chance encounter. It was not a fortuitous creation; it was a summing up and a codification of a long development. The Fuller legend is fundamentally an insult to the intelligence of the founders because it assumes a conception of causality in history—or, if you will, of the proportions of God's acting as exhibited in His providence—which is discontinuous and irrational. It misses entirely the major fact that even before the "Agreement" in the old Cambridge in England, before the formation of the Massachusetts Bay Company, there were sixty years of hard thinking and formulation which, by the 1620s, had come to so fine a point of definition that a philosophical rationale already existed. Within it the enterprise could operate, and without it the enterprise could not have operated at all. Much of the success of Massachusetts Bay—its phenomenal success, that is, in realizing its intention—can be attributed to the coherence of this plan. Thus the platform of 1648, taken along with the masterly theoretical expositions of Cotton, Hooker, Mather, and Stone, is the outward and visible symbol of a matured dialectic. If you wish to celebrate that wherein the platform really was great, that wherein it had vitality in its own day, we must see it not as the prognosticator of the Declaration of Independence and the Bill of Rights, but as the end result, as a review and a codification, of the Puritan Revolution in England.

Here we can finally uncover, I believe, the motive that really inspired the nineteenth century's fixing upon the Fuller legend as the causal explanation of Congregationalism in Massachusetts, albeit the motive worked unconsciously. As long as the course of events could be presented as accidental, as a chance inscription upon *rasa tabula*, then the fully articulated and deep-plotted revolutionary intention of the founders was obscured. It was in fact obliterated. We could then say that the founders of Massachusetts were merely persecuted men, who fled from tyranny because they were against many things that the world agrees were bad, but that they were not actively or aggressively for anything except some vague "freedom." We could say that they were not social planners, but solid citizens who believed in free enterprise. So, being at heart liberals, they came to America with no idea in their heads except to get away from Stuart absolutism, and once here, they grabbed the first thing that was offered, which happened to be Deacon Fuller's charming sketch of how things were done in Plymouth.

In this connection we should begin to appreciate a peculiar manifestation of the Bay Colony's mentality between 1630 and 1646: its extreme, one might almost say its pathological, reluctance to put down in black and white any official announcement of what it stood for. While encouraging the ministers to publish (on their own initiative) disquisitions on the philosophy of the biblical polity, the colony went to obviously inspired lengths to keep from telling England or Europe what it was up to. We need little ingenuity to make out why between 1630 and 1640 the colony found it expeditious to follow John Winthrop's advice of letting laws grow "by practice and custom . . . as in our church discipline." It was not because he was an evolutionary pragmatist, but because he perceived how little was to be gained by exacerbating Archbishop Laud. A formal commitment to the polity that was vigorously being put into practice would be simply to challenge royal intervention.

In 1640, it is true, the situation radically changed. Parliament was summoned, the king was soon goaded into war, and by 1642 it seemed that the moment for which every Puritan for years had plotted and schemed was at last come to pass. The Revolution was about to take over. And then—most unfortunately and most incomprehensibly, according to the New England view—it began to be evident in 1642–1643 that the Revolution was being captured by a centrist party which at first showed every indication of being better organized, more capable of wielding power, than the group we call Congregationalists or Independents. As long as the conflict between king and Parliament hung in the balance, the two groups, the Presbyterians and the Independents, could not afford to split their ranks. The government of Massachusetts, by judiciously indicating its sympathy with Puritanism in general but by reserving itself from any commitments that might subordinate it to an ultimate Presbyterian triumph, retained its freedom of action and kept quietly on its own way. Once more, at the risk of becoming tedious, I must insist that a government which could so carefully pick its way through the quicksands of diplomacy was a government that knew from the beginning at what it was aiming and that had a mature resolution to win its objective.

Therefore the reason why the court finally determined to take a stand was given openly in the summons issued in 1646 for the calling of the synod. Posterity has resolutely refused to believe that the court meant what it said! The drama of the situation is not only that it did mean what it said, but that it was being forced to confess against its will, and was being compelled to undertake the one measure it had tried for sixteen years to avoid or to postpone, namely, the formulation of an established polity. "In as much," the court dared to say, "as times of publicke peace, which by ye mercy of God are vouchsafed to these plantations, but how long ye same may continue wee do not know, are much more comodious for ye effecting of such worke then those troublesome times of warr & of publicke disturbances thereby, as ye example of our deare native country doth witness at this day. . . ." In other words, to such men as Winthrop and Dudley it began to look in 1646 as though the game was up; sixteen years of peace and isolation were about to end in what might be a bitter fight, and the time had come to throw off pretense and prepare for battle.

There is no way of reading this pronouncement, in the light of the situation as it was known to the General Court on May 15,

1646, but that the court was obliged, however reluctantly, to entertain the prospect of a struggle, not with the bishops or with the Crown, but with that faction of their own party which then seemed upon the point of perverting the Revolution. Presbyterianism would create a regime, were it to triumph, that could not tolerate the existence, even across the ocean, of the New England Way. Actually the pattern of events conforms to an old and recurrent design in the history of revolutions: the most radical element is always ready to let the moderate radicals fight the initial engagements. Indeed, it is forced to do so, because the moderates are, at the beginning, a majority of the party. But the true radicals try to keep themselves in reserve until the moment arrives when the center is caught in the toils; then, and only then, is their chance to strike. New England's polity, among the many varieties of Puritan schemes, was the most coherently radical, and had behind it the prestige of a successful administration (having proved its ability to survive by beating down Williams and Mrs. Hutchinson). New Englanders spent the years between 1640 and 1646 waiting for the collapse of the Presbyterians, who to them represented a half-way house. But in 1646 they were beginning to doubt their strategy. Apparently they had miscalculated. Presbyterianism was about to win, and where Laud had never been able to make New England declare its principles, now the threat of a Presbyterian triumph worked what Laud could not. When it came to a final choice, New England must at last come into the open. The result was the document which today we praise, *A Platform of Church Discipline*. It was, in short, a manifesto.

All this is to remind ourselves of what now is hard for most Americans, especially for the children of Puritans, to believe: the Puritans came to Massachusetts Bay not so much to found the United States of America as to execute a flank attack on the Anglican hierarchy. In 1629 the situation in England had seemed hopeless, with Laud coming into power and the king having declared that he would never again call a Parliament. Obviously the Puritans were in for a long struggle, and they would be immensely strengthened if by going to Massachusetts they could set up a base from which, should the time ever come, they could launch an assault upon the bishops. Then, if in the mysterious working of Providence, it were to appear that the overthrow of the bishops must be long delayed, Massachusetts would remain a citadel and a refuge. Therefore silence and procrastination, combined with such diversionary tactics as the publications of New England clergymen, were the proper strategy up to 1640. There was always the hope that if Laud was staved off, then when the break came, the principles of Ames, Cotton, and Hooker would triumph in Westminster.

But in 1646 that hope seemed lost. If Presbyterianism was about to stabilize the Revolution short of the truly radical (or truly biblical) program, and was thereupon to constrain the minority, the Independents, into a new conformity, wherein new presbyter would function as old priest writ large, then there was no avoiding a clash between England and the Congregational colonies. This was precisely what the court meant by saying that 1646 was (for the moment) a time of peace, but that there was no telling how long the peace would last.

In this historical context, the court's determination to draw up a platform of polity was in effect a confession of failure: by committing the colonies to explicit statement the New Englanders acknowledged that they had lost the big gamble. They were now prepared to make do with the minor conquest of Massachusetts and Connecticut, but that much they would not surrender without a fight. Subterfuge was enough as against Laud, but as against their Calvinist brethren they would have no choice but open hostilities. The summons to the synod in 1646 was a preparation for war.

How real was the threat to the New England Way was shown by the Hingham affair—which produced Winthrop's speech on "liberty"—and by the Child petition, which being presented one week after the summons was clearly a Presbyterian counterreaction. Had there been a secure Presbyterian regime in England, to which Child could have appealed (exactly as the Sudeten chieftains appealed to Hitler), the home government would have taken its measures.

Of course, as things turned out, there was no such regime in Whitehall. In our own day we have learned how the earth trembles with the tramp of a dictator's troops entering some Vienna, Prague, or Paris. The citizens of London watched stolidly on August 6, 1647, when Cromwell's troopers rode into London, but the clatter of their hooves on cobblestone streets made music that was distinctly heard in Boston.

Unfortunately, the triumph of Cromwell did not mean quite all that the New Englanders hoped for, the triumph of a uniform Congregational or Independent polity or of doctrinal simplicity. Cromwell had unaccountably become corrupted with the newfangled heresy of toleration. But still, Cromwell would never mount an expedition to reduce Boston. Having called the synod, and having braced themselves to make a stand, the New Englanders had to go through with it, even though the urgency was removed. After two adjournments, the synod finally completed its work. Thus, living in the protection of Cromwell's sword, in August of 1648 it wrote the Cambridge Platform.

To call the platform a confession of the defeat of a great hope and the reconciliation to a lesser success is not to deny its historical grandeur, but rather, I fervently believe, to appreciate it for what it actually was, instead of for what enthusiastic oratory tries to make it. The struggle of the Puritans and the parliamentarians against the Crown, the court, the monopolies and the hierarchy is a vital chapter in the social revolution that finally produced modern England and America. In the specific circumstances under which the platform was written, the document inevitably expresses a stage in that revolution. It signalizes a point of rest in a process which could not be arrested. In that perspective, it is an effort to systematize and codify the reform so that, at least within the provincial limits, there could be a settled regime. But in the next two centuries the revolution refused to stand still. It continued in directions which the founders had not previsioned. It became more secular and more negative; that is, the religious hope was abandoned by surrendering all churches, first, to a policy of toleration and then to religious liberty. The modern revolution concentrated not on building up a positive, centralized society (which was the aim in 1648), but on protecting rights and immunities against the invasion of society. In this weirdly altered context certain principles of the Congregational system—the local autonomy of particular churches, their foundation upon the consent of members, and their right to conduct their internal business without political interference—took on charms that were not quite those they had offered to the founders. These concepts proved to have an immense power, but not of the sort their authors had in mind.

In one sense, then, they builded better than they knew. In another sense, they ought to have known better than they did. The philosophy of a religious uniformity maintained by the state was crumbling fast in England during the late 1640s. The New Englanders tried to detach themselves from history and to stabilize their segment of the Revolution. The platform was their way of saying to the tide of movement that it should come this far and no further.

Of course, they were attempting the impossible. Even as they composed the document, their own children, the first generation of native-born Americans, were growing up, marrying, producing grandchildren, and few of them were experiencing the reinvigoration of will which the system held to be the qualification for visible sainthood and upon which the whole edifice was erected. In their own congregations history was already taking a different and unforeseen turning. The authors of the platform were incapable of perceiving this fact, or were too obstinate to admit it. Richard Mather, the chief penman, did indeed live long enough to see the breakdown of the platform, and to lament the repairs and patchwork that became necessary.

But in still another sense, the founders may have been wiser than we suspect. If the democratic and liberal revolution of the intervening centuries twisted the platform into meanings that the founders did not intend, we have no assurance that the course of history has always been for the best. The most telling criticism of the New England Way launched by the Presbyterians of the 1640s was that it provided no machinery for converting or governing the ignorant majority whom it excluded from the membership, that it was incapable of bringing them under "the wholsom remedy of church-discipline." John Cotton answered this charge in the "Preface," trying not to make too much of it because he did not want to aggravate the issue between Presbyterians and Independents at home. Still, he said, the mass of the people in New England, although not allowed to become members if they show no visible signs of sainthood, are always present at the public ministry of the word—upon which they are invited by counsel, and required by wholesome lawes to attend." Furthermore, they are under the constant surveillance of the elders and the brethren. "What," he asked, "can Classical discipline, or excommunication it selfe do more in this case?"

By which Cotton meant that the pure and restricted churches of the Congregational order were not designed for the protection of immunities; in a society where the civil authority was dedicated to the Christian purpose, such churches would become engines for the regeneration of the whole community. The platform was still informed with the positive, aggressive expectation of Protestantism, with the certainty that the kingdom of God can be more closely approximated on earth than men hitherto had attempted. It made some allowance—though not too much—for the fact that the best of saints in this world are merely "visible" and so still subject to imperfection, but it did not hesitate to call for coercive discipline by the community upon those whose imperfections did not suit with the due form of government, either civil or ecclesiastical. The platform did not intend that the ignorant and unconverted, being excluded from the membership, could then go off in a corner and organize any kind of church they might devise. It did not intend that nonmembers should have the right to stay away from church services. The founders entertained the social hope, and their aim was a united, cohesive body politic, led by the saints, shepherded by the clergy and regulated by energetic governors, and fully prepared to use the lash of authority upon stragglers or rugged individualists.

We are not called upon to censure history. The Puritans always held that the course of divine Providence is inscrutable, and they wrote history—most notably as did Governor Bradford—in a contrite and humble spirit, seeking to decipher the meaning of events but never presuming to say that anything should have fallen out differently from the way it did. By the end of the seventeenth century even Increase Mather could begin to surmise that possibly God was working toward greater ends by forcing upon the saints a policy of tolerating religious difference than He might have entertained by blessing an intolerant, coercive uniformity. Yet the fact remains that when we go back to the platform, and when we read it for what it meant in 1648 rather than for what it has come to mean in 1948, we become aware that by the latter date a certain glory has departed from it. No one here would again advocate that the magistrate assume the power of punishing heresy, since few of us any longer know what is heretical; none of us expects him to put forth coercive power against schismatical churches, because we are all schismatics. But on the other hand, our society is not noticeably holy. Visible saints are few and far between, and while rights and immunities of churches are guaranteed both by law and by the now prevailing ethos, no one can say that the political and social expectation of the platform has been in the least realized.

I have said that upon the first centennial of the platform the consensus of informed opinion would be that it had not worked very well. I believe that in 1848 the suggestion of observing the anniversary was vetoed on the ground that the document was incompatible with free and democratic Americanism; at any rate, about that time, Leonard Woods wrote from Andover:

> The Platform is an ancient document; and though it was the product of men of powerful intellects, after much thought and experience, and though the Puritan fathers deemed it well suited to the wants of the churches in their day; it evidently needs a careful revising, in order to fit it more fully for general use at the present day.

Few of us would probably want the particular revisions that Woods had in mind. Yet it is worth imagining ahead for a moment as to how, conceivably, the platform will appear to the eyes of 2048. What has endured amid change for three centuries may well endure through still greater changes. Certainly, almost from the beginning, from within a decade after the drafting, the platform has called for constant revision; yet oddly enough, each revision has always been able to present at least a show of legitimacy. The Half-Way Covenant, the principle of democracy, the separation of church and state, have all been found compatible with the platform; they have even been shown to be contained, at least potentially or inferentially, in the original formulation. My own suspicion is that we have pushed to the limit those deductions which worked for individualism, inherent rights, and local autonomy. We have developed those implications at the expense, indeed with a total sacrifice, of historical objectivity, and so we have deliberately blinded ourselves to the social or corporate conception which is equally in the platform, which is explicitly in it.

Because the platform is a symbol for our society—of Western European society, or at least of Protestant society—at the precise moment when a balance between the corporate and the private welfare was being struck, it is altogether possible that another century of unfolding tradition may find future inheritors of the platform rediscovering in it ideals which the last two centuries have steadily neglected.

John Bunyan's Pilgrim's Progress

TO CHARACTERIZE *Pilgrim's Progress* as a classic of "devotional" literature is to misunderstand it. There is nothing devotional about it; in every intention it is a program for action and not for meditation. Only as Protestantism became less and less a principle for conquering the world, and more of a mode for coming to terms with it, only after Puritans surrendered their ambition to dominate society and contented themselves with the subjective assurance that, though exposed to temptation, they could still cultivate their gardens or their countinghouses without sin, only after they found methods to rationalize the making of money as a way, the pre-eminent way, of doing God's will on earth—only then did Protestants and Puritans begin to read *Pilgrim's Progress* in the privacy of their chambers as a work of devotion and inspiration. One can understand, given the historical context, how in nonconformist England or in Puritan New England of the eighteenth and nineteenth centuries, hundreds of workmen, farmers, and merchants found nightly reinvigoration by reading Bunyan, and went out in the morning refreshed with the assurance that by making a shoe, or plowing a furrow, or raising the interest rate, they were conquering Apollyon.

An address delivered as part of a series of Lenten lectures held at Phillips Brooks House, Harvard University, in February and March 1948.

But Bunyan had not written in any mild or consolatory spirit. Although the Restoration was a fact and the political program of Puritanism had been defeated, still Bunyan did not conceive of himself as the spokesman for a mere dissenting sect, and he did not accept the relegation of his theology to the status of a denomination. Nothing is more amusing than the way in which persons who have discarded the dogmas of Puritanism—persons as diverse as Bronson Alcott, George Bernard Shaw, or John Buchan—repeatedly announce the startling tidings that Bunyan is a writer of universal import. Actually he wrote in full confidence that as he perceived the world, so it actually was, and to him those who contented themselves with the merely devotional, or with the merely artistic, would be incapable of enduring the ordeal of Vanity Fair. Lord Hategood was to Bunyan not merely the harshness of a Philistine world, against which delicate souls could inwardly steel themselves by reading about Christian and Christiana, but an actual power, a *gauleiter* or a commissar, who put Faithful "to the most cruel death that could be invented." The worst mistake one can make about Bunyan is to read him, as did Macaulay or James Russell Lowell, as something quaint or as a delicious morsel of naïveté.

Furthermore, to discuss *Pilgrim's Progress* in a series of lenten observances is to offer it the final insult. To the man who wrote, "By law and ordinances you will not be saved," Lent was a law and an ordinance. Bunyan endeavored to show that every moment and every act is of equal importance in the drama of salvation; therefore those who set aside formal intervals for an extraordinary effort of piety were confessing a spiritual bankruptcy. Lent was Popery, and Popery, according to Bunyan's confident Protestantism, had grown crazy and stiff in the joints and now could "do little more than sit in his cave's mouth, grinning at pilgrims as they go by, and biting his nails because he cannot come at them." Heavenly truths are a gift of God, and "no man attaineth to them by human industry"; mechanically to set aside a portion of the calendar and expect that by so automatic an appointment zeal can be engendered is to be like Talkative: "All he hath lieth in his tongue, and his religion is to make a noise therewith." When men make observances coincide with seasons, they may be certain that they have become formalists who plead "custom" for what they do; such men, when they come to the Hill Difficulty, are sure to end up either in Danger on the one side or in Destruction on the other.

In short, we think of *Pilgrim's Progress* as a classic, either of devotion or of literature, because we do not understand it, or would not believe it if we did—assuming, for the moment, what Bunyan would question, that we can understand it without believing it. Despite all his warnings, Bunyan's artistry betrayed him and his book lives as a drama. We call it an allegory, and feel free to speak of it as we might of *The Faerie Queene*, *The House of Seven Gables*, or a detective story. Since it is at least next door to fiction, why not, on occasions like Lent, pick it up? To read it as a curiosity of a vanished era is to gloat over such charming metaphors as: "Even as the mother cries out against her child in her lap, when she calleth it slut and naughty girl, and then falls to hugging and kissing it"; but by this manner of appreciation we insulate ourselves against having to consider the point which the metaphor enforces, the by-no-means quaint thesis that as men are currently constituted, they are capable of crying out against sin in the pulpit even while abiding it in the heart and house.

However, we can plead somewhat in our own defense that in Bunyan's day, and with readers of his own persuasion, the book almost immediately achieved an ambiguous kind of popularity, which compelled him, six years after the "exposition of method" he had prefaced to Part I, to commence Part II with a further defense which is in effect a reluctant confession of how far his success had miscarried. There are some things, he was driven to arguing, that by their very nature make "one's fancy chuckle, while his heart doth ache." He had run the hazard that the chuckle of fancy, although legitimate, could not be separated from the concern of the heart; most of the appreciation of Bunyan within the last century has tried, and failed, to reawaken the chuckle, and even so perceptive an admirer as Shaw, although hailing certain stirring passages because they "make the heart vibrate like a bell," is reticent about the ache. All this might amount to no more than a failure of historical perspective, to be remedied by renewing our sense of the seventeenth century, were it not for the ironic fact that modern science, biological and physical, has posed anew an artistic problem that has everything in common with Bunyan's. For Charles Darwin the expanse of nature—the sun on the river bank, the bird on the bough, the worm in the earth—becomes a marvelous and ingenious symbol which must be read simultaneously both for the play of surface phenomena and for the laws of life (the not very rational but the scientifically indisputable laws of selection and survival) at work behind the appearances. The physicist commences with a visible universe, all its elements defined and classified in a table of atomic weights; but he must also perceive that such formulations are masks for deeper formulae, the quantum mechanics and the mathematics of fission, formulae that defy the canons of reason and are accessible only to the professional elect. The artist today cannot escape, though often he tries, the central challenge of the age, by which the concrete and particular fact cannot be denied reality and yet must be treated as not sufficient in itself, as the manifestation of a truth or a law which, if ascertainable, will probably prove repugnant to the norms of rationality. The Puritan, of course, was not worried about the scientific issue, but in the moral universe his insight was essentially that of the biologist and the physicist: that is, he insisted that the existing world is terribly real, and yet he viewed it as standing for a meaning to be found out only by analysis. Nothing is easier than to say that he was a crude Platonist viewing the world as allegory, but in fact he was by tradition just as much an Aristotelian, and so always insisted that things are first of all the particular things they happen to be, and only thereafter symbols of the law. And when the accounting was made, the law turned out to be an insult to reason, such a scandal to logic as predestination and reprobation, which presented as many logical complexities as do natural selection and atomic fission. Within a few years of Bunyan, Isaac Newton persuaded Western culture that particular facts are simply cogs in a universal and wholly rational mechanism, so that the problem which was at the heart of *Pilgrim's Progress* could be dismissed as vulgar superstition. Our present failure to comprehend Bunyan, after the Newtonian mechanics have at last become provisional, is a failure to comprehend ourselves; after Darwin and Einstein, we have been forced to realize that the confidence of the Enlightenment was premature, and so we are obliged to face once more the awful paradox by which men must speak in concretes and yet by feigned words "make truth to spangle and its rays to shine."

The Puritan version of this paradox was, of course, crude, but at the risk of making it even cruder, we may attempt a blunt paraphrase: an unfortunate, a maddening fact of existence, yet (since all actual existence must be finite) an inescapable fact, is that eternal and abstract truth always comes to the human perception in some specific dress. The attractiveness of the dress thereupon becomes an invitation to love, but if the mind is so beguiled by love that it does not pierce the disguise and discover the proposition, it wanders among empty similitudes. On the other hand, if the soul becomes absorbed in the proposition alone, and so fails to love the specific which embodies the truth, it perishes no less. By this complex method of conveyance men receive revelation itself; but even with the Bible in their hands, through their incapacity for understanding the double-edged nature of language, they take its metaphors for the substance and repeatedly are undone. When Faithful expounds the metaphor of the unclean beast as a description of Talkative, Christian replies, "You have spoken, for aught I know, the true gospel sense of those texts." There is one unchanging and unmodifiable sense, but the expression, in the concreteness of existence, can be—inescapably must be—various. "Things deep, things hid, and that mysterious be"—such are the verses of Scripture, the phenomena of science, and the actions of men. The route from the City of Destruction to the Celestial City is essentially the same for all, and roughly the same landmarks are encountered by all, but each pilgrim meets them at different times and under different conditions; Christian goes through the Valley of the Shadow of Death in darkness, but Faithful has sunshine all the way, and Christiana gets past with relative ease because she has Mr. Greatheart for a conductor. The Interpreter's House sets forth the themes of systematic theology—atonement, faith, repentance, election, justification, reprobation—but the particular charades for any one doctrine are innumerable. Christiana is later shown the same tableaux, but, such is the fecundity of representation, still others can be got up, like the man with the muck-rake; there is no limit to metaphor, and illustration can be multiplied forever—which is plausible enough if one reflects that, in order to achieve the specific, Being must become first one thing and then another. For a world to take shape, it too must become a metaphor, and therefore any or all of its parts will, to those who are in on the secret, bear metaphorical relations to other parts. Only in pure chaos would "types, shadows, and metaphors" be unthinkable—or else in the Godhead Himself. Hence existing human beings confront, in the universe of experience, a terrible and never-ending paradox.

In his Apology for Part I, Bunyan addressed himself in advance to his critics, assuming that in his day they would universally condemn what modern commentators have most praised, his realistic imagery. He imagined his contemporaries crying out against his feignings: "They drown the weak; metaphors make us blind." He insisted that readers should perceive how full his book actually is of abstraction: "Must I needs want solidness, because by metaphors I speak?" To prove that the concrete may be used in the framing of propositions, he invoked the Bible or the experience of everyday life, wherein metaphors constantly serve as bait to catch the imagination and so attract the mind. But even while couching his anticipatory apology, Bunyan showed an awareness that he was indeed running the danger of sacrificing the abstract for the concrete, and that for his readers this might equally prove a danger:

> Take heed, also, that thou be not extreme,
> In playing with the outside of my dream.

Bunyan did not have to protest, as does the modern theorist, that art must be grounded in the concrete; he took that much thoroughly for granted, and on such an assumption argued the still more difficult position, that the concrete pertains to the general.

> Put by the curtains, look within my veil,
> Turn up my metaphors. . . .

To turn up his metaphors is to enter into a truly strange world, stranger than any of the weird sights along the pilgrim's path, so monstrously strange and terrifying that we need not ask why thousands of Bunyan's readers have rested content with the outside of his dream. A taste trained by the modern novel or by modern poetry is hardly qualified for the forthright sort of looking within the veil to which Bunyan invites it. Our complexity cannot cope with his simplicity, and his complexity is too subtle for our simplifications. The easiest way is to call him an untutored allegorist and to let him go at that. In college courses, Bunyan is taught as a forerunner of the English novel who attained to realistic passages, but who, unfortunately, wrote in a genre which is no longer to be taken seriously. Symbolism yes, but not allegory!

There is, of course, another way of salvaging Bunyan, and much, if not most, of the recent approving accounts is—not to put too fine a point upon it—sentimental gush, or as Shaw expressed it, "patronizing prattle." In England there has lately grown up a vogue for seeing in Bunyan the incarnation of broad-bottomed, bully-beef-and-ale England, the England of Squire Western, Winston Churchill, and Ernest Bevin. Undoubtedly this version calls attention to something that is actually there, something not sufficiently appreciated in the nineteenth century, but it also errs by leaving out an essential element. He was a self-educated tinker, but he was also a man who lived in anxiety. And why was he miserable? I think the answer is writ plain for any who will take the trouble to put by the curtains of his metaphors; to see him as mainly the solid English yeoman, just as to see him primarily as a teller of tales or as the author of devotions, is to see him in a role congenial to what Reinhold Niebuhr calls the easy conscience of modern man; it is to do what Bunyan pretended no one does—"None throws away the apple for the core." It is, for the sake of the literary core, to throw away Bunyan the theologian.

The easy conscience of modern man would have an easier time with *Pilgrim's Progress* if only Christian had labored all the weary journey with that burden on his back, if he had lost it only at last when he reached the Celestial Gate or had had it washed away in the river that flows before the Gate. But Bunyan's—and the Puritan's—point is that the river of death does not exist in order to cleanse filthy souls; it exists for the ultimate discovery, that "you shall find it deeper or shallower as you believe in the King of the place." As for the burden of sin, that ceases to be a problem almost at the beginning; it is got out of the way by the time the real pilgrimage commences. As soon as the Interpreter has taught him the elements of theology, Christian feels the burden tumble off his back; a mark is set upon his forehead, and the prevenient roll, with a seal upon it, is put into his hand to be delivered at the Celestial Gate. Entrance upon the journey is easy—"We make no objections against any, notwithstanding all that they have done before they came hither." Christian's difficulty is not his doubts about getting there, but the actual getting there. His anxiety is not concerning whether he will or won't be saved; it is the anxiety of living with the certitude, of working out the given. How far is it to the Celestial Gate? "Too far," say the Shepherds, "for any but those that shall get thither indeed." There can be no pilgrimage for those who are not actually going to succeed, no such thing as a story of failure. Ignorance comes to the very Gate of Heaven, but what he experiences along the way constitutes no adventures. The anguish of living is not uncertainty; it is living in relation to the already accomplished. "I was clothed with the armor of proof," says Christian. "Ay, and yet, though I was so harnessed, I found it hard work to quit myself like a man." The wages of battle is not victory, because victory is as early as it is late. The quest is not for the Gate but for the right to the Gate; Christian fights the good fight to find out "what in that combat attends us," and this no man "but he that hath been in the battle himself" can tell.

Study of the Puritan mind has convinced me—though I should be hard put to produce "scientific" proof—that there is a close, an inevitable connection between the predestinarian theology and the literary method of Bunyan's allegory. In *Pilgrim's Progress*, as in *Grace Abounding* or in *Mr. Badman*, Bunyan is not giving a narrative; he does not attempt biography or autobiography as we comprehend the terms. He gives instead the analysis of a timeless situation in order to discover what elements enter eternally into it. In this trait of mind he shows himself most thoroughly the Protestant and the Puritan. One might say, assuming the phrase to be an adequate description of the theology of the book, that it is a treatise on justification by faith—which would be, as far as it goes, true enough, and yet would leave unanswered the question of what in the book is specifically Puritan and not just Christianity in general. The falling off of the burden and gift of the roll do indeed tell Christian that he is justified by his faith, certainly not by his deeds; for all he has done so far has been to get himself a wife and children, then run away from them with his fingers in his ears—a flight that has been indignantly denounced as selfish indulgence—and plunge himself into the Slough of Despond. Surely not, as a politician might say, an impressive record! But what is so peculiarly of the Reformation in Bunyan's treatment, as opposed to either Catholic or evangelical formulations, is the assumption that an event which takes place outside of time must be experienced by man somewhere inside time, even though the experience involves a realization that the event must lie as much before as after the moment of experience. The tremendous strength of early Protestantism was its persuading of frantic humanity that they need not constantly be buying indulgences, rushing to the confessional, or burning candles, because there is a point where the thing actually is settled, where time and eternity do touch. This did not mean, for true Protestants, that with assurance the struggle was over and no sin thereafter mattered; on the contrary, it meant that the real fight had only begun, because man is a creature in time and of time. If justification by faith had meant a reward given at the end of a journey, after a life of effort had proved the man's faith, faith would be another name for works; if it meant that for the faithful conflict was unreal because election was certain, there could be no such thing as a faith whereby men might be justified. No wonder Ignorance, when these mysteries are expounded to him, prefers ignorance to such "fruit of distracted brains." But Bunyan had no intention of overcoming Ignorance by persuasion. Ignorance, either in the book or among the readers, could remain ignorant only by willful insensitivity once he had perceived by dramatic realism that neither in the City of Destruction nor in the Slough of Despond could Christian rid himself of his burden, but that he could be relieved after he had visited the Interpreter's House and learned that the world and all its creatures are symbols of significances which, once lodged in the mind, are "as a goad in thy sides, to prick thee forward in the way thou must go." What in theology is a logical riddle of fate and freedom becomes in the realm of art a resolution of assurance and effort.

If the problem for faith, therefore, is to learn what is already known, to work out what is already given, to live with what is already accomplished, Bunyan would be obliged to strive for metaphors not to catch the kind of fish who bite on anything, but to snare those who "must be groped for, and be tickled too." If the undifferentiated truth is so incommensurate with human reason that all its formal statements must perforce be logical riddles, how else is the Puritan writer, with his acute sense of the ineluctable modality of the visible, to convey his meaning except in "dark and cloudy words"? Or rather, no matter how solid the words or how earthy, what can words ever be except dark and cloudy to those who have looked upon the mystery? "Not Honesty in the abstract, but Honest is my name; and I wish that my nature may agree to what I am called." So the duty of the serious reader is to leave the laughter and literary criticism to boys and fools, and instead, "Do thou the substance of my matter see." Otherwise, by all the normal principles of reason, the archetype of the true pilgrim would be Ignorance, and his the proper pilgrimage as we would have to conceive it on solid and substantial earth:

> I know my Lord's will, and I have been a good liver; I pay every man his own; I pray, fast, pay tithes, and give alms, and have left my country for whither I am going.

What possible justice can there be in condemning such a man? Is it any answer to argue,

> God saith, those that no understanding have,
> Although he made them, them he will not save?

Hopeful understandably lists among the incidents that have reminded him of his sins, "If mine head did begin to ache"!

In the same spirit Hopeful hesitantly replies, when Christian asks him if he is following the discussion, "I would know where we are." We are, I believe, close to perceiving that if we are the sort of fish who must be groped for, we must see in *Pilgrim's Progress* the biography not of a character, like Tom Jones or David Copperfield, but of man outside time, which is to say, of the innermost man who, like the Freudian Id, never grows old and learns little by experience. Only then will Bunyan's fancies "stick like burrs," and only then will we see that his dialect contains "nothing but sound and honest gospel strains." The book is, to use an overworked term, psychological analysis; it is a study of the fluctuations that follow upon illumination, of what Kierkegaard calls living in an absolute relation to the absolute. How joyful was this man when he recovered his lost certificate (which of course cannot be lost), "for this roll was the assurance of his life and acceptance at the desired haven!" But how, we still are asking, can predestined assurance even seem to be lost? That is not the point, answers Bunyan; it is after—not before, but after—Christian has his roll that he first confronts the Hill Difficulty. "Do you not find sometimes," asks Prudence, "as if those things were vanquished, which at other times are your perplexity?" A prudent question indeed! But it takes more than Prudence to handle it. The delicate plain called Ease gives much content, "but that plain was but narrow, so they were quickly got over it." In the midst of perplexities, even when we struggle up to the very Gate of Heaven, we shall find that the men whose raiment shines like gold and whose faces shine as the light will tell us that they can give us no help in such a case, for the waters are deep or shallow according as we believe in the King of the place.

In the light of this analysis, we may perhaps see more deeply into the shrewdness of George Bernard Shaw's remark that in *Pilgrim's Progress*, "the whole allegory is a consistent attack on morality and respectability, without a word that one can remember against vice and crime." There is no personified representative of the thief or murderer, the adulterer, blasphemer, or usurer. One and all, the unregenerate, like Mr. By-ends, maintain principles that "are harmless and profitable." They are men warned by affliction, who take forethought to secure life and estate, sincerely venerate a religion "that walks in his golden slippers, in the sunshine, and with applause," and all of them make a show of pilgrimage, some of them enduring as far as, and even beyond, the Delectable Mountains. (They often make a pious observance of Lent!) They live sanely amid solid, three-dimensional objects: "Houses, lands, trades, places, honours, preferments, titles, countries, kingdoms, lusts, pleasures, and delights of all sorts, as whores, bawds, wives, husbands, children, masters, servants, lives, blood, bodies, souls, silver, gold, pearls, precious stones, and what not." There are no out-and-out criminals. There is no Whoredom, but only Morality, Legality, Civility. Whoredom is an achievement of Morality, along with honors, preferments, wives and husbands. The customs of Christianity and of Vanity Fair are "diametrically opposite," and when Little-faith is robbed, his jewels are not taken because in that country they "were not accounted of." Bunyan went to considerable pains thus to underscore, from every possible approach, the lesson that Christianity is not merchandise, with the result that he became a household classic among the most merchandising kind of Christians that history has yet thrown up.

There are those who contend that Bunyan was born a literary artist and then was cast away among Puritans; they argue that he was condemned by his time and place to compose allegories, but that nevertheless, because he was invincibly an artist, he broke through his form and succeeded in becoming a realist. They devise critical distinctions between the kind of allegory which is an extended metaphor and the kind in which personifications are crushed under the weight of secondary meaning. Bunyan is conceded to have developed an extended metaphor, but only because he stayed closer to reality than to secondary meanings, and obviously the moral is that allegory on the whole is not a profitable genre. I think Bunyan would be the first to admit that he did not always walk successfully the razor's edge of this aesthetic. "I, for my part, have been in the fray before now; and though, through the goodness of him that is best, I am, as you see, alive, yet I cannot boast of my manhood." There are barren passages where he becomes too explicit, and in others he waxes so concrete that his Apology must be read as self-criticism. It is indeed hard to take joy in the inconsequential behavior of the young mother with her child and yet keep firmly in mind the theological rebuke that she incarnates. The second part, the pilgrimage of Christiana, written after Bunyan was out of prison, has generally been regarded as something of an anticlimax: try as she will, Christiana can hardly come up to a strenuous journey through time, and she remains a sprightly widow flouncing about the village, her adventures not strung out across a geographical expanse but limited to her innumerable crossings of the Common or to her daily shopping expeditions in the High Street.

Still, granting these shortcomings, Bunyan's strength is simply that the discriminations of theorists were not his guides. His effort was to put the temporal into relation with the eternal, and that he wavered between them follows not from his effort to keep the metaphor close to reality but from the violence of the tension to which he was subjected. He transcends allegory not because he was a thwarted realist but because he was a man employing time to defeat time, and telling a narrative which at heart is not a narrative. So he made the fact that the sinner is justified at the beginning, that the saint commences with a certitude "of my going in after all," that Despair can torture in the dungeons of Doubting Castle only those who have the key of the Promise already in their bosoms —he made this anticipation of the climax actually dramatic. He gave aesthetic suspense to a foregone conclusion. And therefore he remains a challenge to all hastily conceived programs, meliorative or revolutionary, in which salvation is to be somehow manufactured, a challenge not to their effort but to their motive. Let them answer this conundrum if they can: the only thing you can ever hunt for is what has been given you. Mr. Money-love proves that a man who gets results by becoming religious thereby gets what must be good; Christian is confident that "even a babe in religion may answer ten thousand such questions." Mr. Money-love, says Christian, makes religion a "stalking-horse" for his enjoyment of the world, thus using a standard metaphor of the Puritan preacher, but pushing the analysis deeper than any sermon. The Puritans lived on intimate, if not always comfortable, terms with paradox: in their business and their farming they were utilitarians, and if they used means to get an end, God allowed them so to operate; but they had to be aware constantly that in divinity the end is given first, and that the fascination and terror is furnishing it subsequently with means. In the strength of such an insight, the balance of the concrete and the abstract takes care of itself—as in our own day Franz Kafka has once more shown—to the disturbing of the complacent opinion which had agreed that allegory no longer would do.

This sort of speculation was not congenial a hundred years ago to Edgar Allan Poe, who jolted pious and respectable Americans by telling them that *Pilgrim's Progress* was a "ludicrously overrated book." I think that as they were reading it, Poe was right. It would be idle to argue that a book is a great book only if readers accept the theological prepossessions of the author; if so, the book is at best a sectarian tract. Still, to be read, *Pilgrim's Progress* has to be understood, and Calvinism has always contended that the invincibly ignorant are proof against every persuasion. Wherein Bunyan's real success consists may become more evident if we single out Henry James's comment on the sometimes unfortunate, even grotesque, excesses of Nathaniel Hawthorne, who, James said, was perpetually looking for images which could be put by main force into correspondence with spiritual facts. "In such a process discretion is everything, and when the image becomes importunate, it is in danger of seeming to stand for nothing more serious than itself." The question which every reader of Bunyan must answer is whether the images stand in such danger. To me it is apparent that they are not importunate. Bunyan did not look for images; he excluded them. The intensity of his conviction took care of the discretion. He did not need a set of critical principles to tell him the difference between a false note and a true, for to him nothing could for long be serious merely in and for itself.

Again we are led from the problem of technique to that of meaning. We may legitimately correlate Bunyan's stylistic success in uniting his symbols and his theme with the fact that when Christian contends with external foes, he is always a hero. When the ordeal is internal, he fails. When there is a physical, objective enemy—Apollyon, the court and jailers of Vanity Fair, the floggings by Giant Despair—Christian never flinches and returns blow for blow. But this valiant hero also falls asleep and stupidly forgets his roll; in the Valley of the Shadow of Death the blasphemies proceed from his own mind; he follows Vain-confidence against his own judgment, and he leads Hopeful with him. "Good brother, be not offended; I am sorry I have brought thee out of the way." Must the elect, even with the mark on their foreheads and the scroll in their hands, repeatedly beg forgiveness of those that love them and adhere to them? If they put their companions into imminent danger, can anyone be trusted? Is an outer triumph always the sign of an inner dislocation? Does he who overcomes Apollyon have to confirm his valor by falling into stupidity, confusion, and cruelty?

Evidently he does. How then does he avoid irrevocable and absolute failure? Surely the chances of going astray—either in life or in fiction—are all too numerous, and once Christian is not engaged in combat or suffering, he is as wrongheaded as a man can be. *Pilgrim's Progress* would be an infinitely less powerful, or puzzling, book if at this point it surrendered Christian to some heavenly guide and introduced at all his bunglings a lovely agent of the grace that was predestined to look after him. Then it would be more susceptible to the now fashionable condemnation of allegory, and could more neatly be bound in the vellum of obsolescence. But Christian never finds it that simple: by pursuing Vain-confidence, he stumbles into the precincts of Giant Despair, and must thereupon suffer the consequence of his own folly. The inexorable logic of the symbol is terribly consistent, and Bunyan's anxiety was so compelling that he never needed to go out and hunt for images: none could become importunate by standing only for itself because for him symbols were thrown up by the agony of his suffering and his repentance. Christian, it is true, is never destroyed, but not because an allegorical angel hovers over him; he is saved because, in the midst of folly, he can always recognize his own foolishness for exactly what it is, and can always give it a name, the right name.

Another way of putting it would be to say that although Bunyan as a preacher was a self-conscious workman and, as the two versified Apologies make clear, knew what technical devices he was using, he was not so self-conscious that the problem of discretion, in Henry James's sense, was ever a problem for him. He was not arbitrarily choosing images to stand for something other than themselves; he was suffering under the images that the spiritual terror thrust upon him. "The solving word," said William James, who perhaps had more in common with Bunyan than did his brother, "for the learned and the unlearned alike, lies in the last resort in the dumb willingness or unwillingness of the interior character and nowhere else." Dumb willingness is something that is apt, upon being logically expounded, to become even more dumb; but Christian with a scroll in his hand does not need exposition: he simply has the willingness. This is the truth that is unsuspected by Worldly Wiseman, who will not meddle with things too high for him, or by Talkative, who sees no difference between crying out against and abhorring sin, or by Ignorance, who has to ask how we can tell whether our thoughts of ourselves agree with the Word of God. Literal-mindedness undoes them all. They take the word for what it says and the world for what it seems; they do not search behind appearances, they follow the literary trend and think allegory is outmoded. Either they identify the thing with the thought or they separate the concept from the object; they are idealists, naturalists, imagists, or impressionists. Says Paul Valéry:

> Among the victims of liberty are forms and, in every sense of the term, *style*. Everything that requires a training, . . . all that leads, by way of discipline, from the liberty of refusing an obstacle to the superior liberty of passing beyond it, all this is endangered, and glibness smears the world with its works. A real history of the arts would show how many novelties, how many so-called discoveries and audacities are merely disguises worn by the devil of the line of least resistance.

These emancipated individualists do not understand that the multiplicity of appearance flows from the fountain of simplicity. They settle on one form of existence, one profession and one attitude, and they become that one, never any more than one; they are, to the exclusion of all other traits, either obstinate or pliable, timorous or ignorant.

Bunyan's mastery of what Henry James meant by discretion is nowhere better exemplified than in the seldom-appreciated fact that the procession of unregenerate characters makes a progression in a rising crescendo: Christian begins with Obstinate and Pliable, works his way past Worldly Wiseman, Formality and Hypocrisy, Talkative and the denizens of Vanity Fair, By-ends, then Atheist, and so finds that up to the very last he is dogged by Ignorance. For in Ignorance all the characters are summed up, in him they culminate; they approach him as a limit and a norm. His is indeed the supremely false pilgrimage, but his is the most difficult to confute; he gets the farthest, he crosses the waters and even knocks on the Gate for the admission he assumes will be given him. Only Ignorance can offer the final demonstration that even from the Gate of Heaven, as well as from the City of Destruction, there is a way to Hell. That indeed would be the one thing Ignorance could never know!

What Ignorance possesses instead of knowledge is inward assurance: "My heart tells me so." But what is this, if not what Christian also has? What is there in the sinner that is not in the saint? So similar are the assurances that no subtlety of hypocrisy can come so close to holiness as does simple Ignorance, and yet the difference is fundamental. What never fails Christian, in contrast to all the others, is the intuition of the self. Something within him, he himself, appraises his own stupidity and measures it by a never-varying rule. He never lets himself off. All the depraved characters are what they are because of a deficiency; they are *deprived* of something because they have stifled the spontaneous intuition which is Christian's salvation. Therefore Christian knows them all, as they cannot know themselves or each other. Christian has what William James incautiously attributed to all of us, the gift of knowing "off-hand that such philosophies are out of plumb and out of key and out of 'whack' and have no business to speak up in the universe's name." According to Bunyan the universe speaks to Christian first through the knowledge of the burden on his own back, and then through the knowledge of why he must still press on after that burden is lightened, through all the suffering of the way, even though the roll of assurance is in his hand. None of the others, from Pliable on, knows himself, and none of them knows what he is doing, and none of them knows that he doesn't know, and the most sublimely oblivious is Ignorance, for he insists, "I will never believe that my heart is thus bad." Knowledge, full knowledge of the self, not the unclouded respect for himself which is Ignorance's delusion, but knowledge of the whole self, in its grandeur and its loathsomeness, this alone will save the hero. This alone can be, both in time and out of time, the meaning of election. Come along with us, plead Christian and Hopeful of the men in shining raiment, as they are at last within sight of the Gate and are about to descend into the waters; the men assure them that they will abide—"But, said they, you must obtain it by your own faith."

Education under Cross Fire

I call therefore a complete and generous education, that which fits a man to perform justly, skillfully, and magnanimously all the offices, both private and public, of peace and war.—*Milton*

This education comes to us from nature, from men, or from things. The inner growth of our organs and faculties is the education of nature, the use we learn to make of this growth is the education of men, what we gain by our experience of our surroundings is the education of things.—*Rousseau*

IF EVER AN IDEAL molded a society, it is the American belief that the more education a child can get, the better. If there is an American credo, this is its primary article. In 1837 Horace Mann, the prophet of the American system, declared that already time had ratified the soundness of "universal education through the establishment of free schools." Michigan's Chief Justice Thomas Cooley wrote in the Kalamazoo decision, "We supposed it had always been understood in this state that education, not merely in the rudiments, but in an enlarged sense, was regarded as an important practical advantage to be supplied at their option to rich and poor alike." Education, he insisted, voicing what by mid-century was the axiomatic identification of school with democracy, is not some-

Written for *Years of the Modern*, an exploration of the crisis of modern man and society in the aftermath of World War II.

thing "pertaining merely to culture" which only the wealthy may enjoy, but something essential to American society.

The growth of an America that in Mann's day had barely entered upon the most massive material expansion of history can be charted in the mounting statistics of the "advantage": nine million in the common schools of 1878, sixteen in 1898, twenty million in 1920; a hundred thousand in the high schools of 1878, seven hundred thousand in 1900, and then seven million in 1940; in 1914 one college student for every twenty-five persons of collegiate age; in 1940, one out of every seven on some sort of campus. Horace Mann, extravagant idealist, never dared dream of so stupendous a universality.

The America of the future will not be the America of the past without an educational graph that continues, both absolutely and relatively, to rise. "Not only," said the Biennial Survey of 1918, "should college education be open to everybody, but nearly everybody should have it." It is only since that date that this proposition has been widely questioned. Henry Adams, a disgruntled man, dying that year, declared the wonder of education to be that it did not ruin everybody, teachers as well as the taught; but John Dewey, who at the turn of the century attempted to assume the mantle of Horace Mann, said that a society for which stratification into separate classes would be fatal "must see to it that intellectual opportunities are accessible to all on equable and easy terms." If, then, by the middle of the twentieth century there is reason to scrutinize this historic affirmation, in the very existence of that doubt our Republic now faces a dislocation in a basic tradition.

It may help, therefore, if we can arrive at a definition, or at any rate a description, of what role education has in fact played in this democracy, at least since, under Andrew Jackson, the society began to call itself democratic. Leaving aside the explanations of a hundred supposedly definitive (although competing) textbooks of "educational sociology," I propose the blunt observation that there was early thrust upon the American educational system a dual obligation, and that the endeavor to satisfy simultaneously both these demands is now resulting in a state of tension best described as advanced schizophrenia. Two loyalties, heretofore considered compatible, have begun to diverge, and the antinomy amounts in effect to an epitome of the age.

On the one hand, American schools exist to service society. They replace the dying elders. This truism would hardly need comment did not the most widely used textbooks of teacher training—products of Schools of Education where the obvious is never left unaccounted for—begin their exposition of this social function with a preliminary demonstration of the appalling disadvantages of perpetual life—with which elementary calculation we must begin. But the question, which is not so obvious, is: for *what* society does the school train society's recruits? The present uneasiness over the plight of education arises from the fact that only in the last decade has this question been seriously thrust upon the American people.

In colonial New England, where our public school tradition originated, service to society meant training ministers. A child learned to read and write so that he could ultimately preach sermons. Those not destined to such dignity went a limited distance along the educational way, and upon reaching their limit—as the majority quickly did—fell off into being farmers or merchants. True, Puritan education, still medieval in form, included John of Salisbury's ideal of the education of princes, or at least of magistrates, within the more comprehensive aim of forming priests. The New Haven Hopkins Grammar School was dedicated in 1684 to preparing youth "for ye Colledge and publique service of ye Country in Church and Commonwealth." Thus magistrates were students who had gone (or should have gone) a good distance on the road, but who stopped short of the final goal; nevertheless, they had not, in order to become servants of the Commonwealth, been separately instructed. The educational hierarchy, from dame school to Harvard College, was so constructed that those who persevered to the summit automatically became ministers. After God had carried us to New England, said the founders of Harvard, and we had obtained the necessaries of livelihood and a civil government, "One of the next things we longed for, and looked after was to advance Learning, and perpetuate it to Posterity; dreading to leave an illiterate Ministery to the Churches, when our present Ministers shall lie in the Dust." To train ministers was thus the purpose of education. It was not concerned, for example, with suggesting to young men that they fly kites in a storm, to discover, by any act so ridiculous as knocking their knuckles against a key on a string, whether there be a consanguinity between lightning and the mysterious stuff of electricity.

In the nineteenth century the conception of a free society preempted that of a literate ministry. New states beyond the Alleghenies wrote into their constitutions: "Knowledge and learning generally diffused through a community being essential to the preservation of free government. . . ."[1] Education must be universal, said Mann, because while it is good that the wise discover new truths, it is better that truths already discovered be spread among the masses. "Diffusion, then, rather than discovery, is the duty of our government." In its fine simplicity, this sentence is the classic statement of what for over a century has been the controlling aim of American education.

Of course, there was a philosophy behind it. Mann was close enough to Puritan sources—although a "liberal" in theology—to conceive the mission of universal diffusion upon the premise of original sin. Republican institutions, he argued, offer scope for the nobler propensities of mankind, but at the same time they stimulate the "lower order of faculties belonging to the human mind." Freedom, in short, excites appetites and arouses passions. If these are not tamed—Mann deeply impressed this doctrine upon our educational inheritance—then the very liberty which is our glory "will hurry us forward into regions populous with every form of evil." Only one institution restrains us from this looming disaster; Mann paid tribute to the clergy as checks upon depravity, but to him it was clear that in the nineteenth century education alone could save republican society. It alone could catch the child in his impressionable and innocent years, and mold him to the Republic's desire.

The shift of emphasis from Horace Mann to John Dewey indicates, no doubt, an immense intellectual revolution; yet Mann, despite his theological idiom, is closer to Dewey than to the founders of Harvard. Both he and Dewey call upon the schools to make a kind of citizen who, because of his training, without any supernatural assistance, will behave in ways useful to society. Discarding the last vestiges of the notion of sin, Dewey in 1916 called education "a continuous reconstruction of experience"; in the psyche of the student, his theory and Mann's would work the same effect. The drying up of a sense of sin did not break the progression of American theory from Andrew Jackson to the present. Education

[1]The Constitution of Indiana (1816).

serves society by equipping children to take a decent and efficient part in the national prosperity; if Dewey's version stresses the efficient more heavily than the decent, in either case the terms are interchangeable, and inefficiency merely becomes the new form of sin. In both conceptions, education is not preparation for a remote future, not a preliminary acquisition of tools to be used by the mature preacher, but a device through which society insures that freedom will not be abused. The student is not about to enter society; he has already been seized by it, and school days are already communal experience. Because the schools alone instill into impressionable youth the norms that hold the society together, that prevent the chaos which otherwise would be the consequence of freedom, education can—nay, absolutely must—be made universal.

So the drive behind the American ideal of a universally diffused education has not been just a fine sentiment; it has been a vital thrust of the whole community, an achievement of cohesion. Only with this perspective can we comprehend the otherwise miraculous growth in the last fifty years of the schools of pedagogy. The Normal School and the Teachers' College are manifestations of a deep-seated persuasion; they owe their ready triumph over legislative committees and school boards to the fact that these were already imbued with it. So much fun has been made of the "educators" that it would be impertinent to compound an impotent satire. What should be emphasized is the promise they have given of making the schools efficient, on the widest possible scale, in everything from music appreciation to the cooking of cabbage. America would indeed triumph over the defeatism of the past if classroom activities might be so geared into actual life that the graduate, furnished with a reconstruction of experience, could enter smoothly into the responsibilities of adult citizenship. Without recognizing the depth and sincerity of this expectation, we cannot begin to understand contemporary America. No doubt the Normal Schools have also maintained a skillful lobby, and now hold so effective a monopoly that they constitute a major industry; but they could not have imposed a single regulation requiring such and such a "course unit" as the prerequisite to promotion, had there not already existed in the minds of legislators a profoundly democratic conviction that the schools should be so conducted as automatically to produce exactly what America wants.

It is easy enough to construct a satire on educational sociologists merely by quoting their textbooks, their "blueprint," for example, of the "Optimum Citizen" and of the "Domestically Efficient Person." Burlesque itself can hardly improve upon the latter: she should "be able to bathe, dress, and otherwise care for the baby," and also "be able and disposed to keep the home free from flies and vermin." What more logical, therefore, than to give courses on these recondite subjects, measure them in hours and credits, and offer M.A.'s which in turn lead to raises in salary? It is important to remember that such forms of instruction carry out, in meticulous detail, the American conviction that education must qualify persons for real life; flies and vermin do not, after all, belong in the American home. Again, it was Horace Mann, struggling against the now inconceivable amateurishness of the Massachusetts schools, who delivered in 1838 a radical lecture, "Special Preparation, a Pre-Requisite to Teaching." Precisely because all children are not alike, he said, but differ according to "substructures of temperament and disposition," there is every reason why education must not become stereotyped, and consequently why teachers must have professional training. "Every teacher ought to know vastly more than he is required to teach." A hundred years later, the natural working out of this observation was legislation that imposes upon the teacher, before he or she be certified, so many units of "educational psychology."

Far-reaching though the effect—or the strangle hold—of the Schools of Education has become, another development within the schools themselves, especially within those of "higher" learning, offers a still greater exhibition of how they have been adapted, or adapted themselves, to the requirements of society. In ordinary parlance, this is called "specialization." It cannot be diagnosed only as an occupational disease. Not so much did the vast increase of knowledge produce this result as did the American conception of how knowledge can be made available to the democracy, of how it might, if the word is permissible, be packaged. The transformation at the end of the nineteenth century of the college into the university was a response of the American spirit to the over-ruling injunction of the age. When duty whispered low, Thou must, the colleges replied, We can, and articulated themselves into departments, and then into "fields" within departments. The American record of proficiency in two world wars, let alone in household appliances, is testimony to the success with which the educational system not only met, but even anticipated, the challenge of modernity. Its end-products were happily able to cope, well enough to wage successful war, with the paper work of bureaucracy, the logistics of steel, and (with some immigrant assistance) the fissionability of uranium.

By 1880 or 1890 the need was for skills. How strong was the pressure is illustrated less in the physical sciences, where specialties inevitably developed, than in the humanities. The old-fashioned course for the senior year on moral philosophy, taught by the college president, suddenly became the Department of Philosophy; for a brief period held together by a few magnetic personalities, it soon found itself parceling out its functions as though it were chemistry. Specialists in social psychology, intellectual history, anthropology, mathematical logic, semantics, and basic English took over investigations that had languished under a too purely contemplative love of wisdom. In literature, the result was even more disastrous: dates, sources, influences, textual criticism became the subject matter of modern language instruction, and a proficiency in philology was made the qualification for an ability to teach Shakespeare and Keats to American youth.

There were great teachers who resisted these tendencies, and who still spoke intelligibly to laymen, but they usually suffered from a paucity of students. The candidate for the Ph.D. chose to work under a professor who could recommend him for a specific job. There remained fewer and fewer on the faculty who felt, as Morris Cohen put it, "responsibility for the student's total view of the universe." The university became an assemblage of experts who respected each other's preserves. Hence the professors of education had a mandate to bring order into the primary and secondary schools by planning the curriculum and telling teachers how to teach—though, of course, not *what* to teach! The democracy was pleased, because on the lower levels means were adapted to ends, and on the higher the desired professionalism was secured. To the extent that education in a democracy must service the immediate needs of democracy, the American schools up to World War I more than fulfilled their obligation. The record was something to be proud of; it had not been imposed by authority, as in Prussia, or been attained as in England by virtue of class distinctions. Jude the Obscure was inconceivable in America. Commencing even in the Puritan theocracy, where the rendering of scholars serviceable to the community as well as to God was first suggested, the ideal of diffusion ran through the centuries with an ever-increasing purpose, and the twentieth century promised to realize it to the full.

2

If this relationship to society were the sole dimension within which the problem of education were posed today, if the only criterion were "service," it could safely be entrusted to the experts. Most histories of American education conceive it within this single frame, and formal discussion concerns itself only with ways and means for "implementing" Horace Mann's diffusion. The ease with which the professionals take their mission for granted reveals what an immensely inarticulate major premise it has become. Even the revolt against specialization that has appeared in the last decade, the movement for "general education" or for the "common core of culture," justifies itself on the plea of social utility. Apologists explain that because the contemporary scene has become complex, there must now be found principles of unity, so that all Americans may converse. The Harvard report, *General Education in a Free Society*, argues that to counteract multiplicity we must pitch upon an island of unanimity in order to save our communal sanity. While the high school "reflects dimly like a clouded mirror the diversity of our society itself," it is also evident that democracy "depends equally on the binding ties of common standards." Hence the report recommends inserting into the curriculum an "organic strand" of general education.

On the surface, all this seems no more than the swing of the pendulum in a direction opposite to that of a half-century ago. If the issue in education today were no more than a shifting of ballast, it could be comprehended in a merely historico-sociological context. American education would appear to be overhauling itself in order to render still more extensive services to society than it did in the past generation when it rushed into precipitous agreement with Professor Dewey that instruction should be a "reconstruction of experience."

But between the lines of these pronouncements there is to be detected another theme, which can hardly be dissociated from certain other phenomena in the realm of education that do not altogether accord with the story of ever-triumphant diffusion. The advocates of common purpose glance aside from their proposals to the low salaries of teachers, to crowded classrooms and inadequate installations, and toward the indifference, the astonishing callousness, of the populace toward these deteriorations. They cannot argue their case without at least skirting the undemocratic proposition that all students are not biologically capable of the utmost education. They do not sound the tocsin for universal diffusion; they lament the vulgarizing effects of the radio, films, television, the comics and the tabloids. Nor can the spokesmen for unity dissociate their campaign from the problem of "academic freedom." Their manifestoes are haunted by the memory of portentous cases, the array of which grows with the years, and their claims for the organic strand suddenly become confessions of a failure of accord between the schools and the people. In the background lurk the spectres of teachers' oath bills, legislative hearings, unrenewed contracts for nonconformist instructors, and reputed decisive actions of trustees. There is the distant echo of Veblen's growl that businessmen have replaced the clergy on governing boards. The movement toward unification of the cultural heritage cannot be interpreted simply as an intramural reform of the course offering; there is a suspicion of lines forming for a showdown. There is a broad hint that, possibly for the first time in the existence of the Republic, the pursuit of knowledge, far from being an obedient servant, may find itself at odds with the society that has supported it.

To understand the situation, we must look at the history of American education from a point of view different from that inculcated by the historic rationale. In this light, the school system has a different story to tell, one that is only incidentally related to its servicing of society. While it has indeed been occupied with the preparation of citizens, it has also devoted itself to an activity that might be best described as domesticating the disreputable. Or, if that seems too strong, as bestowing reputation upon unreputable ideas that it could not otherwise ignore. The schools have seldom performed this function well, and never gracefully, but however timorously or belatedly, they have done it. Yet—and here is the irony—this unplanned intrusion, rather than their success in attaining universality, constituted their inward being. They have experienced a constant renewal, a succession of new leases on life, or escapes from stultification. Again and again, confronted with a new doctrine, a shattering discovery, a shocking literary fashion, the schools have, after an interval of resistance, come to terms with it, and eventually undertaken to teach it.

The arch-example of what a quarantine against the fructifying contagion of the outside world does to education is undoubtedly the English universities of the eighteenth century:

> Feuds, factions, flatteries, enmity, and guile,
> Murmuring submission, and bald government,
> (The idol weak as the idolater,)
> And Decency and Custom starving Truth,
> And blind Authority beating with his staff
> The child that might have led him; Emptiness
> Followed as of good omen, and meek Worth
> Left to herself unheard of and unknown.[2]

The intellectual history of Britain in this era is a dynamic chapter, but it can be told with barely a mention of the colleges. Intelligence flowered in coffeehouses and taverns, in salons, and in Grub Street. The Royal Society was a focus for science, but the schools ignored it. The universities in all conscience served a useful function and they also turned surplus younger sons into dull curates. But the life of the mind was something else. It required in the nineteenth century a reform imposed by a Royal Commission to turn the currents of discovery once more into the universities.

A republic, Horace Mann contended, cannot afford institutions with limited objectives. It has no place for schools that draw aside from the currents of life. There is not enough money, even in a rich democracy, to maintain a mandarin ritual, and there is no market for the product. For better or worse, American graduates must run the gauntlet of American life. This nation has not yet reached the stage—call it civilization or decadence—wherein it can waste education upon younger sons alone.

Thus, paradoxically, the American schools discovered, in the first place, that they were linked to a democratic society by the neces-

[2]Wordsworth, *The Prelude*.

sity of insuring freedom. In the second place, they found that they could not, even if they tried, circumscribe their notion of what constitutes freedom. The challenge has come to them from the outside, from quarters not academically respectable; often it has come from Europe, and their resistance has been fortified by xenophobia. That the American schools have proved, on the whole, receptive is possibly a contribution to our culture more important than their conquest of astronomical numbers. In every case, the impact forced an internal shake-up. It opened up new ranges of experiments or of courses—it even raised up new teachers. By this process American education has been invigorated, not by buildings, stadia, or even by increases in administrative staffs.

Periodically, the schools forget this, but they have never been allowed to vegetate in comfort. They have been obliged, often to their chagrin, to catch up. Whenever they have settled down with the satisfied certainty that they were manufacturing the optimum citizen, they have been rudely jolted from without. They have had to atone by incorporating into an expanding course program what at first they scorned. They have discovered that even while servicing the society, they were forced to explore topics which, at least when first broached, seemed by the official standards of that society to be simply scandalous.

The Harvard community of the 1830s may be taken as a miniature model of the American experience. Having stabilized an intellectual revolution, sloughed off Calvinism and converted itself to "liberal Christianity," the college was devoting itself to the service of society by raising up urbane scholars, of whom Holmes and Lowell were the paragons. Yet at the acme of its complacency a number of the undergraduates found themselves acquiring two separate educations—the one vended by the faculty, and the other surreptitiously acquired from their reading of imported books by Coleridge, Carlyle, Cousin, and the German romantics. This generation, one of them remembered, were never really interested in their college work, although their careers were determined by it, but were much more devoted to "pursuits outside the curriculum." Through the historic proclamations of Emerson this band became articulate, whereupon the great pundit of the Divinity School, Andrews Norton, excoriated them as "the latest form of infidelity." One of the infidels, who for years had been struggling to keep alive a church in the business district of Boston, replied in 1839 that he could no longer speak the language of his professors. His generation, he explained, having been brought "into contact with a great variety of minds," with "men of discernment and acuteness" outside the college, had there learned that the formal liberalism of Harvard was half-hearted and its metaphysics obsolete. They beheld vistas to which Coleridge and Carlyle, considered by the faculty despicable and dangerous, were better guides than Professor Norton. Emerson delivered the sentence by which not only Harvard education of that time, but all American education since, must be judged (remember that he spoke of the "clergy" as the representatives of scholarship rather than of piety): "I have heard it said that the clergy are addressed as women; that the rough, spontaneous speech of men they do not hear, but only a mincing and diluted speech."

In the lexicon of 1949, Transcendental talk may not seem to have captured the rough conversation of men, but it came closer than that of the Harvard faculty. For thirty years after *The Divinity School Address*, Emerson was an outcast from Cambridge. By now the moral is clear: by excluding Emerson, Harvard injured only itself; hence it does sorry penance by naming the hall of philosophy after him and teaching him in "survey" courses. He is even read, if not understood, in the high schools, and students find it quaint that he was ever considered subversive. Today, of course, the pace is faster; the schools are not granted decades in which to accustom themselves to radical ideas, but must act within months. While educators draw up blueprints for the optimum citizen, students are bombarded with ideas which, from the point of view of the blueprint, excite a lower, or at any rate a different, order of faculties. If diffusion means the diffusion only of mincing and diluted speech, especially if it means only the jargon of professional educators, there will always be found channels outside the schools for making audible the spontaneous conversation of men.

In science, as in literature, the impetus to discovery came from outside the academy. The schools here responded with more alacrity, since the utilitarian appeal was stronger, but the process of accommodation was much the same. Again, the problem was not so much one of diffusion as of knowledge itself. "Hard hands," wrote Abbott Lawrence in 1847, while offering to endow Harvard with a scientific school, "are ready to work upon our hard materials; and where shall sagacious heads be taught to direct those hands?" By agreeing to furnish the heads, American education was again servicing society, and Lawrence was insistent: "Let theory be proved by practical results." Still, experience soon demonstrated the practical worth of theory, and pure science was fostered by applied. The democracy accustomed itself (not too easily) to indulging scientists in the disinterested, even if expensive, quest of discovery for its own sake, on the chance that they would turn up a profitable theorem. The astonishing hospitality of the schools to Darwinian evolution, as contrasted with the hesitations of the pulpit, and to evolution's progeny, sociology and anthropology, indicated the strengthening within the system of a conception of knowledge as something which might be pursued without always calculating the tangible benefits. Since the turn of the century, the efflorescence of this ideal has progressively been less and less inhibited by the elder one of a universal diffusion subserving a merely efficient citizenship.

The historian of the future will assuredly behold in the decade of the 1920s an explosive era in the history of the American mind. By continuing to call it the Age of Wonderful Nonsense or of bathtub gin, we willfully conceal from ourselves how drastically it severed modern America from the nineteenth century. The schools and colleges notoriously failed, at first, to grasp what was happening; Mencken's barrage against the pedagogues was altogether in order. But in the subsequent years, the profession has again done penance, and more vigorously than in the 1830s. Though this is oversimplification, it is still not quite extravagant to say that the multitudinous reforms of the last decades amount to a conscientious effort of the academicians to systematize and to regularize the impact of the Jazz Age. Which is to say that once again they have been preoccupied with the secondary but persistent function of American education, of domesticating the disreputable. In a democracy, education feeds upon, or is fed by, the hurly-burly, the sprawling turmoil, of an ebullient culture.

3

On the very page where Horace Mann proclaimed that diffusion and not discovery is the duty of government in education, he also declared, "A love of truth—*a love of truth*; this is the pool of a moral Bethesda, whose waters have miraculous healing." It did not occur to him that the quest of truth would lead into those realms of appetite and passion against which it was the purpose of education to guard. In his mind there was no possibility that the regions populous with every form of evil would ever be confused by a republican society with the regions of scientific, economic, or literary investigation. Nevertheless, in his formulation and in a myriad others after him, American education was serenely dedicated to the service of two masters: "the advancement and diffusion of knowledge." Down the years, diffusion—measured in numbers, buildings, laboratories—carried advancement on its back. Discovery floated on the tide of expansion. But today the spokesman for education does not hit upon Mann's confident accent; instead, he is more apt to sound as though bracing himself for a grim ordeal, and to say, with President Seymour of Yale, "We seek the truth and will endure the consequences."

What consequences must be "endured"? What is the implied threat? Were it only that conventional or received opinions must be upset, the past century assures us that such crises can be weathered. Is it that demagogues and investigating commissions raise the cry of subversion? There are strong bulwarks against such attacks. The obligation to be independent, said President Killian in his inaugural address at the Massachusetts Institute of Technology, lies upon all our institutions of higher learning. All educators know this, and know that the devotion to intellectual discovery is not only nothing to be ashamed of, but is rooted deep in the truly American tradition. Though newspaper headlines make much of this or that episode, periodic attacks upon academic freedom are nothing new, nor would the recent outbreak be anything more than a recurrence if it were not revelatory of forces at work beneath the surface, forces deeper and more pervasive than merely demagogic frenzy.

The real threat to education is the fact that America is entering upon a phase of social evolution different from any we have known. "In a period of armed truce," President Killian continues, "the fundamental principle of academic freedom is subject to stresses which we have not met before." Others more outspokenly call it "cold war." Cold or hot, war is war, and does not encourage heresy. Energies must not be dissipated. The prospect before American education is baldly this: the spontaneity of the environing society, which has hitherto provided the impetus toward the advance of knowledge, which has supplied the courage for adventure, may be stifled. A nation committed to static defense, to a dread of innovation, to anxiety, may gird itself for global conflict, may gear its laboratories to industry and its classrooms to the military, but will it do so by paralyzing the sources that hitherto have imparted the incentive to exploration? If the wind is no longer to blow where it listeth, will American education remain education in a free society? If Mann's innocent sentence, that the duty of government is diffusion and not discovery, is to mean that, under pressure, discovery must be curtailed, then diffusion, no matter how effectively it be preserved, ceases to be the diffusion of education. If the grinding of the wheels means that the ineffable qualities of discovery must be sacrified for the brute quantities of diffusion, then the educational crisis is indeed more than a matter of programs and numbers. The illiteracy rate may be reduced to zero, but a diffusion that does not carry with it the excitement of discovery, though it may have clear prescriptions for the optimum citizen, will become an assembly line for the production of serviceable robots.

Apprehension deepens into trepidation when, along with such reflections, we consider what effect the economy itself appears to be working upon the educational establishment. Although it now seems that the total number of school children—which in the late 1930s, for the first time in our history, declined—may for a while increase, the relative ratio as against the total population is going down. Obviously connected with this fact is the shortage of teachers. Benjamin Fine estimated in 1947 that over the previous seven years, 350,000 abandoned the profession. The reason might be supposed simply to be that they were not paid enough, but Professor Seymour Harris takes us to a deeper and more ominous level of explanation: as the rewards of those occupations which require educated employees have shrunk, we find ourselves with an oversupply of them, and we can no longer recompense them on a scale commensurate with that of tradesmen and laborers. Thus, by a logic which requires an economist to comprehend we seem to have too few teachers because we have too many.

Uneasiness on such purely economic grounds has been anything but quieted by the government's post-World War II generosity to the veterans. That program is itself a supreme witness to the deep hold upon the American mind of the historic conception that a state's duty is to make education as widely available as possible; it incarnates the pervasive conviction that whoever has a claim upon society best receives recompense for lost time and the confronting of danger in the form of education. Thousands of youths who in 1941 would have been content with a high school diploma, upon perceiving that a college education was a help toward acquiring the superior comforts of an officer, came home from the services resolved to get a college degree. In the four years since the V-Days, the economy has absorbed these graduates more easily than economists anticipated, but the rate of production continues. Who would dare to promise that in the next years all of those whom the democracy has rewarded according to its traditional lights will automatically step into the "advantages" they expected? In the midst of the Depression, out of the heart of Middletown, rose the cry recorded by the Lynds: "I think we've been kidding ourselves in breaking our backs to send our children to college. There just aren't enough good jobs to take care of all the college graduates." That in the America of Jefferson and Mann and Lincoln such a lament should so much as be whispered proclaims the end of an era. If this is a sign of the times, it amounts to sounding a retreat from the democratic ideal of education universally diffused. By a curious twist in history, democracy itself is brought to the point of suspecting that the ideal of diffusion, which for over a century was assumed to be synonymous with the very being of democracy, is no longer obvious, or is even admirable.

Within the schools themselves, this "retrograde" movement—if the word be not too strong—is being hastened by a corrosive conviction that education simply cannot be given to all in equal degree. The Schools of Education devise finer and more intricate, and possibly reliable, methods for measuring "primary mental abilities." Psychologists and "counsellors on careers" accentuate the withering doubt, that the masses are not universally educable. Few of them—as yet—say it too loudly, but out of their classifications the implication emerges. The noble old American faith appears riddled. The prospect is no longer for indefinite expansion, but for shrinkage and contraction, for reconciliation to the notion of an inferior training for the many, while guarding the superior for an elite who must be prevented from becoming so numerous as to force down the level of wages. By no stretch of the term can such a program be called democratic, and should the nation bring itself to proclaim this philosophy, it will have difficulty convincing even itself that it is any longer a democracy. "Restricting the body of knowledge," says Albert Einstein, "to a small group deadens the philosophical spirit of a people and leads to spiritual poverty."

It is, therefore, as a part of this pattern of constriction that assaults upon academic freedom take on their more serious meaning. These are not merely the results of jittery trustees, congressmen, and chambers of commerce; they are steps toward the curtailing of the content of research and instruction. They announce that there are forces now at work in the American democracy which are far from assured, as was the age of Jackson and of Lincoln, that education can do harm to nobody, and that the more of it anybody can get, the better citizen he will be. In the motto I have prefaced to this essay, John Milton spoke for the Puritan revolution of the seventeenth century; as that revolution became the industrial development of the nineteenth, the conception reached down from the middle classes to the populace in general, and so the doctrine of education for citizenship was extended to all. But as America is suddenly thrust into the position of a very great power—of *the* great power—fears arise lest the American way of life be endangered. Thereupon, the assumption that education prepares citizens is transformed into a demand that it prevent Americans from entertaining or even examining subversive ideas. The investigators undoubtedly are patriotic men, but the result of their investigations is certainly a limitation upon the free play of mind, an effort to confine education to certain limited, definable, and frankly nationalistic ends.

Hence the American educator in the year 1949 is caught in a tension of forces which play upon him with peculiar severity because upon the schools coverge the issues of civilization. A shift has been insensibly wrought in the meaning of the traditions, and it is no wonder that educators are bewildered. On the one hand, the tradition of social service, which has hitherto been one with the belief in universal diffusion, is being transformed, before our eyes, into a program of restriction and limitation. But the tradition of a disinterested devotion to knowledge for its own sake, which originally had distinctly aristocratic connotations, contends for democratic freedom in the face of the democracy's hesitation. The conception of a complete receptivity to all ideas or fancies, no matter whence they come, which Rousseau opposed to the classical Miltonic conception of education for the offices of peace and war—this conception now insists that curtailment is death, that career must be open to talents, that everybody must be trained to the utmost of his capacity. And this conception now thrives, not alone upon some Rousseauistic fervor, but upon the hard experience of the last century, which has persuaded the researcher and the teacher that a steady growth of knowledge is health, and that the slightest inhibition is fatal.

The predicament of the conscientious educator is indeed agonizing, the more so as he is convinced that it is an epitome of the whole civilization. He is the victim of historic forces that have altered their characters. Hitherto diffusion and discovery were pursued simultaneously, because they were entirely complementary: in fact, diffusion supplied the margin within which discovery could operate. But a reversal of diffusion will certainly bring the threat of a narrowing of the field for discovery. An economy of contraction—whether it be the result only of an overproduction of scholars or also of the retrenchments imposed by an armed truce—is not compatible with a policy of intellectual expansion. Discovery is outgoing and improvident, and will risk any idea or experiment; retrenchment is not. Discovery requires ever new materials to work upon; a nation frozen into a cold war will not readily supply them. America, above all nations in recorded history, has thus far embodied the reason working experimentally and experientially; it had a continent to exploit, and no limits to its wide-flung shores. So it built schools and colleges. If it has suddenly become in effect an island economy, and the space between its coasts has violently shrunk, then the pressures will surely be exerted upon the educational system. It, along with the rest of the culture, may try to seek safety in rigidity.

If the history and experience of America mean anything, they mean that such a course foretells disaster. History is littered with the corpses of civilizations that reached the limit of expansion, dug in behind walls and moats, and there yielded to decay. There is still no evidence that America is irrevocably caught in a determined cycle of rise and decline. The instruments in our hands, the resources, the difficulties already surmounted, are immense. No society ever reached the end of its expansion with so much trained intelligence to command, with so many potentialities for understanding, and thus for transcending its predicament. American education has paid dividends so incalculable that the nation has not yet begun to tap them, and has accumulated the mightiest reservoirs of knowledge ever put at the disposal of a great power. It is not written in the stars that discovery must necessarily perish, even though it now seems possible that discoverers may have to fight for the right to discover.

In this situation, the educator, if he is to preserve his self-respect, has little or no choice. If the end of the era of indefinite expansion has indeed come, then he must stand, more firmly than ever he felt he would be called upon to stand, for the freedom of investigation, for the principle that nothing, not democracy itself, and not even the American way of life, is so sacred that it cannot be studied, analyzed, and criticized. Furthermore, the results of such criticism must continue to augment the content of education. The accumulation of knowledge cannot be arrested; the educator will be, it is assumed, loyal to his country, but he will manifest that loyalty by meticulously remaining faithful to the pursuit of learning, and to the transmission of learning to posterity, no matter how many conflicts this devotion may lead him into. Unless he is to surrender entirely his function, and to become merely an instrument of national policy, he must keep alive a passion for knowledge that is first and foremost its own excuse for being, and take the position that under present conditions, this insistence is his major responsibility to the future of democracy.

Of course, much depends on events, on the hazard of peace and war, but still more depends, in American education, upon the teachers themselves. Inside the schools, in the libraries and laboratories, in techniques and scholarship, in the hard-won freedom of speculation, in the American itch of curiosity, they have enough to draw upon, enough energies to maintain the pace of discovery. There is no guarantee that the powers making for constriction are invincible, and there is no assurance that a slackening of numerical diffusion must inevitably signify the end of innovation. It has not yet been conclusively demonstrated that this democracy is incapable of understanding what is happening to it, that it will abjectly submit to an undemocratic conception of education simply because economists argue that this is the only recourse. It may not accept the new definition of the socially useful, and it may not forever subject its teachers to hysterical tests of "loyalty." There is a kind of invigoration that comes with contending against society for the welfare of society, and of this paradoxical strength American education now stands in desperate need.

It is altogether possible that the great democratic God, to whom Herman Melville prayed in similar extremities of doubt, may disregard such seemingly incontrovertible facts as quantitatively accurate measurements of primary mental abilities. There may be—who knows?—enough average qualitative ability, along with a little give-and-take, to keep education going as a democratic venture. Or there may be, if only the educators will keep it alive. In the present posture of affairs, the future of American education—and so of the republic itself—hangs, above all other considerations, upon the courage, the devotion, and the vision of the teachers themselves.

What Drove Me Crazy in Europe

IN EVERY SESSION where Americans and Western Europeans meet—ECA conference, North Atlantic Pact, Fulbright board—the American representatives sit opposite a row of university-trained Europeans. The American delegate may be—he generally is—a man who, as we say, "happened to go" to college, although he won't give that fact much thought. His fatal error—I have seen it frequently—is to assume that his opposite number is the same sort of fellow.

The European didn't just "happen" to go to the university. He is a man with a status. He is aware of it. When you get to the basic patterns of thinking—beneath specific opinions or arguments—you find that he reasons, or still more feels, as a man conscious at every moment of status. Furthermore, he knows little or nothing of American scholarship. There are exceptions, but in general his fundamental structure of mind has not been altered, although he may have been much grieved, by what has happened in Europe in the last generation.

Those who make the decisions in Europe also make the opinion, and these determiners, in politics or in business, are a corps of university graduates. Unless the structure of European society is to

Perry Miller served as guest professor at the University of Leiden for the academic year 1949–50. This and the next two pieces are his reflections on that experience.

be violently altered, we shall have to deal, in all our interchanges, with this corps. There may be here and there a party leader or a manufacturer who has come up without attending a university, but the undersecretaries and the experts, the *fonctionnaires*, the bank presidents and industrialists, the burgomasters and most of the councillors, carry an academic dignity. They are divided into parties and interests, but when it comes to larger points of view and to inarticulate premises, these people are, throughout Europe, astonishingly alike. Whether Dutch, French, German, or Swiss, when they have to meet the American mentality, they exhibit the same features. Each university does cling proudly and even fiercely to its distinguishing "tradition"—and yet education on the Continent, from the North Sea to the Mediterranean, is standardized.

This may seem an odd charge to come from an American, and I must stress that I am trying to speak only of certain qualities which we encounter in negotiating with Europe in general. One difficulty is that this uniformity manifests itself not in the many areas of which Europeans are conscious—and they are extremely self-conscious—but in those of which they are unconscious. Consciously, they make much of their disagreements; the American must stay in Europe long enough to read between, or behind, the words before he appreciates their similarities.

Precisely in this area of the unarticulated major premise resides the deep and ubiquitous anti-Americanism that the visitor gradually senses behind the most charming cordiality and hospitality. Or rather, "anti" is too strong: it is much more a settled and frozen image of America which is so deeply embedded in the educated mind that it does not need to be brought out, least of all in the presence of the American. Because it is seldom explicitly uttered, and still more seldom examined, it becomes a conditioning factor in all instruction, whether in law, theology, or even in medicine.

Many Europeans—my colleagues and friends—will stoutly deny this charge of academic standardization. They will cite the great variety of national traditions, and then the inveterate individuality of even the most provincial academy. I can only insist that to the American eye the pattern demonstrates its uniformity by showing everywhere just those deficiencies of knowledge, or of insight, which now are most desperately needed for the success of our communion. Whether the European comes from Toulouse or

Utrecht, Zürich or Paris—whether he be conservative or socialist, Christian or freethinker—he says the same things about America and he asks the same questions. By the insistence of their repetitions, Europeans demonstrate how much they apprehend all things within the rubrics of their training—how, even with the best will in the world, they can comprehend America only within those rubrics.

Let me say at once, I am not trying to exalt America against Europe. We must not forget that amid the European schools, often working under heartbreaking difficulties, there are very great scholars; neither can we forget the tremendous assistance American science received in the last decades from the immigrants we were so fortunate as to have to receive. But I am compelled to ask, however reluctantly, whether the European educational system, rather than the American, has not become set in a rigorous and intransigent mold. I am forced to declare that there are respects in which the Continental method has become a hindrance to the Continent's survival. It is, in short, fossilized.

2

Recognizing, then, that this is dangerous ground, where discussion too easily degenerates into insult, I can collect my observations under two heads: the lack in European schools of anything resembling the "college," and the absence in the pedagogy of anything resembling the point of view Americans have imbibed, willingly or unwillingly, from the "social sciences."

By the experience of the college I do not mean sports. Most European students are adequately athletic, although they do not have massed cheering sections or proper field houses. What I do mean is that the serious student, after a high school that consists of intensive drill in memorization and very little else, enters the university at about eighteen (for the European, as compared with the American, still a very tender age), is confined to a single "faculty," and never, intellectually speaking, gets outside it. Then and there he is committed for life to theology, law, or medicine; the pressures of society do not permit him to gamble with his career by wasting academic effort on anything but professional training. He cultivates his tastes for the arts or indulges curiosity about other subjects on his own. Many of the students come from households with libraries, or from circles in which there is a premium upon the evidences of what we may call, in the restricted sense, "culture"; these will have in their rooms a collection of paperback books, and they do read them. The room may be of a tawdriness that would horrify the janitor of an American dormitory, but the books represent a wider range of reading than most of our undergraduates can show even under the compulsion of a variegated "course program." But the university itself takes no responsibility for these concerns; it is a professional training ground, and it imparts standard and formal disciplines. In the university, the professor tells the student, and on examinations the student repeats what the professor has told him.

If you think I am exaggerating, try to expound the conception of the college to European academic groups, especially its relation to the graduate school. I have tried it, to persons whose eagerness to comprehend and whose perplexity were written on their faces; even when they hear the words, they cannot grasp the fact. That a man should spend four years in a College of Arts and Sciences, pursuing simultaneously a miscellany of courses—which he will never "use" in his profession—seems in Europe an extravagance comparable only to the legends about Americans throwing into the garbage half-eaten steaks. I could bring any conversation to a dead stop by asserting that yes, I positively do believe a year spent studying a little something (even if only a little) about, let us say, Renaissance Florence, Racine, elementary physics, and a queer business called anthropology—that I do believe this is "education." In that sense, the world simply has no meaning in Europe.

To put it another way, few Americans can really understand how profound a manifestation of the European malaise is the vogue of existentialism. Especially the cry of humanity it raises against the identification of the person with his profession, of the postman with the function, above all of the professor with the professorship. One comprehends the depth of this protest only when he learns with what solemnity the professor does take himself (although there are exceptions), and how the society encourages him never to forget that he is Professor Doctor. There are pompous and pedantic professors in America who also fail to hear the rough and spontaneous speech of men, but let us thank heaven for all the pinpricks this society administers to their complacency. I am proud of my calling, but I come back from Europe treasuring as an indispensable portion of the national heritage the American disposition to think the professor slightly ridiculous.

Out of the European universities come, indubitably, cultured persons. The ordinary student is more at home with literature, painting, and music than the average senior over here. What becomes confusing is that these amenities are cultivated, not because they are real knowledge, but as badges of class and status. They are graces and accomplishments, like needlepoint among Victorian women. This was all very well in the last century, when the Buddenbrookses of Europe were playing a basic role, and so could pardonably embellish it; in the changing society, when these classes employ their culture as a means of marking themselves off from their inferiors, the emphasis becomes sinister. Since the acquisition is unrelated to the lecture room, the university does nothing about bringing these interests into vital relation with any body of knowledge. Hence the careful student of Europe today discovers, with a horror of which Henry James felt the preliminary tremors only as late as 1914, that the so-called culture of Europe does not go very deep. The American often leaves his campus still vulgar and uninformed, but we do have the opportunity, more by good luck than good management, of impressing upon him the glimmerings of a notion that learning is not something apart from life.

3

The universities of Europe were fixed in their present structures by the time of the Renaissance. Then, when winds of doctrine were blowing in gales, the universities spread their canvas to catch every gust. To settle the doctrine of the enclitic *De* was to rally the forces of society. To cope with the departments of knowledge, the universities were organized into "faculties," usually the basic five that corresponded to the areas then discernible—theology, letters, law, medicine, and natural science. The last two still are feasible organs for administering the increased learning (hence the good work done in them, particularly on the higher levels of theory), but the other three are totally inadequate to the twentieth century. There is a constant and pathetic effort to pour new wines into old and insufficient bottles. Hence the burgeoning of "institutes," of little projects for teaching and research in fields that do not quite fit into the hierarchy of the faculties. These are generally organized around some great (or ambitious) professor, and may survive him; in effect they atomize the life of the university, sequester books in disparate collections, become vested interests, and make the whole conception of scholarship something tucked away in corners. The "departmental system" forces many distractions upon the American university, and rubrics multiply; but even if it leads to the offering of useless courses, it does allow scope for a healthy experimentation, all under a moderately efficient management. (Not that I hold a brief for *all* administrators.) Here again we have to thank not our prescience but the brute fact that American universities grew up this way because of the pressures of American society. They were never permitted the utter isolation of the self-righteous.

By the same token, the visitor is quickly struck by, and remains to the end puzzled by, the deliberate isolation of the European students from the society around them. Gradually he becomes aware that this is organically connected with the architectonic nature of the instruction itself. Of course, Americans sometimes think of college as the best years of their life, and commencement orators speak of going out into the world, but these matters are relative. Compared with the Europeans, American students live in the center of the world. Our orators talk nonsense: the numbers of students who earn at least a part of their way (European professors and students *always* ask about this practice, with a dreadful fascination), the undergraduate political clubs, our mores of relations between the sexes, and a thousand other things make it impossible for a youth in America to be quarantined against business, politics, and the radio. In Europe the "tradition"—baneful word!—is that the student at the university, acquiring title to the status he will enter about the age of twenty-five or thirty, dwells within a parenthesis in time. He is out of society and a privileged character. In the Dutch universities, where the tradition is most resolutely maintained, this immunization is dramatized by having all student functions—evenings at the Corps, dances, festival dinners—begin at midnight, so that in the morning the student, in full evening dress, is conspicuously going home just as solid burghers go to work. He, of course, will be a burgher later on, but for the time being he is existentially another kind of being, with his peculiar capers.

For that society of burghers the Dutch students have a revealing word, *killemaatschappe*—the chilly outside world. If the world is outside, and is chilly—and if the ultimate doom is implacable—then the period of study becomes a licensed interval, and learning is rigorously separated from living. It took a little time, but soon I began to understand why student after student flatly informed me that in America all education was of course utilitarian, "while we are theoretical." He carries that conviction with him for the rest of his life, let us remember, even when he is negotiating a trade agreement.

In this happy period the student's only task—in a vacuum, how could it be otherwise?—is to learn what the professor says. Especially in the study of law, in which the majority are engaged and out of which come the businessmen and cabinet ministers, where the law is not an accumulation of precedents but the bound book of the code, learning consists of what is in the book. In theology and literature the attitude is much the same. I struggled in vain to drive my own students to the original sources, or to persuade them to check what I was saying against their own interpretation of the documents. "Critical" reading, in that sense, I found an almost unknown conception. At an oral examination—significantly enough, the professor does not give an examination, he "takes" it from the student!—I wearily tried to expound the conception to one of my better students, and received the candid answer, "Yes, but this way is much easier."

I should be grossly unfair, however, if I did not also say that this state of affairs is not satisfactory to many of the students. Those I found the more alert, or the more rebellious, would confide to me expressions of complete dissent—possibly in part because I rather encouraged them. Some of my colleagues will bitterly object to my saying this, yet I found (I think it is a common experience for the American) that as between the world of the professors and that of my student friends, I led an utterly schizophrenic existence. On matters of history and scholarship I could communicate easily with my colleagues. But I had served in World War II, and my subject was the literature of America—which happens to be much concerned, at least in my conception, with "powerful uneducated persons," whalers, Gatsby, and Jennie Gerhardt. Of course European writers deal with "people"—François le Champi and Germinie Lacerteux—but the effect was not the same when the European professor of literature held forth on *la vie et les œuvres* of Sand or the Goncourts.

So, it became something of a sacred trust, and a problem for sleepless nights, when a Dutch student who had escaped in 1940 and spent four hard years in the Navy confided to me that his contemporaries, by accepting their isolation from the chilly world, were merely postponing decisions which he knew could not be postponed, and that few of them knew what he was talking about. Likewise, when the candidate for the *agrégé* in Strasbourg confessed that, although Whitman was a required topic this year—an official post-liberation gesture!—nobody would dare to write upon him as I had lectured upon him and still expect to pass an examination set by the Sorbonne. Or when the president of the theological students at Leiden declared that many of the first-year boys were suffering genuine nervous crises in the cruel transition from domesticity and the routine of the high school to the "freedom"—the highly conventionalized freedom—of the university. He felt that nobody in the community—there is, of course, no "hygiene department" or anything like it—would recognize that these were in truth crises, and he was trying to be of help by reading, entirely on his own, Freud and Jung. So, as I say, I talked one kind of language with my colleagues, which was rich and satisfactory, but I could not carry the terms of their discourse over into that of the students. Neither could I, no matter how much I tried, explain my predicament to my colleagues since they naturally assumed that they knew their own students better than I did.

For my sins, I have often attacked the influence of John Dewey upon the American schools. I believe that those operating in his name have often debased the intellectual coinage. No one familiar with the American situation can fail to sympathize with the many recent efforts to resist the ultrapragmatical drift—although he may not go all the way with Robert Maynard Hutchins. But all this becomes a tempest in an American teapot when viewed from Europe, where there never has been any John Dewey in the first place. It is one thing to have faced his challenge, to have learned everything from it, and then to resist; it is quite another thing never to have heard it.

Repeatedly I found that these dissident students were reaching out—generally by buying from slender resources such casual volumes as appeared in the booksellers'—for works of psychology, anthropology, sociology, social psychology, economics, and what we call generically political science. I was constantly bombarded by eager questions about these subjects, which according to rumor were widely taught in America. It is a fantastic situation when one thinks of European names like Weber, Mannheim, Gunnar Myrdal —not to mention Marx. The explanation is simple: great theorists of the social sciences exist in their little "institutes," but the student in law or theology has too much to memorize against the moment when the examination in his subject is to be taken from him to do more than cursory reading in anything else. And he certainly has no one to give the faintest intimation that these disciplines have any bearing on the corpus of his specialty.

The force of these considerations is, indeed, making some headway in a few academies, particularly, as one might imagine, in urban centers. At Amsterdam, for instance, there has been newly established a separate "faculty" to teach essentially the social sciences. But again, old bottles are being strained to receive modern wine; the professors being organized into a faculty, only students specifically enrolled in it receive the instruction, and those in law or literature—who most need it—do not. There is Professor Tinbergen at the Rotterdam School of Economics, but what the student in the faculty of law at Leiden or Utrecht gets in the way of economics is less than the dullest freshman "Ec. 1" in America. It is not a Tinbergen, who is at home in American scientific circles, who shapes the European image of America: it is the graduate of the faculty of law entrenched in a secretaryship or a bank, the graduate of the faculty of theology in his pulpit. These know vaguely and with distaste that in America the mysterious sciences of which they are initiate are vulgarized and diluted.

The most hopeless task I confronted in lecturing upon modern literature in Continental universities was to explain the power of the recent revolt, inside English and American institutions, against the "history of literature"—the crusades of T. S. Eliot, of Leavis, of the "new criticism," to make possible the reading of a poem for the poem's sake. With some great exceptions, instruction in the Continental faculty of letters struck me as so serenely barricaded behind philology and the morphology of types that the sociological concept was not even there to be revolted against!

It is somewhere in this gulf then, the gulf between the university and the society, that the European image of America emerges and hardens. The student listens with interest to the assertion that in every department American scholarship has been obliged to reconsider the content of learning because the social sciences have connected the most codified learning with conditions and circumstances, but he listens incredulously. Inwardly, he says to himself once more that the Americans are mechanics. He goes into the chilly outside world in the full possession of his stereotype. A charming first-year man at Leiden came to ask me about the possibility of his going to America. I invited him to lunch, whereupon he fell over himself with amazement. He came, and for half an hour descanted on this marvel, that a professor should condescend to find time to talk about a student's personal problem, and give him lunch into the bargain. Then, getting down to business, in the most matter-of-fact tone, he blandly asked me, "Do you think I would be happy in America, where-all-the-people-are-so-superficial-and-materialistic?" I wager that this young man has a career before him in Holland!

It may be a reckless divination, but I am convinced that the connection between the insularity of the university and the universal apathy of European students toward the problem of the future of Western culture is direct and fundamental. The apathy is certainly there; by the end of my sojourn, it haunted me. The cry that we must all stand together for the preservation of "values" excites little enthusiasm among European students. Or where there are stirrings, they never lead to the idea that these are a common concern of Europe and America. There is no conception of America which permits it to figure as a champion of culture. The widely spreading doctrine of Europe as a "third force" is founded upon an image in which America appears as an entirely different, and repulsive, force. The conduct of our liberating armies and of our tourists helps create the image, no doubt; but deeper than these irritations lies the fact that the student has no idea of the meanings the term education has acquired in America, or of the struggle to find those meanings. Frequently I would get a charmingly oblique manifestation of the hidden conviction that invariably fell into the same pattern: Europeans really cannot be impressed with American art or scholarship, the student would say; we can hardly be expected to admire what you do in imitation of us, but show us your skyscrapers or your mass production and we marvel. They say again and again that they are helpless between the two materialistic giants of America and Russia, that Europeans can no longer influence the one great decision of war or peace, and that they can only abide. If you then ask them why they continue studying at the university, they answer that they are becoming qualified for the special position which will be theirs by right of the university degree.

I am the last one to want Europe "Americanized." But in an industrial and mechanized century, some things in Europe must change: a continental economy cannot be managed through such minute entities as France and Italy, let alone Holland and Belgium. America has no choice but to urge the union. No wonder there is deep resentment. A typical European character—who has been in America and ought to know better—took pleasure in assuring me that America is an "episode" in history, which is now coming to a close, whereafter history will resume its march along the great European path. This gentleman, I need not add, holds a degree from a faculty of law.

Whatever other kinds of communication we attempt, the real effort must commence on the university level. There are forces, even if only resentment, making for the inclusion of American subjects—history, literature, economics, social sciences—in the curricula of instruction. There are Europeans who know that the ancient faculties have become strait jackets. My invitation to Leiden came from a committee of graduates who were not an official governing body, some of whom dwell in the chilly outside world. The students are eager to listen. There are immense difficulties in conveying American meanings, but the least of these is the linguistic. The great problem, I can assure you, is one of semantics.

The Fulbright program, which sends teachers and students to Europe, is a splendid enterprise—although there are defects in its administration. I have found that the really effective agents, however, are not so much the Americans in Europe as the European students who have been in America. At Leiden two young men, one of whom had a year at Kansas and the other at Union, were worth twenty times the visiting professor in making comprehensible American ways of thought. Their parents may lament, and their professors not listen—since professors seldom listen to students anyway—but their comrades will. No dollar spent in bringing a student to America is wasted—considering what we waste, this is an advisedly sweeping statement. It is not necessary that they be brought here to be indoctrinated: it is just necessary that they be brought.

One of my most astute Dutch students said to me in so many words that his education gave him no clues as to how to apply his knowledge to a new situation. The American colleges do not impart this knack ready-made, but circumstances have forced upon us the realization that it is a handy thing to have. Even while aware of how much we have yet to do, one can take some pride in what our schools have achieved. Yet this very degree of accomplishment—or the extent to which we have fallen short—stands as a main barrier between the mentality of Europe and of America. On either side there are those who keep the barrier up—out of a lack of imagination and sympathy on this side, out of the inertia of "tradition" on the other. If there is to be anything more than a rickety military alliance—which will fall apart under the first blow—this barrier must be razed.

The Incorruptible Sinclair Lewis

THE FIRST NIGHT out of New York on the *Nieuw Amsterdam*, September 7, 1949, my wife said, "That man going out of the bar looks like Sinclair Lewis." I caught a side glimpse—which I shall forever behold—of that long figure, its head tilted back, its narrow shoulders heightened and compressed, an elastic-jointed puppet held two inches off the deck by invisible strings, so that the longest pair of legs ever attached to so short a body jerked their way across the room in a motion that had nothing to do with the ordinary act of walking.

The obituaries, since his death on January 10, comment on the length of his legs and the convoluted patterns he made by intertwining them. Actually, he was not especially tall, and not preternaturally supple: it was the nervous compulsion inside the man that incessantly contorted his body as he talked or smoked or drank. It also sharpened his face and tormented his skin, drove him restless from place to place (made him hover, at last, over Italy like an exhausted hawk), gutted his loves and his friendships, kept him an obstinate adolescent at the same time that it wore him out; and finally it killed him.

I had the good fortune never to have met him before; hence we had never quarreled. When he had been working (if that is the word

This essay was occasioned by the death of Sinclair Lewis, January 10, 1951.

for what he did in preparation for the worst book he ever pieced together) upon *The God-Seeker*, he had wanted to consult an out-of-print work of mine on New England theology. I offered, through the bookseller, to send him my own copy; he found another somewhere, and never replied. Now I was to discover that this sort of thing Lewis did not forget. Of all the men I have ever known, his gratitude—for such a trifle—was the most profound and the most lasting. The point being that one thing really counted—his work. By which I mean that many observances which count much for other people, ruthlessly and magnificently and brutally did not figure for him. Or rather, he had so schooled himself to not letting them matter that even when he stooped to acknowledge them he just did not any longer know how to cope with them. He and I were friends within five minutes, because we did not have to explain anything.

It took no astuteness to realize that Sinclair Lewis was dying. He had barely recovered from a siege of pneumonia (on this voyage he was not drinking): his hand shook, and the wavering of his legs meant that he was unsteady on them. With him was his brother, Dr. Claude Lewis of Saint Cloud, Minnesota—of whom Red had not seen much in recent decades, who was six years older than he, and who addressed him, to my never-ending astonishment, as "Hal." Dr. Lewis looked a good ten years younger: Red's myth—to which he clung with inexhaustible solicitude—was that he was about to introduce Claude for the first time to the immemorial riches of Europe. He asked my advice morning and evening as to just how gradually and circumspectly he should spring the art galleries and cathedrals on brother Claude, so as not to heap too much into the initiation.

The whole business was infinitely comic: Dr. Lewis is a distinguished surgeon, of eminent common sense, who can and does find his way about the world by his own native shrewdness. And when it comes to the conventional "sight-seeing," Red Lewis was about the most unperceptive and blundering of all the myriads of tourists this country annually exports. (He was as delighted as a boy with the tableau of the assassination of William the Silent in the Prinsenhof at Delft, and hung over the piece of the wall in which they have framed by glass the ricochet of the bullet, but the Grande Place of Brussels made him think only of Kansas City; he was never certain he was eating a good European meal unless he knew he was in the most expensive restaurant in the town.)

Still, all this was a clue: here was Sam Dodsworth casting himself, with outward bravado and considerable inward trepidation, as Virgil to a Dante who in fact was competently on his own. Sinclair Lewis was about to impart to his untraveled brother the immense stores of insight which to him, the much-traveled Odysseus, had become old stuff. One remembered the calculated brevity of the items Dodsworth finally enumerated as the sum total of what he was able to learn out of years of tourism.

I had easily assumed that Lewis made up Dodsworth's list by looking down from a vast familiarity with Europe, as a device in "character study." The creature, not the creator, had obviously acquired no more out of Europe than a knowledge of timetables and the way to say "too much." My education took one vast stride forward when I discovered that the relation of this particular artist to that particular creation was not so disjunctive. It took another—a more tentative step—as I began to comprehend that nevertheless Dodsworth was not mere autobiography, not just an alias for Sinclair Lewis. It came momentarily to a dead halt when daily conversation (I pressed him unfairly) showed that if Dodsworth was in any sense Lewis himself, nevertheless the creator did know in what frame of reference he had set the man and that only thereafter had he become identified with the character. It took a final and immense leap when I realized that, although Lewis could not say it, and certainly would not, in the writing of that book, he had been (and still was) both in and out of it—not so much triumphantly as hopelessly. He had not mastered Dodsworth: he had presented him, and now was compelled to re-enact him.

I found that the secret was much the same when I got him onto *Main Street* and *Babbitt*. I then and there, with great relief, said good-by to the notion (which in the last weeks has been monotonously asserted in the obituaries) that Lewis was a "realist" and a "satirist." It does indeed become a curious comment on our age that lyrics and love songs which in any previous period would have been published frankly and freely as such, had to be composed, in our time, by this highly American artist under such elaborate disguises as his vast accumulation of the minutiae and the lingo of American life. What I have yet to learn—perhaps few of us yet understand or want to inquire too closely—is where did the love come from that could pour upon these things with a passion so concentrated that the only relief permitted it was to lash out against the very objects to which it was inescapably and irrevocably bound?

2

For the sake of the record, let me say that during Lewis's last year, I saw much of him—simply because I was in Europe and able to reach him. We perfected a little fiction between us that my wife and I, his newest friends, were his oldest and only friends. This gambit often grew rather harrowing as his perpetual mulling over the past disclosed the number of former friends who were now estranged, or at any rate out of touch. He received staggering quantities of mail, most of which (when he was with us) he never opened. In October he came to Holland and delivered a lecture at the University of Leiden. (Announced as an appearance for my class in American literature, it was attended by virtually the whole university, and had to be held in the great auditorium.) We drove him to Delft, Haarlem, and Alkmaar, to Antwerp and Brussels. We stayed with him in the spring at Florence, in the Villa di Costa with its vulgar spun-glass balustrades, and we last saw him at Zurich in August.

In December of 1949 he had found, in the Cook's Tourist Office at Florence, Alexander Manson, who became his secretary, chauffeur, nurse, and interpreter. I gather that Aleck and his lovely Tina were with him to the end. I knew that Lewis had tried this "secretary" arrangement before, and that it had ended in repeated disasters; but Aleck Manson is something special: he knows Europe completely, speaks the languages, can repair a car or order a dinner, tell a story or comprehend a picture, and both he and his wife devoted themselves to Lewis with a disregard of self that would take all the recent history of Europe to explain. The beauty and poignance of the story is that Aleck instantly knew, and never for a moment imagined anything else, what Lewis signified as an artist. I am a countryman of Sinclair Lewis, as Aleck is not; and I grew up with his novels a part—a very great part—of my experience; most of those who read this did likewise. It took me all these years, and then the illumination of his discourse, and after that Aleck's by no means blind consecration, to realize what a terrifying thing it is to be in at the death of a lion. I use the word lion not in the flip sense of a target for hostesses: I mean it in the primitive sense of a leonine beast who roars his last defiance from a cave in the rocks.

You may think that this is melodramatic overstatement as against some of the facts. Externally they are shabby enough. During the winter, while he worked on a novel, he managed—with Aleck's help—to keep away from the bottle. As soon as he finished the manuscript, he started drinking, until his Florentine physician forbade him spirits. When I reached him in April, he was guzzling quantities of red wine, and despite Aleck's strenuous efforts, he generally succeeded in knocking himself out by afternoon. At a Florence restaurant he commanded the orchestra to play the sentimental tunes of his earlier escapades; he peeled off and flung about five-thousand-lira notes—Babbitt on a spree—until Aleck could get him out and pour him into the car. By August he was drinking only beer, but he had already had two serious heart attacks and should not have touched even that.

I suppose hundreds of people in three decades have seen Sinclair Lewis drunk; no doubt he made a vast public spectacle of himself. I cannot say what kept him going through the years of creativity; I do know that at the end of it, his back to the wall, facing himself drunk or sober, he did not flinch. There was something positively reckless about it. He was not drinking because he was miserable and wanted solace; neither was he what you would call a drunkard. He was no disenchanted, alcoholic Scott Fitzgerald, drinking compulsively. There may not have been much joy in what Red was doing, but there was still plenty of defiance. Remember, this was not Walter Scott collecting his retainers about him in feudal glory; this was not Zola declining in the realization of an enshrined place in the Academy. This was just an American who had written himself out, to whom the Nobel Prize was no canonization but merely one of those things that happen, for whom the dignity of the artist had no external supports, and who yet somehow maintained it, as Poe and Whitman did, on the terms which this nation imposes upon its artists—terms that Lewis gladly, as a matter of fact, imposed upon himself for fear he might otherwise take himself too solemnly.

This was something that ran deep and strong in him—his hatred for pomposity. I don't mean his treasuring the hypocrisies of Main Street or the sanctimoniousness of Elmer Gantry: that was something else entirely. I mean his attitude toward himself as a writer and toward writing in general. It was too serious a business to be taken solemnly. In the last months he had a game he would play with Aleck—it went on interminably—in which he was the stuffy, grandiose German Professor and Aleck was the trembling *Privatdocent;* the point of the game (aside from letting Lewis show off his German, for he was vain about his smattering of languages) was that the Herr Professor Dr. Geheimrat made a damn fool of himself. It was a way of throwing bricks at high silk hats. It was a Mark Twain gesture, it was deeply and embarrassingly American, but it was also more: it was a myth-maker thumbing his nose at those who would reduce myth to literalness.

3

Being a professor of literary history, I wanted to find out what he derived from. The answer was instructive: Dickens. He knew Dickens by heart. There was little to be gained by asking him about what had come in between, about realists and naturalists. He had read here and there, but most of them meant little to him, except for Shaw and Wells, who to him were primarily writers that showed what might be done with Dickensian exaggeration in a modern situation. The most valuable and most plausible thing in his account of his own beginnings (you must understand that I seldom asked him a point-blank question) was the perfect naturalness and inevitability with which, it had seemed to him, a young writer of about 1910, with Dickens as a model, would proceed to make social comedy out of America.

Yes, he recognized that by now the generation of the twenties, himself the foremost, were being defined in historical terms and treated as radical departures, as collectively a great break with the past. He had no such sense of the story at all; as for most of the "influences" which, according to our historians, brought about the revolution, he was unaware of them or else heard about them only after their effect on his own work had been detected by some ingenious critic. He would agree that up to a point it had been a matter of the time and place; as he talked about the coming of the deep-freeze, television, and the high-powered automobile to Gopher

Prairie, he saw that he had caught Main Street just at the turning point, at a now vanished point, and that his book was already a matter of history—and then he would take flight into fantasy, showing that he had never been and could never be capable of thinking in terms of history. He was in love with mythological and typological creations like Micawber and Gradgrind, and all his effort had been to evoke such genii out of the American bottle. It was a constricted and stoppered vessel he had—as he saw it—to work with, which is one reason he vented so much rage upon it. His incantations had to be more labored than those of Dickens, who was in a position to summon up, with a wave of the hand so to speak, a Pecksniff or a Mr. Squeers. In America there had to be a vaster quantity of documented fact before Lewis could extract from it a Babbitt or a Gantry, just as there had to be all the knowledge of the river before Mark Twain could set Huck Finn afloat upon it.

Lewis listened to, and sometimes was impressed by, what the critics said of his books as providing a panorama of the civilization, but for him Babbitt and Gantry and Arrowsmith were creations; he was still trying the old art when he wrote such pathetically documented things as *The Prodigal Parents* or *Cass Timberlane*. He was still trying it even last winter, and told me with affected complacence, as though one should say that Winston Churchill had dropped in yesterday, that in the new book Mr. and Mrs. Dodsworth had reappeared.

In this view—I believe I am not overstressing it—the lecture he gave for my class at Leiden was immensely revealing: most of the students were bewildered, because it was not anything they expected or wanted Sinclair Lewis to say. He worked on it carefully, and his notes reside now in the university library. It was his last effort at any such sustained discourse—in Florence he made one or two perfunctory appearances on platforms, when it took all of Aleck's immense diplomacy to keep him from attempting to deliver an address in Italian! At Leiden his argument was that America is not new, it is actually very old. He proved this first by dwelling on the antiquity of the Indian culture; how that was linked to the present American civilization so as to furnish us with its venerability never became quite clear. Second, he insisted, Americans all brought with them the civilization of Europe, and consequently their culture is as old as any European. He then blamed the Europeans for the antics of the Americans: because they expect us to act like wild Indians, we are obliged to put on a show for them. If you listen to the second half of a sentence uttered by the visiting American, he said, it will be a logical, sensible statement, but the first half will contain some "Oh boy" or "Gee whiz" or "What the hell"—to assist the European in keeping up his illusion.

This from the author of *Babbitt*! If I was amused, my students were puzzled, because the primary (and almost the only) assumption among literate Europeans is that the recent literature of America is a sociological report on the horrors of a materialistic order, that all our artists hate it and want, like Lewis, to escape to Europe. In part, Lewis's speech was sheer perversity: he got fun out of scandalizing the European stereotype. He, like all of us, was troubled over the charge that the American literature of protest, with himself as Exhibit A, was confirming Europeans in their anti-Americanism. But there was something else at work in him when he wrote this lecture, which I think is fundamental in his best work.

I stumbled upon it early in our friendship by telling him that as a boy in Chicago I had wanted to devote myself to the ancient history of the Near East. Nothing I ever said to him made his eyes shine so much. He too had wanted, more than anything in the world, to be an Egyptologist. Don't ask me if this is true (although Claude did remember that the boy Hal had spouted a lot about Babylonia): my point is only that he announced this to have been the great dream of his youth, and swore that it was the adventure yet to come. While his strength was visibly failing, even after the heart attacks commenced, he descanted on how he and Aleck were to set out in the fall, work their way through Sicily, then go to Egypt and Damascus and Assyria, and at last penetrate to Persepolis. I do not know how much history he read, but he loved to pontificate about Rameses II and the queen of Palmyra.

Was it a trauma of escapism? Maybe. In ordinary terms, I think it was something simpler: it was a thin little boy in Sauk Center dreaming (over an unfinished book) about the gorgeous panoply of Ashur-bani-pal. Remember how many times the majestic syllables of ancient history are invoked in his ironic addresses to America, how "Ur of the Chaldees" had for him a magic sound, and how it seemed the supreme comment upon the tin Lizzie standing before the Bon Ton store that for this the pyramids were built and Hannibal crossed the Alps.

I said good-by to him one night in Zurich; Aleck was taking him the next day to Turin, and he and I knew that we would never meet again. The next morning, before breakfast, he telephoned: he wanted me to tell him whether Rangoon is a port for ocean-going vessels and the precise dates when Generals Lee and Grant died.

4

I suppose he knew that he would never get to Egypt. He probably would have been as restless before the pyramids as he was in the cathedral of Antwerp, and would have distracted his attention from the sublimity of the pile by finding some ridiculous detail off to one side, or by looking at his watch and worrying about whether he could get back to the hotel on time. But that is not what concerns us. One of the most perceptive of my friends in Leiden came from his lecture exhilarated; when I asked her what she liked about it, she replied with unhesitating emphasis, "His fanaticism." That, she said, is what Europe needs, and she went on to contrast him and Dodsworth with Henry James: where James made so exquisite an effort to comprehend the special essence of every European place, to stretch his sensibility into the fine web that would catch the slightest reverberations, Lewis (like Dodsworth) stood intransigent and incorruptible. For this listener, and several others, his lecture had not been what he may consciously have intended it, the rebuttal of a flimsy European stereotype about America; it was much more: it was a revelation of the sources of his energy as an artist, of the act of dedication he had performed so thoroughly that he could never, whether flamboyant or, as now, sick and battered, do anything but exemplify it. My friend said that she was reading *Babbitt* with new eyes.

The difficulty is that too few in America have read him with such eyes. Perhaps I might put my contention more bluntly (although it loses much if stated so flatly): it is all very well to call Lewis a realist because he heaped up the furnishings of the Kennicotts' parlor or because he could mimic to the last grammatical atrocity the jabberings of the man who knew Coolidge, but at the heart of him Lewis was what we must call, for lack of a better word, a romancer. He loved telling stories, and even in this last year, in the ebb of his powers, could start with almost anything and make the draft of a novel out of it. I have never heard anything so fascinating, and it made the Dickens clue trebly revelatory.

Lewis could have earned a comfortable living writing stories for magazines; in fact, before *Main Street* he was doing exactly that. He might well have become another Hervey Allen or a Kenneth Roberts. What kept him from being just a spinner of yarns was not something more sophisticated in him—not any doctrinal adherence to, or even comprehension of, the tenets of realism or naturalism—but something more primitive. The scrupulous documentation was the working of a conscience. This organ does not operate so strenuously in easy living or in facile writing; it becomes tormenting only when there is some deep psychic dislocation, some wrong done—or some hurt felt.

5

I gather that few of Red's friends got along with him for any period without certain stormy scenes. I had mine the night before his lecture, when we were invited for dinner by the Rector Magnificus of Leiden University. Professor van Groningen is a civilized, gentle classicist; his wife is witty and, fortunately, comprehends the world. They both had behaved with quiet heroism in the war, and are what in Holland is known as "conservative" on the Indonesian question (which means that they regret the American policy), but I never had any difficulty discussing it with them.*

This night, I started the dinner off by remarking that the Amsterdam paper had called Claude the younger brother. (There is no way I can tell this story that reflects the slightest credit on me.) At the table, the van Groningens intimated their attitude toward Indonesia, whereupon Red launched into a patriotic tirade, of the sort he had voluminously burlesqued, in which the embattled Indonesians became American patriots at Valley Forge and his Dutch hosts supercilious Tories in London of 1776. I completed the ruin of the

* The conflict between the Netherlands and the insurgent Indonesian Republic came before the U.N. Security Council in 1947. United States policy supported a sovereign "Republic of the United States of Indonesia"; during the settlement of 1949, strong American influence was exerted upon the Dutch to accept United Nations authority and to give sovereignty to the United States of Indonesia.

evening by asking the rector to have Dr. Lewis escorted through the faculty of medicine on the morrow, managing by an inspiration of stupidity to say that Claude had heard his brother before and did not need to hear him again. The resulting scene was Red Lewis at his most histrionic: we were all denounced and assured that the lecture would never be delivered. The situation was saved only by the wit of Mevrouw van Groningen, who told funny stories, mostly at her own expense, while Lewis sulked like a child, until he came out of it, put his hand on my arm, and said of his hostess, "Wouldn't Frans Hals have liked to paint her!"

Somehow, my wife and I got them back to the hotel. Claude pulled me aside and whispered as he went up to bed, "He's been like that since he was a boy."

Lewis was contrite, but of course wouldn't admit it; he took us into the bar, and then the confession came. It's been that way from the beginning, he said. I wanted to write, and I've worked like hell at it, and the whole of Sauk Center and my family and America have never understood that it is work, that I haven't just been playing around, that this is every bit as serious a proposition as Claude's hospital. When you said that Claude did not want to hear my lecture, Lewis told me, you set up all the resentments I have had ever since I can remember.

If much of this sounds petulant, it was. It was also the story of the artist in America. It was a revelation of the sources of what the perceptive Dutch woman found his redeeming fanaticism. It may have been bad manners but it was freedom, passionate and consuming. It was the *élan* that went into the writing of the great novels of the twenties, which makes them, in the guise of ferocious attacks upon America, celebrations of it. For at the end of the lecture on the next day, he said something which I believe he seldom brought himself to avow, which certainly he never put in print: "I wrote *Babbitt* not out of hatred for him but out of love."

Schlegel's Julius once said to his Lucinda that man is a serious animal and that we must attack this abominable propensity from all sides. "To that end ambiguities are also good, except that they are so seldom ambiguous. When they are not and allow only one interpretation, that is not immoral, it is only obtrusive and vulgar." I am afraid that in the books of his later years Sinclair Lewis wrote much that allows only one interpretation. All this immense

America had to be poured through him; there was too much of it, and finally he took merely to reporting it, as Whitman, when his vitality flagged, catalogued it. But Lewis never got altogether away from the ambiguity that informs his five triumphs of the 1920s.

Over and over again, after he had mailed the manuscript of his last book, when he would try to enjoy Italian scenery or the Swiss Alps, he would come back, with the reiteration of obsession, to asserting that he had written twenty-three novels about America, that nobody could ask more of him, that he had done his duty by his country. "I love America," he would shout into the unoffending European atmosphere; "I love it, but I don't like it." As a closing statement on the career of Sinclair Lewis, this assuredly does not, whatever else you say about it, allow of only a single, and certainly not of a literal, interpretation.

Europe's Faith in American Fiction

IT WAS a relief, I must confess, to get into a world where the people I dealt with took it for granted that literature is an index of civilization. In America I have to spend time and energy maintaining that thesis. I don't complain, but I often wonder, as do my colleagues, whether I might make more progress were I less obliged to prove that my calling is not frivolous. In Europe I did not need to explain my mission; I had come to expound American writing, especially of this century. Not only in university circles but in community after community, the response was overwhelming, and I soon found myself able to charm audiences merely with a magic incantation: Hemingway, Dos Passos, Steinbeck, Faulkner.

Sometimes, earlier names would also serve. In the autumn of 1949, as soon as I was ashore, I was invited to Leeuwarden, ancient capital of Friesland, a town of perhaps 80,000, in contrast with which Des Moines or Albany would seem metropolitan, to observe in public ceremonial the hundredth anniversary of the death of Edgar Allan Poe. Solid citizens—bankers, lawyers, the queen's commissioner, and the provincial government—suspended their affairs for an afternoon and gravely devoted four hours (with an intermission for tea) to hearing orations on Poe and readings of his poems. For the first time since I was thirteen, I recited "The Raven" aloud. Translated into Frisian by a poet who appeared to have stepped out of some primitive North Sea saga, it sounded beautiful!

During the intermission came the inevitable question: "What are they doing in America on October 7?" (I believe that a Baltimore newspaper did run a "story," and that one or two literary magazines commented—that was about all, wasn't it? What happened in Des Moines or Albany?) Was I to reply, "Yes, we do have a great literature, and I am delighted that you appreciate Poe; but in America, you know, we don't shut up shop for an afternoon to pay him homage"? They are polite people, and their rejoinder would be more implied than baldly stated; still, it would be clear enough: shouldn't I go home and proselyte my own people rather than preach to those who needed not my ministrations?

In Europe there is today a tremendous vogue of American writers—mainly of the modern novelists, but including also the plays of O'Neill, Wilder, Williams, and Miller. In the intellectual history of Europe the impact of these writers during the last two decades is comparable to the domination of the *philosophes* in the eighteenth century, to the contagion of the German romantics in the early nineteenth, or to the later influence of Turgenev, Tolstoy, and Chekhov.

The evidence is voluminous. I stand in no danger of attributing a pro-American bias to Jean-Paul Sartre; yet he has said that the encounter of the French mind with Dos Passos, Hemingway, and Faulkner effected a revolution comparable to that of its meeting with Joyce. Even in Algiers, one of the first publications of the liberation in 1943 was *Écrivains et Poètes des États-Unis*, reissued in Paris in 1945. Because French opinion still guides the taste of Western Europe, essays of the last five years—of Pierre Brodin, Claude-Edmonde Magny, Jean Simon, and above all of Maurice Coindreau (who also has copiously translated Faulkner and Caldwell)—are extensively studied. The direct influence of the Americans upon the styles and techniques of French writers is already a matter of record: of Dos Passos upon Sartre, of Hemingway upon Camus. In Italy likewise: Vittorini, Berto, Pratolini acknowledge the debt.

But as I experienced it, influences on this more sophisticated level are the least part of the story. Hundreds of ordinary people have read the books; they came to my lectures not to learn about strange names but to test their insights. The most striking evidence is the sale of the novels, either in paperback English texts or in translations. Again and again, some businessman, lawyer, or architect—

in France, Holland, Switzerland, Italy—would shyly, half-proudly and half-hesitantly, show me his shelf or his case of American fiction. The shyness was in part deference to my professorial status, which of course is the European manner. But it was also something more touching, full of tact: it was a muted asking whether I, as an American, would resent his gathering impressions of America from these arresting but decidedly uncomplimentary portrayals of the national scene.

The problem thus imposed itself: what should I say was the real significance of this "school" of writers? What did they mean, not so much for Europeans as for Americans?

For there is a fact about these collections in so many European homes: they are almost entirely concentrated upon those writers whom, for shorthand purposes, I may call violent. The names are always Lewis, Dos Passos, Hemingway, Faulkner, Steinbeck, Caldwell, Farrell. There are also copies of James M. Cain and of others whom Edmund Wilson dubbed "the boys in the backroom," but seldom any representation of those I would call our "realists"—Ellen Glasgow, Edith Wharton, Ruth Suckow, Willa Cather. Henry Miller was everywhere taken seriously, along with Dashiell Hammett. Often I found Sherwood Anderson comparatively unknown; after I talked about him, the local bookstore immediately sold what copies it stocked of *Winesburg, Ohio*. Occasionally Dreiser was no more than a name, but those who read him at my urging recognized that he also belonged to the literary image which they consider so distinctively American. And for my account of the recent "revival" of Henry James, attention usually was gracious but perfunctory.

Furthermore, I had difficulty explaining that in America there has been a concerted critical effort to sift the authentic from the imitation, and that not all of us suppose, every time the postman rings twice, he is delivering *Light in August*. In fact, another dimension was added to my problem by what seemed an appalling inability, often an unwillingness, even among those most friendly to the literature, to make a rudimentary effort at evaluation. As long as a book flaunted the stigmata of American violence, it was accepted uncritically as the real thing. There is always, of course, some such difficulty in the migration of a literature (remember how many second- or third-rate French and German writers have had vogues in America!), yet here the issue is slightly different: there exists so remarkable a receptivity to the genre that almost anything which pretends to be "tough" will be read. The difficulty is not in getting attention: it is in moderating, in the name of standards, a disposition to embrace everything that employs the clichés of this species of Americanism.

However, if this be a difficulty, it is not an obstacle to communication. After one has at least half-persuaded an audience that some of these books are "better" than others, he still has to face the insistent question: are the novels, particularly the best of them, reliable reports on civilization in America?

There are, fortunately, European interpreters to help in answering that question. André Gide's imaginary interviewer asks if one should not conclude from this fiction that American cities and countrysides offer a foretaste of Hell; to which Gide says, do not believe a word of it, for each of these authors is achieving a consciousness of his own nature by reacting. Jean Simon pleads with us not to be too severe in blaming French taste if it grasps indiscriminately at every such American utterance, because this passionate curiosity proclaims how profoundly America symbolizes French hopes.

But the ordinary reader, the eager student, has not always had the benefit of such warnings. He has simply read the books, and is fascinated. He knows that America will largely determine the future of Europe. Hence my friends and students asked the question not idly but anxiously: these writings, they would say, are all vehement attacks on the American way of life; if we are not to take them as meaning that American civilization is a foretaste of Hell, how are we to take them? If *Main Street*, *The Great Gatsby*, *An American Tragedy*, *The Sound and the Fury*, *The Grapes of Wrath* are not factual reports on the workings of the economy, what are they? And if they are accurate, do they not portend what a Europe dominated by America must expect? If so, should not Europe dread that future, and resist?

2

There are certain qualities of the European mind that make such discussions difficult for Americans. Often I had to struggle with literary stereotypes much prized among cultivated Europeans, which stand in the way of their understanding American writing. As with Poe at Leeuwarden: like most of my generation, I have had a long struggle with him; if I have rejected the Poe over whom I swooned at thirteen, I have come painfully to appreciate him as a conscious craftsman, an editor who increased the circulation of his magazines, and above all as a critic of society. I presented this Poe in Friesland (and elsewhere), causing only bafflement; I found that the Poe honored throughout Europe is that construction of the French imagination who is quite another being from the historical person. I asked the poet who had rendered "The Raven" into a Frisian even more mellifluous than the original, what in Poe attracted him. He replied, in sepulchral tones that would have become the bird itself, "He is ominous."

In part I blame the academic instruction, wherein literature is often taught as a dead succession of schools, influences, and types, into which schematized conception the reader tries to fit Lewis and Hemingway. Furthermore, classification of writers not only into nationalities but into regionalities comes easy to the European. Hence Faulkner is ticketed as "Southern"; I had hard work contending that his use of Southern materials is incidental, that his work is not an official report on agricultural and racial conditions, and that he is not to be read as one reads Daudet or Giono on Provence.

Not unrelated to this habit of mind is a deeper one, which Guy Métraux put concisely when he said that education in Europe (especially in France) seeks always for *l'homme en général*, so that the pragmatic, empirical, unsystematic temper of American writing is not fully grasped. When studying the American novel, European readers try to annotate the "universal" and "general" traits, rather than to accept a total and a singular experience.

Then, there is still a deeper worry. Europe is a tired and exhausted continent, living on the edge of despair. It has lost the sense of how an ebullient literature comes into being: it has forgotten what went into the making of a Rabelais, a Rousseau, or a Byron. Readers expect from their writers a documentation of political hopelessness, such as they find in Sartre or in Koestler. They suppose, therefore, that Dos Passos does no more than reproduce a panorama of horrors, or that in the Mississippi of Faulkner, rape, incest, and lynching are daily occurrences.

Let me say, parenthetically, that the novel is, on levels that really count, a more vital factor in Europe's image of America than the moving picture. Thousands do indeed queue up to gaze at our westerns and our glamour girls; intellectuals like J. E. Morpurgo lament that the films present only a sybaritic regime. Yet the film-derived idea of America, supposing it widely accepted, is inert. But the fiction, I assure you, is pondered in those circles from which leadership must emerge. A culture that hails Poe as a citizen of the world accords a similar welcome to Faulkner and listens attentively to what he says in Oslo.

3

Despite the conceptions and misconceptions, despite the effort to read Americans within European rubrics, the books exert another sort of fascination. The European student wonders what and why. He has a sense which he cannot deny that in them there is still a quality deeper than sheer violence or sociological documentation. His question is redoubled: are the murders, the sexual obsessions, the disintegration of Hurstwood, the banality of Main Street, the agonies of the Joads—are these the realities? Nor is the question always asked out of anti-American prejudice. Even where the violence or dullness is taken literally, until the image of America seems a chamber of horrors, there is always a recognition of vitality. Even when the American novel seems to say that all is frightful, it curiously and paradoxically intimates a hope. In some inexplicable fashion, it has a resurgent quality. My auditors wanted to ascertain just what this amounts to. They wanted desperately to know.

In the end, the problem came down to trying to explicate not vocabulary or techniques, but the experience out of which these works were written. The books have been exported. Could I, or anyone, carry across the Atlantic the vibrations that engendered them?

First, I discovered that I had the task of expounding simultaneously two Americas: of sharpening my own and my students' discrimination between them. The one that gave no trouble either to them or to me is the America which has derived its thought as well as its peoples from Europe. You can present a coherent, and seemingly complete, history of the intellect in these terms; an empty continent has been steadily furnished with waves of European ideas: Calvinism in the seventeenth century; Evangelicalism, Newtonian physics, and Locke's philosophy in the eighteenth; in the nineteenth, the romantic cult of nature and of the individual, Darwinian and Spencerian sociology, naturalism; and more recently Marxism, Keynesian policies, and Freudianism. In this view the American element consists of what the native wit makes out of imported materials, and it has generally taken the form of a simplification, or the accentuation of a particular aspect. Thus Jefferson's Americanism consists of his substitution, in Locke's triad of life, liberty, and property, of "pursuit of happiness" for the third item. Emerson's genius amounts to so rephrasing the romantic philosophy of nature that it should lead to the imperative of self-reliance. Edwards is the American form of Pietism; Cooper is the American Scott, and Dreiser is an echo of Zola. Dos Passos and Faulkner must fit in somewhere, just as Wilder's plays are adaptations of "expressionism." Everywhere in Europe there exists a great courtesy toward this America. If you insist that occasionally, as in Whitman, the reworking of imported concepts came close to originality, the praise is unstinted.

Americans who conceive their intellectual and artistic achievement solely in these terms are what Europeans call "nice Americans." They display a suitable sense of the cultural tradition, and a becoming modesty before its avatars, being themselves professed colonials and provincials. The learned world is interested; it approves of Emerson and Cooper; it also assumes that if a nice American remains long enough in Europe, he will come to appreciate not only the vast accumulation of treasures but how much more complex all problems are than they seem in the bright light of the New World: that admirable as is Jefferson and Whitman's democracy, it is a hasty oversimplification of innocence.

But is Ernest Hemingway a nice American? Was Scott Fitzgerald? What has that notion of America to do with Sister Carrie, Isaac MacCaslin, or Eugene Gant?

4

It is possible to tell the story of American literature in another way, which pertains to a nation that has nothing whatsoever to do with an extension of Europe. Instead of derivation, there is reckless exaggeration and ridicule; a mythologizing, a cult of immensity. It appears in Franklin's suave agreement with the Englishman who declared the Great Lakes unnavigable because they are full of whales; yes, Franklin gravely asserted, this is true, for leviathan pursues the cod, and "the grand leap of the Whale in that Chase up the Fall of Niagara is esteemed by all who have seen it, as one of the finest Spectacles in nature." This America is Natty Bumppo wiping his nose on his sleeve; it is Sut Lovengood tearing down a steep point, in a kangaroo lope, holding his flask high above his head: "If I were jis' es smart es I am mean, an' ornary, I'd be President ove a Wild Cat Bank in less nor a week. Is sperrits plenty over wif yu?" It is Moby Dick, sliding along the sea "as if an isolated thing," invested with a gentle joyousness and a mighty mildness, "still withholding from sight the full terrors of his submerged trunk, entirely hiding the wrenched hideousness of his jaw." It is Davy Crockett grinning the coons off a tree; it is Huck Finn's river; it is the Great Bear of Arkansas, a creation bear, who in a fair fight would have licked Samson in the twinkling of a dice-box: "My private opinion is, that that bar was an unhuntable bar, and died when his time came." It is William Faulkner's bear: "It did not emerge, appear: it was just there, immobile, fixed in the green and windless noon's hot dappling, not as big as he had dreamed it but as big as he had expected, bigger, dimensionless against the dappled obscurity, looking at him." It is Henry Thoreau, who found all English literature tame and regarded Concord as a port of entry.

Define the quality of this America as you will, our novels abound in it. It is not naturalism or realism; it is the whale and the bear. Not alone because they are replete with sex and violence do they attract readers in Europe; the worst mistake you can fall into is to suppose they do no more than stimulate jaded palates. Nor is it merely that they are "vital." Indeed, by contrast with European works, they are just that: in Huxley, Proust, Gide shines a finer intelligence than any that gleams in Lewis or Hemingway, yet beside these they appear pallid, without force. Coindreau and others emphasize the "epic" character of *As I Lay Dying*; if Jean Simon demurs, he still finds in it *une bouffonnerie macabre*. Yes, vitality is part of the appeal; yet that is not the bottom of it.

I found Thomas Wolfe not so generally perused as the others;

but I could excite a strange, responsive look in every group I addressed—as though they were hearing distant yet joyful shouts—by quoting his famous sentence, "I believe that we are lost in America, but I believe we shall be found." At home I had never exactly heard trumpets blow when reading that passage; in Europe it became not destructive but assertive. It acquired a ring as it went on to say that the forms we have fashioned are self-destructive and must be destroyed, but that "I think these forms are dying, and must die, just as I know that America and the people in it are deathless, undiscovered, and immortal, and must live."

What makes such words inspiriting in Europe is that on every side their writers are saying, as Malraux puts it, that a dying (or at least a menaced) society can no longer confront the future in terms of freedom, but solely in terms of destiny. In the American writer there is a reckless amateurism which bespeaks a fundamental freedom; it is manifested conspicuously in his refusal to take himself solemnly as a writer, his inability to pontificate about "Art," his determination to appear to the world as a playboy, a deep-sea fisherman, or a Mississippi farmer, who incidentally writes books. For a time, Europeans took the Americans at their own evaluation; but now the suspicion has dawned that there is a deep connection between this insouciance, this fecundity of invention which Continentals imitate, and the assertion with which Faulkner accepted the Nobel Prize, that man will not merely endure, but will prevail. Faulkner's "man" is definitely not the abstraction *en général*. "They are obsessed," Malraux has said, "with fundamental man."

The stuff of the novels is sordid, terrifying, hateful: village meanness, improbable binges, the brutal impersonality of New York, the passions of a mob. But the treatment is unfettered. In the night of *Nigger Jeff*, Dreiser saw the tragedy and the grief: "I'll get it all in!" he cried. "I'll get it all in!" My audiences often needed tutelage in the structure of *The Sound and the Fury*—in what Sartre has called Faulkner's "metaphysic of time"—so as to perceive that it was not just a narrative device, but an experiential sense of history; then they reached for it with avidity. To speak of Hemingway and of "that simplicity sure of itself" (the phrase is Jean Simon's) was to communicate a sense of joy. Bemused observers like John Lehmann, looking at the prevalence among our novelists of a hatred for their own civilization, ask if the result should not be "cynicism and despair," yet own to the fantastic otherness. As a teacher, I never found work so ready to my hand, nor the rewards so rich.

5

This is not all my story; nor can I yet entirely answer that question addressed to me at Leeuwarden or at a hundred other places. As early as *The American Scholar*, Emerson said that the spirit of the American freeman had become tame and insipid. Thoreau lashed out at the impositions of conformity, and called ours a desperate odd-fellow society. Cooper returned from lecturing Europe upon the virtues of democracy to find the democracy in the clutch of politicians he allegorically named Aristabulus Bragg and newspaper editors denominated Steadfast Dodge. Faulkner gives us the Snopeses, and Lewis, of course, discovered Babbitt. If there is an America of the whale and the bear—which is no offspring of Europe—then the European asks about still a third America, which is painfully evident to him, which also seems to have no European lineage: an America that does not glide through the seas with a mighty mildness of repose.

What about this America of men in offices and women at bridge tables, which knows little about the first America; which is ignorant of, or suspicious of, the second; and upon which the second heaps its scorn and contempt? This is not so much the mechanical and enameled America of the films; rather it is one to which the whale and bear are symbols as alien as to Europe itself. It is orthodoxy and complacency; it manifests itself by imposing oaths of loyalty: it is timorous, and displays what Lionel Trilling calls "the political fear of the intellect."

The perceptive European will agree that Faulkner is a great writer, and will make the effort to comprehend him in American terms; then he asks about the sales, and I have to report how scanty was the circulation of his early and best work, as well as to confess how shockingly little Dos Passos has been recompensed. I have to note that Thornton Wilder suffered from a too early popularity—wherefore the depth of his *Ides of March* has simply not been gauged; while Hemingway's novels have become best-sellers only as his work deteriorates. I have conversed with Americans, since my return, who, upon learning that I lectured on the novelists in

Europe, inform me that they have lived their lives in this country without seeing anything to justify those denunciations. Meanwhile the European learns that vast segments of our people are reading (when not gazing emptily at television) phony historical romances populated by lush-bosomed heroines, are studying how to win friends and influence people (wherefore they learn how to alienate their friends in Europe), and devouring treatises on peace of mind, when everybody knows there is no peace. Europe extends an ample hospitality to Hemingway and Dos Passos: may this not, after all, be the story of Poe once more? Is that America which has been the target of the Americans' own attack the dominant one? Suppose that the novelists' representation is not always photographically or sociologically precise: is it not, in the deeper sense of art, true?

The enigma and threat of this third America is not its violence; rather its pusillanimity. There can be seen something splendid in a society that raises up gang wars or such conflicts as *In Dubious Battle*—as long as there are artists, concerned with fundamental man, to detect the grandeur of the struggle. But the dull uncomprehension of the tourist, the callousness of liberating troops who buy their women with chocolate bars and cigarettes, a strident shouting for democracy which has lost the meaning of democracy—what has this to do with the fanaticism of Sinclair Lewis or with Faulkner's hymn to the glory of man? If there be a preponderance of Americans who, even after they have been satirized, attacked, and insulted, do not so much as get angry, but at best dumbly contemplate their assailants and at worst stolidly ignore them, what wonder that those Europeans who have caught in our literature a glimmer of hope must thereupon demand whether that hope will be stifled in its own country. Will not the self-destructive forms, as Wolfe called them, destroy the promise?

I aspire to be an honest expositor, and I count myself a patriotic American. Had I to contend in Europe with only the old-fashioned ignorance or obtuseness—with only what Lowell called a certain condescension—my task would have been easy. Fenimore Cooper's hectoring of Europe was thoroughly in order in 1830; only ten years earlier, Sydney Smith had delivered his famous sneer: who, in the four quarters of the world, reads an American book or sees an American play? The wheel has come a very full circle. The important point is that we can, through the American novel and play, communicate with free men everywhere. Because this is a literature of criticism in the name of the fundamental man, it is a literature of freedom. Outright censorship, whether by commissar or priest or a board of trustees, can be fought; but Lionel Trilling has named a still more "ominous" opponent. Our literature has vitality, and more than vitality, because it is the record of a civil war—of a fight waged by the human spirit against its direst foes, against monotony and standardization and cold charity. The second of my Americas has, so far, withstood the third. For this reason it signifies hope. So long as it continues to carry the war into the enemy's camp, we shall not be lost at home, nor shall we fail to encourage those in Europe who urgently need such heartening.

The Social Context of the Covenant

I HAVE a good friend—a very astute man—who was born and brought up in Rome, who now lives in America and is an American citizen but who frequently revisits his native city, where he is admitted to various impenetrable circles. He came back this summer with the intelligence that the shrewdest diplomats inside the Vatican—those who lay down, with the timeless wisdom of the Church, the longest of long-range calculations—figure that in another fifty years the materialistic culture of the United States will have exhausted itself. The natural resources will be gone, confusion and then torpor will spread over the society; then it will become evident that America is not and never was the Roman Empire of this age, it is only another Parthia.

My friend remarks that not since 1789 have the planners of Vatican diplomacy been correct about anything, and that may be some consolation. Still, it is not only the crafty prognosticators of Rome who foresee in America some such development. You hardly have to be a Spengler or a Toynbee in order to ask yourself, at least from time to time, whether this American way of life is not rushing at a steadily accelerating pace toward a massive megalopolis which finally, of sheer dead weight, shall grind to an agonizing

An address delivered at the annual meeting of the Congregational Christian Historical Society, held in Boston at the Old South Church, November 10, 1954.

stop, and then crumble into ruin by the force of inertia. If you want to entertain prospects of doom, you may well argue that we shall not be destroyed by the instantaneous explosion of a hydrogen bomb but that we shall decay by a slightly slower yet even more terrifying process—a process of which the blinding smog that now hangs over the once bright city of Los Angeles is the premonitory symptom.

Wracked as we are by such anxieties, we are apt to lose all perspective about ourselves, to jump to the conclusion that we are entirely unique, that no previous generation in recorded history ever faced so awful a prospect as we do. Sometimes, in fact, our proximity to destruction ministers subtly to our pride: we secretly gloat that no other human beings were so selected to live dangerously, were so privileged to behold the end of all things. Hence in our arrogance, we do not notice that we have come into a mental and spiritual predicament astonishingly analogous to that of the seventeenth-century Congregationalists who believed, whether in England or in New England, that the fate of a nation is contained within a covenant. We imagine we alone have learned to worry; we thus prevent ourselves from appreciating the profundity, the bitterness, the grandeur of the terror that haunted the founders.

You are kind enough to invite me to address you because you believe that my attempts at historical investigation of the origins and development of "the New England Way" have helped your understanding of yourselves. I hope this is true; you will forgive me for sounding a bit conceited when I say that one reason I started, about thirty years ago, these researches was a dissatisfaction which, even as a very callow student, I felt with nineteenth-century treatments of the seventeenth century. I could see even then, and see even more clearly now, that the scholarship was indeed excellent and thorough. This is a fitting occasion to express my immense admiration for, as well as my incalculable debt to, such mighty scholars as John Gorham Palfrey, Henry Martyn Dexter, Williston Walker, George Fisher, Frank Hugh Foster. If I have been able to contribute anything over and above what these learned men formulated, it is only because I came of age after the First World War, in what has by now come to be generally termed an Age of Anxiety. The optimism of the well-bred mind in the nineteenth century was so pervasive, irresistible, you might even say unconscious, that men of this stamp were hopelessly cut off from the innermost mood of the Covenant theology. In America, concepts of individualism, free enterprise, self-reliance, the right to make money, of indefinite and inexhaustible prosperity, had become so identified with the eternal law of Almighty God that by no stretch of the historical imagination could these well-intentioned researchers share in the dread that lay at the heart of the Puritan experiment. They felt, and rightly, that even though emancipated from Calvinism they could sympathetically understand the mentality of individual Calvinists; what they could not comprehend, for they had no clue for comprehending, was that the individual drama in a Puritan community was enacted amid an enveloping concern about the social destiny. I think I may say that such opposition as my books have encountered—or rather, such deficiency of full appreciation even on the part of those wanting to be friendly—seems to me attributable in great part to the fact that many of my readers, especially those somewhat older than I am, have remained in the clutch of that stubborn, persistent, indomitable optimism that inspired the gigantic growth and prosperity of this country.

Students are constantly coming to me with this question: "If the Puritans believed that everything was predestined, not only their salvation but the moment of their death, why did they ever exert themselves? Why did they ever *do* anything?" To an uncompromising optimism, this seems the logical question. Professor Foster found adequate explanation for the decline and ultimate disintegration of the New England theology in the thesis that it was vitiated from the beginning by a concept of human inability, that this was bound to produce a general apathy. One of the tiresome criticisms of Jonathan Edwards with which I have repeatedly to deal is the charge that he was "inconsistent" because, while arguing against free will, he nevertheless preached such hortatory sermons as "Sinners in the Hands of an Angry God."

I admit that for Edwards the problem was real, though not quite in the sense in which moderns make the objection. But what is hard to get moderns to comprehend about the founders of New England is, first, that for them the doctrine of predestination did not have as a psychological consequence the surrender of all volition but rather that it was a powerful stimulus to activity; second and more important, this tremendous exertion being made in a social context, the incentive was therefore strengthened by an awful realization that without it the whole enterprise might fail. Hence they could not work out their particular salvations in a fear and trembling about only themselves; redemption of the soul was inextricably tied up with the question of whether the remnant of virtue and piety was enough, and could be kept enough, to save the community.

John Winthrop put the issue to the settlers in the famous sermon aboard the *Arbella*, delivered in mid-ocean and before the community had even been established, printed in 1630 under the title "A Modell of Christian Charity." There, as I am sure is known to all of you, he told the people that they had entered into covenant with God, professing this enterprise upon stated terms; if the people keep the covenant, Providence will reward them, but if they fail the bond, Heaven will rain plagues and afflictions upon them. Out of this concept grew that form of sermon so widely spoken in New England which I have called the "Jeremiad," the history of which I have recently sketched.

As I tried in that book to point out—and I still think this contention substantially right—as the conception of the community being in covenant with God was progressively employed as a weapon to get public support for limited rather than communal ends—the ambitions of a particular segment of the clergy, to be exact—it rapidly lost its effectiveness. When it had become nothing more than a hollow ritual, Jonathan Edwards junked it and developed an entirely new form of arousing the populace, a sermon designed to excite individuals and masses but not specifically concerned with the temporal well-being of the whole society. When I first endeavored to reach back across the gulf of the eighteenth century and to excavate the forgotten theology of the covenant many people thought I was performing an act of mere antiquarianism, and they pitied me. Recently my friend Richard Niebuhr said to me that while I might consider myself responsible for calling the attention of modern American theologians to the covenant, still my work was valuable mainly because it thus did start a new application of thought to the idea: this development is otherwise not indebted to me because, Mr. Niebuhr said, "You don't take the idea seriously, you don't believe in it; we do."

If a historian writes in behalf of a cause or a party and so makes history support his living commitment, he is accused of partiality; if he strives for objectivity, he is accused of not believing anything. I am not sufficiently familiar with current movements in theology to say just what a revivified covenant is accomplishing; however I am not at all surprised that certain Christians, especially those most sensitive to the urgencies of this troubled age, should discover more meaning in the Puritan doctrine than a dead and archaic mechanism.

For the question that the doctrine irresistibly poses has become our question: How can a society save itself? History is assuredly strewn with wreckages of societies; hence we have a superfluity of lessons as to the ways in which a community can go to pieces. We have none as to how it can escape, once a collapse appears inevitable. And it would seem, as I have remarked, that from one angle, Puritan thinking would teach that there is nothing at all the citizens of a foredoomed state can do about the inevitable. A volume of John Cotton's—I think the most readable of his publications—was printed in London in 1641 as *The Way of Life*. In a preface, the editor announced in conventional language what he supposed was the theme of the collected discourses:

> What small power have we over our owne spirits! how little are we able either to turne them, or to keep them so when they are well; but let the heart bee brought into never so gracious and sweet a frame, let grace be accompanied with peace, and peace with joy; yet how little can we doe with our grace, if God leave us to work in the strength of it! now how soone will our graces die, and our comforts wither?

This would certainly seem to inculcate an extreme inability, a passivity so absolute that even when men have received an influx of divine grace they are still powerless to accomplish anything by and of themselves, that they are incapable of keeping up even their hope and comfort. Because John Cotton did so pointedly stress this sort of reflection, Anne Hutchinson concluded that he was the only one in New England untainted with the heresy of salvation by works and thus tried to erect in his name the banner of so utter a dependence upon the Holy Spirit that the leaders had to denounce it and her as Antinomian. Her notions, said the General Court in

1637, are obviously unsound as well as dangerous because they "tend to slothfulnesse, and quench all endevour in the creature."

John Cotton, as you know, eventually joined with his colleagues in condemning Mistress Hutchinson; he himself pronounced the sentence of her excommunication from the First Church of Boston. Historians speculate about his motive, and there is reason to suspect that he yielded to strong pressure. Had he persisted in defending the Antinomians, he would have been cast with them into the infernal regions of Rhode Island. But on the other hand, it is highly probable that Mistress Hutchinson did appropriate some of Cotton's most extreme utterances on the uselessness of good works but that she did not pay sufficient heed to his disquisitions on the social aspects of holiness. Had she marked and digested the latter sort of teachings as well as the former, she would have known better than to expect him to support her after she had become a public nuisance!

In this same *The Way of Life* Cotton discusses, without resorting to the technicalities of the federal theology, the problem of Christian sociology. In ordinary situations, he says—as he continues, it becomes clear that the theory of the normal situation is hardly ever exemplified in actual fact—God regards the society as one with the people. "If they be innocent, so is the whole Nation before him; if they be humble, reformed, and upright, such is the whole Nation." In other words, sanctification is not only a condition achieved or attained by this, that, or the other individual; it is also corporate; or as Cotton puts it, "the whole lumpe is sanctified." Hence if a nation of righteous men seek God, no matter where they live, "he will heare in Heaven and all the country shall fare the better for their sakes."

But unfortunately, in all too many cases—indeed in most cases—the circle of righteousness is not identical with the national frontier. When the discrepancy becomes too great, then the minority of good men can no longer save the majority. There are, Cotton specifies, two ways in which they fail. When they offer themselves as substitutes for the others, when they try to take the affliction upon themselves, God will thrust them out of the gap. He will inflict His vengeance despite them. But the other, and the more fatal, way in which the saints lose their usefulness is when they themselves become "wrapt up in the contagions of the sinners of the times and places they live in." Here let us stop for a moment and marvel at what an intolerable dilemma Cotton presents to the chosen of God. Unless they happen to be members of a society where holiness is virtually universal, they have the alternatives of recognizing that their virtue is too little to save the community, or else, by complying with the national ethos, of so acquiring the sins of the time and place as justly to be included in the national condemnation! In the one you must resign yourself to unpopularity and ineffectiveness, in the other to conformity and destruction.

If then the "mourning of Gods people," to use Cotton's phrase—by which he means their spiritual resolution—be the mourning of the whole land, then "as the people of God shall behave themselves in times of publick dangers, so will the state of things stand." And now, when this is not the case, what do we do? Do we despair, do we say that the catastrophe, the declension, the collapse is fated, that nothing we perform can arrest it? Have we no social ability whatsoever? No, says Cotton, there is one thing we can achieve: "Bee well acquainted, not onely with your own sins, but be not strangers to the sinnes of the Town and Country you live in." I think it not too rough a modernization of Cotton's injunction to say that in times of public crisis we are not to submit or to sit apart, we are to become active critics of our society. The best patriotism in such emergencies is not conformity, it is speaking out against those abuses which have brought us into the dire predicament.

> Complain not therefore of any declension of times, or decayes of things that are good, or breaking in of things that are kinde (though they ought unfainedly to exercise us) but follow close to wise and faithfull preservation of our selves from fellowship in these evils, and as much as in us lies, reforme what is amisse in our selves and ours; and let it be a strong motive to us to fall faithfully to this work, because if we shall so doe, such a mourning of a few will be counted the mourning of a whole Land.

I think it likely that this sermon was delivered in England, before 1633 when Cotton fled to New England; the manuscript had probably been left behind, and so could be published there in 1641. In that case, John Cotton was really talking to his people about the attitude they should hold toward a state that was imposing upon the saints a corrupt and destructive, as they believed, church system. The whole passage is a kind of double talk about nonconformity; I suppose those who do not love the Puritans can see in it only another piece of casuistry and hypocrisy. Why doesn't he come out in the open and say what he means?

Well, he does say what he means. Cotton is not a radical, a revolutionary. Actually, as he later was to show, in political philosophy he is, by the standards of his day, a conservative. But he is a decent, conscientious citizen faced with the spectacle of his country, which he dearly loves, embarking on a policy, maintaining a line of conduct, employing methods, which he is certain will lead to disaster. What then does a man do, we ask? By virtue of that very concern for the health and reputation of the nation, he refuses to conform. And this logic, let us remember, was possible in a universe conceived as conforming to Calvinist principles. Nay, more than that, this resolution not to conform, this courage to stand by the resolution of nonconformity, was not at war with the theology; it was in fact a direct consequence of it. This is the fruit of Christian freedom. Thus the righteous man stands for his freedom, when politicians and majorities demand that he comply with a system and a discipline he knows is wrong.

Equality in the American Setting

IN PREPARING for my part in this conference I made a point of inspecting reports of preceding sessions. I gather that, on the whole, specialists assembled to discuss "aspects" of the theme used the theme as a point of departure for expounding their own specialties. Whether this sort of thing constitutes a meeting of minds or only a procession of eccentrics, I would not venture to decide; I can only say that if it is the latter, then I am honored to contribute my mite of eccentricity to the general spectacle of Human Equality.

My problem, however, when confronted with so massive a concept—on which the wisest sages have uttered many profundities, most in contradiction of each other—is that I am obliged to ask myself just what is my eccentricity? Equality may well appear a "social" concept, and, therefore, ought to be analyzed only by social scientists. I am sure there are several such on these panels, and they may well feel that they alone have an *expertise* adequate to the subject, and that I should be left, in the general circus, with no more part to play than that of clown. Still, I have an immense respect for clowns, especially when they contrive to upset the

An address delivered August 30, 1955, at the sixteenth meeting of the Fellows of the Conference on Science, Philosophy and Religion in Relation to the Democratic Way of Life. Held at Columbia University, the theme of the conference was "Aspects of Human Equality."

revered and solemn dignifications to which, in more sober moods, the human mind too readily submits. Thus clowns are constant reminders of our fundamental equality in absurdity. So I dare to begin my performance by announcing that equality is not at all a social concept, and should not be profaned by any sociological treatment, or indeed by any analysis from the practitioners of what are today called—horrid phrase—the "behavioral sciences." This indulgence in eccentricity, which to behavioral scientists will no doubt seem sheer perversity (if so blunt a word be left in their vocabulary), will not prevent them from winding within the cocoon of sociologyese a subject about which ordinary men, men in America, entertain an agonizing concern.

Surely, the subject or problem of human equality can be discussed—perhaps most cogently and rewardingly—in terms of the law or of the history of law. Neither should anyone come near the theme without considerable awareness of what modern physiology and psychiatry have to say; I am persuaded that those who know their Freud and Jung have more to speak on the topic than would Plato or Aristotle themselves, could we revive them and invite them to sit down with us. Obviously, the philosopher has much to observe to which all others should reverently listen—though so few of us are, as is my esteemed friend, Richard McKeon, philosophers.

And, it is to be assumed, historians have a great deal to tell us, if only because they set forth what college catalogues are fond of calling "backgrounds." But I am unrepentantly convinced that historians may have still more to contribute if they are at least slightly tarred with the brush of philosophy—though I can assure you, from distressing personal experience, that he who in this country exhibits the slightest smear of philosophy in his historical compositions is bound to be charged, at one and the same time, of being a muddled historian and a philosopher *manqué*.

So then, if the sociologist, legalist, classicist, philosopher, historian are all so involved with their private eccentricities as to be not quite fitted for pronouncing the ultimate word on this vexed interest of mankind, whom have we left? The poet, perhaps? Not all poets are by any means poets of equality—witness, above all, Shakespeare. As Ulysses says in that speech from *Troilus and Cressida* which in this sort of symposium has been so often cited—generally by those who profess a "conservative" bias—that had any but Shakespeare written it, it would long since have become a bore:

> Take but degree away, untune that string,
> And, hark, what discord follows!

Nevertheless, there have been, possibly there still are, poets of another kind, who have constituted themselves Poets of Equality. Wherever these appear, they are usually accused of succumbing to the vice of "mysticism," and on that score are relegated by other poets and many critics to the purgatory of impractical vision. But—if a poet verges upon mysticism, or even if he is accused of verging, he becomes in a sense a theologian. He may even achieve the honor of being condemned by theologians for daring to trespass on their preserve! I, alas, am no poet, and still less a theologian; but I have studied and striven to chronicle an episode or two in the development of Western poetry and theology. Since I discover in myself an aptitude, were it improved, more for comprehending Chinese characters than for grasping the mysterious polysyllables of sociology, I am obliged to talk about human equality from this highly eccentric, not to say fantastic, point of vantage.

Settlers of the plantations which ultimately became the thirteen United States—or at least the vocal leaders—were to a man of Ulysses's opinion. The pioneers of Virginia and Maryland were too busy, too distracted, or—with assistance from the ague and the Indians—too short-lived, to develop in the first decades an elaborated social theory, but their enactments and occasional remarks show how axiomatically they accepted a philosophy of gradation. As one of their spokesmen said in 1666: "There should be degrees and diversities amongst the sons of men, in acknowledging of a superiority from inferiors to superiors." The Dutch in New Amsterdam would have agreed, but more important for the spiritual history of America, so did the Puritan founders of New England.

I say more important, not out of a desire to enhance my eccentricity, or to magnify the New England element in American culture beyond what its numbers and migrations warrant, but simply because under the peculiar conditions of the settlement, the issues were in that region made more articulate—the dedication to a specific ecclesiastical program required the leaders more to expound their conception—than elsewhere. And we know how thoroughly *a priori* their thinking was, because even before the Great

Migration, in 1630, reached the shores of America, Governor John Winthrop, in a lay sermon delivered in mid-ocean upon the deck of the flagship, made the point explicitly.

Adopting the standardized form of the Puritan sermon, which a devout layman like John Winthrop would know as well as any cleric, the governor propounded the doctrine which is the center of Puritan political theory—or which, I should say, was assumed by all Puritan leaders at this date, 1630, to be the unshakable premise. "God Almighty," said Governor Winthrop, "in His most holy and wise Providence, hath so disposed of the condition of mankind, as in all times some must be rich, some poor; some high and eminent in power and dignity, others mean and in subjection."

The temptation is strong to linger upon just what crafty consideration induced the governor, out there in the Atlantic, to make his principal exhortation to the Great Migration hinge upon this deliberate diatribe against egalitarianism. (The text was sent back to London for printing, and was reimported to Massachusetts Bay, so that all might heed.) We may surmise—it is only a surmise—that he already anticipated how many of the migrants, not only indentured servants or other less saintly companions but even the saints themselves, were excited by dreams that the new country—where there would be no courtiers, no duke of Buckingham, no feudal estates, no appropriated monasteries—might offer them a chance to become as good, in wealth if not in ancestral prestige, as those they had been obliged in England to regard as their betters.

Be that as it may, Winthrop makes clear in this remarkable document that while the inequality he inculcates may be supported by an appeal to nature—it is, he says, "in conformity with the rest of His [God's] works"—still, it is primarily a consequence of those peculiar institutions which God has graciously imparted to man as partial compensations for the Fall of Adam. At the moment of this Great Migration, Puritan thought—which is to say most Christian thought, and more particularly all Protestant thought, and then to say most especially the thought of English Nonconformists—was prepossessed by a sharp distinction between the two formulations of law: that which they called the natural law and that which is "positive." As Winthrop astutely said, "There is likewise a double law by which we are regulated in our conversation one towards another."

Now the important consideration to be noted—I think it germane to every paper in this conference—is that Winthrop explains how the law of nature retains eternal validity, yet that this validity is qualified by the all important consideration of its having been issued to man in a state of—or as he wonderfully calls it, "estate of"—innocence. Which is to say (Winthrop does not, in so many words, say precisely this, but it is his premise), equality of man with man was of course the rule of nature; but with the Fall, with the transmission from generation to generation of the taint of corruption, inequality becomes necessary to protect the body politic from the ravages of sinful egotism. Therefore, the division of society into a hierarchy of rank and station—not so much of the naturally superior chieftains to their clansmen but the more subtle and artificial subordinations among superiors themselves, such as magistrates, citizens, and inhabitants—is a consequence of that "positive" law promulgated after the Fall, after it had become clear that a continuance of the natural equality of Eden would result only in the slaughter of all good Abels by the wicked Cains. In that sense, as Winthrop was free to confess, the conventional scheme of social stratification is indeed "artificial." But if this were opposed to nature, it was not so much as artifice to the spontaneous as it was the realm of salvation opposed to the kingdom of brutishness. Or, to go back to Winthrop's own words, the opposition lay between "the law of nature, and the law of Grace, or the moral law or the law of the Gospel."

I compress infinite reams of Protestant thinking into this bald rendering of Winthrop's meaning: equality is indeed the original law of nature, received from the pristine mandate of the Creator; but inequality is the subsequent revelation, delivered after the Fall, when mankind could no longer hear the language of nature without becoming incited to such deeds of natural assertion as would produce social chaos.

I suppose I do not need to point out, as others in this conference will, how a profound belief in original sin tends to strengthen the hands of those who argue for conservatism, especially where conservatism is taken to mean a denial of human equality. In fact, many of those most eloquent in the cause of conservatism—even when forced to accept as their slogan that contradiction in terms which calls itself "the new conservatism"—appeal to the Puritans as their legitimate, even if not their genealogical, forbears. It might be easier for this conference if we could accept some such rule of thumb: those of us who believe in the sinfulness of man, in his *original* depravity, deny human equality; whereas only those of us who believe in the innate goodness, however limited, of the species, dare proclaim our adherence to the ideal—and this in spite of sociologists and physiologists.

Still, I should like to make my point as briefly as possible, out of Governor Winthrop and out of the theologians upon whom he depended: if original sin is the ground upon which a society of unequals takes its stand, and because of human depravity that society strives to maintain its gradations, then the real temptation to sin, in the present predicament of human nature, is not resort to the idyllic dream of equality arising out of the law of nature, but the endeavor to impose the specific orderings of society which can claim no more justification than the concept of positive law, or that of, as Winthrop phrased it, the moral law.

Hobbes's doctrine of the state as a desperate remedy against the vicious tumultuousness of human nature does seem to derive from the Calvinist concept of the race. But there is a crucial difference in any Christian formulation—such as Winthrop's is—from Hobbes's: the real temptation is no longer the law of nature, but the law of Grace. That which invites to an abuse of charity is no longer the fiction of equality, but the organized, legalized, institutionalized inequality. The governor who, in mid-Atlantic, preaches the subordination of inferiors to superiors, knows in his heart of hearts that men will remain sinful, even Puritan men. Though he must exercise his authority, he is not jubilant over the prospect; to the extent that he is not, we may call him no conservative.

In 1645, Governor Winthrop had his most severe brush with the democracy of saints, as they impeached him for exceeding the limits of his office and he beat them by winning a complete exoneration. Then he delivered, from the prisoner's box this time, his second great treatise on political theory, his famous speech on liberty. The distinction he now invokes is between the state of nature and the state he would call "civil or federal." In the natural state, men are indeed equal, and each may do as he pleases; but men being what they are since the expulsion from the Garden, the exercise of this liberty makes them only the more brutish. In civil liberty—that is, within the realm of positive law—freedom is given "to that only which is good, just and honest." This liberty is obtained, Winthrop tells the citizens, when "you quietly and cheerfully submit unto that authority which is set over you, in all administrations of it, for your good."

This utterance has for over a century seemed to liberal and egalitarian sensitivity a shocking demand that citizens yield to their officials an implicit obedience beyond anything Louis XIV might have expected. But the modern mind can hardly conceive the humility out of which Winthrop spoke this apparent arrogance. He certainly was not demanding that the people pay an unquestioning subservience to himself. He was pointing out that for them to arrogate to themselves the administration of the positive or civil law was to produce chaos, because of the omnipresence of depravity; being what they were, they would try to administer positive law as though it were natural. But Winthrop was not pretending that he and his fellow magistrates were exempt from the curse. He argued for the inequality of the civil state in fear and trembling, knowing as a convinced Christian, and long before Acton, that power corrupts.

In all Puritan thinking, as to some extent there must be in all Christian thinking, a double anxiety was always present: if, on the one hand, there was a fear, similar to Shakespeare's and Hobbes's, that utter discord would follow any untuning of the string of degree, on the other, there was a besetting worry that too strong a government would impose such a tyranny upon the people as would endanger their salvation. Obviously, the Puritans were forced along this second line of apprehension by what they knew of the papacy and of Catholic countries, and more immediately by their experience under the repressions of Laud and Strafford. But whatever the origin, the idea was firmly fixed in their minds, just as firmly as Winthrop's doctrine of social submission. As John Cotton said, "It is therefore most wholesome for magistrates and officers in church and commonwealth never to affect more liberty and authority than will do them good, and the people good." At the election in Hartford in 1638, two years after his band had left Massachusetts, the spiritual leader of the Connecticut settlement, Thomas Hooker, expounded the same thesis: "They who have power to appoint officers and magistrates, it is in their power, also, to set the bounds and limitations of the power and place unto which they call him." Filial piety has proved as strong in Connecticut as in Massachusetts, so that in modern times claims have been made that this discourse proves Hooker to have been more "liberal" than the theocrats of Boston, such as Winthrop and Cotton. But it was Cotton who said: "It is counted a matter of danger to the state to limit prerogatives; but it is a further danger not to have them limited: they will be like a tempest, if they be not limited." And it was Cotton who put the idea into the most vivid image: "If you tether a beast at night, he knows the length of his tether before morning." In Puritan doctrine, while the uninhibited exercise of natural equality within the positive state made men bestial, the unlimited prerogative of the sovereign was itself a beast.

It is all too easy, when we trace the evolution of ideas in America out of the seventeenth century, to forget that these founders were religious men. Many varieties of professing Christians may indeed accuse the Puritans of having lost the essence of Christianity, but the Puritans did not think so. John Cotton concludes his discourse on limitation with: "Oh, the bottomless depth of sandy earth! of a corrupt spirit, that breaks over all bounds, and loves inordinate vastness. That is what we ought to be careful of." They did not suppose for a moment that the right to worship as one chooses, whether or not the way of the society, was a right either of natural or of positive law, but they were absolutely convinced of "the priesthood of believers." That great proposition, which over three centuries has proved a mighty engine of equality, was not entertained by the early Protestants as an egalitarian ideal, but they entirely appreciated one of its innermost meanings: no potentiality of the spirit must be permitted to be suppressed by the artifices of society. Every potential believer must have the chance to actuate the faith that is in him, and these accesses to activation must be open to all, peasant as well as noble, servant as well as master.

For this very reason the founders of New England had gone further than the majority of English Puritans were prepared to go, to devise a reformation of the church that would positively guarantee such equality of opportunity. The reason this particular group had to get out of England, rather than stay and fight alongside those who later became parliamentary forces, was because they were already convinced that the true biblical polity was neither

Episcopal nor Presbyterian, but Congregational. So, even while Winthrop was driving home the lesson of inequality in society, he knew that he was leading an enterprise committed to a system of churches within which officers and people would all be equals in the fellowship of Christ.

The founders of New England vigorously rejected the charge often brought against them by their critics, that their Congregational way was "democratical." Still, they had to face the charge, and were put to many ingenious twists of logic to prove that particular societies created by a covenant of all the members, wherein each signer had precisely the same rights as all others, wherein the citizens chose and ordained the officers, or discharged them if not pleased with them—that these minute body politics were not democratic nor egalitarian. Hooker's colleague in Hartford was reduced to characterizing the polity as "a speaking aristocracy in the face of a silent democracy." However, this was in effect an admission that the democracy, if only within the potentiality of silence, was effectively present.

The story of how the Congregational order became, step by step, conscious of the fact that it was indeed a democracy, and how ultimately it learned to boast of the fact, has been told many times. By the second decade of the eighteenth century, the Reverend John Wise of Ipswich, defending the original constitution against what he believed to be "Presbyterial" innovations, was the first to bring the implication into the open. A democracy, he said, is the form of government "which the Light of Nature does highly value, and often directs to as most agreeable to the just and natural prerogatives of human beings." Therefore, Wise reasoned, man's "original liberty" ought to be as fully cherished as is compatible with due restrictions, and likewise "the Natural Equality of men amongst men must be duly favored."

There is, however, one interesting reversal in theological and social emphasis that appears in John Wise's explicit democratization of the polity. If by Calvin's and Winthrop's logic, Adam was created so as to be equal with all other men, and then before any other men appeared he fell, thus bringing death into the world, then the fact of death like the existence of government is a badge of innate depravity. Were we perfect, we would have neither, and so would again be equals. But the cautious way Puritan theologians handled this argument suggests that they could see how dangerous it was, how easily it might work against them. Thus William Hubbard of Ipswich, preaching the election sermon in 1676, assured the colony that it was the will of God for some to be advanced as high above others in dignity and power as the cedars of Lebanon are above the low shrubs in the valley, that it is not time and chance but divine appointment "that some are mounted on horseback, while others are left to travel on foot." Then he comes to the naturalistic argument, and has to refute it: "Nothing therefore can be imagined more remote either from right reason or true religion, than to think that because we were all once equal at our birth, and shall be again at our death, therefore we should be so in the whole course of our lives." But John Wise, only some forty years later, noting that our bodies are frail and subject to accident, draws the opposite deduction: "The noblest mortal in his entrance on to the stage of life is not distinguished by any pomp of passage from the lowest of mankind; and our life hastens to the same general mark: death observes no ceremony, but knocks as loud at the barriers of the court as at the door of the cottage." It might seem that hidden in the center of Protestant theology there is a tangle of death, sin and equality which could be further snarled when patriotic Protestants announce themselves, for political reasons, egalitarians.

Wise, it is true, was in advance of his time; there is no evidence that he had any appreciable effect upon his own generation, or that his radically democratic ideas were utilized by propagandists for the Revolution of 1776, even in New England. In fact, it still remains obscure just how, if at all, the Congregational theory—with its initial propositions of communal covenant and equality within the covenant—got transferred to the larger realm of the whole society. But still New England is of interest because it did work out, even though reluctantly, the hidden directions of its primitive polity. Amid the violent theological disturbances of the eighteenth century, essentially the same ideal of polity became incorporated into the thinking of most American Protestants, especially the Baptists; through the influence of the "New Lights," it invaded and transformed the Presbyterian churches. Even Episcopalians, unless they were doctrinaire royalists like Jonathan Boucher, were not immune from the infection: vestries in colonial Virginia were in effect caretakers for a Congregational polity—a fact which goes far to explain why so many Episcopalian planters could become revolutionaries without straining their consciences.

Now, what I would like to insist upon is that there was a logic in the whole evolution—which I have shamelessly oversimplified—that proceeds in a roughly ordered fashion out of the original premises, and that the final result does not necessarily require a rejection of the Protestant originators. The conventional thing is to say that by the time of the Revolution a conception of man as inherently good had so effectually driven out the Christian (or at least Protestant) view of him as depraved, that the road was open for the Continental Congress to announce (with some help from John Locke) that all men, being naturally virtuous, were created equal and were endowed by their Creator with certain unalienable rights. This version of history—which we may identify with such noble spirits as Vernon Parrington—then plays into the hands of those who today have miraculously rediscovered the doctrine of original sin, and who thereupon dismiss Jefferson as unrealistic, and so once more propose that we not only recognize but legalize inequality among men.

This version leaves out of account many matters of fact. It ignores, for instance, the utter horror with which Puritans—firm believers in natural depravity—regarded Hobbes. Also, it pays no attention to the number of orthodox Calvinists in the America of 1776—all professing in substance *The Westminster* or *The Augsburg Confession*—who rallied around *The Declaration of Independence* and fought or prayed for the triumph of its second paragraph. Possibly some critics will say that these Protestants, particularly those who were still officially Calvinistic, were in fact hypocrites, who paid only lip service to historic symbols. This may be true about a few of the Congregational clergy in eastern Massachusetts who were already well on the way to becoming Unitarians, but there is no evidence that the orthodox ministers of the Connecticut Valley or the Presbyterians of the middle states had any more difficulty embracing Jefferson's manifesto than did the liberals. John Adams later said that the "black regiment," the Protestant clergy, were of more value to the cause than any regiment in the field. Though these prayed for grace, they had so fallen into the habit of addressing not so much Jehovah as Nature and Nature's God, that such a Tory as Jonathan Boucher felt justified in charging them with having become idolaters of Nature. In that sense they could at long last accept without a qualm the assertion that all men are created free and equal, and that they can, therefore, never alienate their rights to life, liberty, and the pursuit of happiness, especially when the latter right meant most immediately the pursuit of trade routes or of frontier acreages from which the British government tried to withhold them.

No doubt there is much truth in this version. But the main thing to be said against it—or if you will, alongside it—is that it shows no real understanding of Protestant, Puritan, New Light theology. To repeat, one way of translating Luther's "priesthood of believers" is to say that no potentiality shall be allowed to perish. Run the risk of hypocrisy and deception if you must, as indeed you must, but still it is clear that any earthly power which comes between the possibility and the actualization is infinitely more sinful than the wildest riot of an infatuated democracy. Whether that power come as King Charles and Archbishop Laud, or as Presbyteries of New Jersey demanding subscription, or as agents of George III imposing stamps or a tax on tea—that presumption of the positive against the natural law is the great beast who must eternally be kept, as John Cotton said, tethered. Winthrop told the Migration that they must consent to inequality, but he ended his magnificent oration with the injunction that all participants must be knit together as one man. For the people to lose sight of the grand objective by distracting dreams of equality would be to wreck the enterprise. But Winthrop and his successors were as much aware of the danger from the other side, from the abuse of power. So then, when power was now patently being abused, the danger from proclaiming equality was as nothing compared with its usefulness as a defense against this monstrous depravity.

If I speak with more asperity than the theme calls for, it is because I have been long exacerbated by the platitude one so often encounters, that the great revolution of the eighteenth century as against the seventeenth was the substitution of an optimistic and positive doctrine of man for a pessimistic and negative one. Perhaps this may be the case in certain quarters of Europe, though I often wonder who gives the more terrifying picture of human depravity, Calvin or Voltaire. And I suppose that the thesis is applicable to a few of the deistic or deistically minded leaders of the American Revolution, most notably Tom Paine—who was not at all American, who came from a circle of European sophistication, and who, whatever assistance he gave to the movement for independence, was motivated by reasons of his own and spoke through his own imagery.

We come much closer to the sense in which the argument for equality was a viable conception for Americans when we turn from *Common Sense* to, for instance, the speech delivered in June 1775, by Colonel George Mason to the Fairfax Independent Company in Alexandria, Virginia. "We come equals into this world," Colonel Mason said, "and equals shall we go out of it." (Thomas Paine, I submit, was giving very little thought to the conditions under which men go out of this world!) So, after proving by infallible logic that men are born equally free and independent, and create societies by compacts, Colonel Mason came around to his real point:

> But when we reflect upon the insidious arts of wicked and designing men, the various and plausible pretences for continuing and increasing authority, the incautious nature of the many, and the inordinate lust of power in the few, we shall no longer be surprised that free-born man hath been enslaved, and that those very means which were contrived for his preservation have been perverted to his ruin; or, to borrow a metaphor from Holy Writ, that the kid hath been seethed in his mother's milk.

This subject has been so voluminously worried by historians and students of political theory that I hesitate to enter the snarling arena. But the lesson of Mason's paragraph is evident enough, and plausible enough: for many, if not for most, of the leaders of the American Revolution, the statement of equality—equality in birth and in death—was not so much a program for the reorganization of society as it was a theological and poetic vision to be invoked against "the insidious arts of wicked and designing men." Or put it another way: whereas the founders of the colonies had been concerned lest the appeal to natural law pervert the reign of positive law, and yet at the same time had completely understood that the positive regime also offers its own temptations to bestiality, by the time of the Revolution it had become legitimately possible for honest Christians to appeal to the law of nature, in which equality was the primary postulate, against the positive laws and regulations of England, which had been proved to be insidious, wicked, designing, and so at last were to be rejected with the assistance of a metaphor borrowed from Holy Writ. This is a very different thing from proclaiming a revolution on the grounds that all men are naturally good, therefore equal, and therefore, on the premise of their intrinsic virtuousness, entitled to rebel against a king they do not like. It is rather to say that a king who so abuses positive law as to outrage the natural is a wicked creature with an inordinate lust of power. Equality then becomes not the goal of the revolutionaries but an instrument for wreaking divine vengeance upon impious rulers—so that they, like King Ahab, may be brought to the universal equality of death.

Though the scholastic distinction, so dear to the Puritans, between the natural and the positive did not survive into the eighteenth century as anything more than a figure of speech, the descendants of Puritans who did retain some feeling for the original definitions, had on the whole little difficulty in seeing the Revolution as an appeal to the natural in order to redress a sinful abuse of the positive. There is abundant evidence to testify to the effectiveness as a mobilizing device of the days of humiliation and prayer called for by the Continental Congresses. Puritan loyalists like Governor Hutchinson had a hard time, indeed an impossible task, trying to prove that royal decrees and the Intolerable Acts were justified in their own terms, in terms of commerce and empire not in those of nature. Their cause was lost before they started; but then few of the patriots had time to realize how thoroughly their cause was won before they, too, started, and so they found themselves after the victory in the embarrassing position of a conqueror who has employed an auxiliary to which he owes his success, and must now put up with the annoying ally. The patriots' auxiliary had been Mason's and Jefferson's invocation of equality as a natural right against the positive, the artificial inequality of British rule. Very well, the enemy was gone. England was removed. The negativism of nature had exorcised the positivity of artifice. But then, here was society chained to a doctrine whose major tactical advantage had been negation, but which now threatened, with a tremendous religious sanction behind it, to become in turn the *positive* principle of an independent republic.

Many, most notably Jefferson, who had made the bargain with their eyes open, realized what they had let themselves in for. "The First Republicans," as Stuart Gerry Brown calls them, never repented the deal. But those who lived long enough, and some who like Jefferson perceived the portent, had their consciences put on the rack when the cult of equality produced, not Mason's dignified rhetoric but the histrionic person of General Andrew Jackson. It was all very well to use nature as a negation upon a positive George III, but what do civilized (and Christian) gentlemen do when out of nature come, in defiance of all scholastic categories, a Jackson who is even more positive, a Caesar who derives his powers from the enthusiastic consent of the governed, and so is not a wicked and designing man, but a devoutly pious egoist whose purpose, at least as announced, is to let no potentiality be suppressed, and who, in pursuance of that equalitarian purpose, wrecks the Bank of the United States?

I shall not try in this short space to describe the American experience with Jackson, beyond saying that unless one comprehends the era, he understands little of the present ambiguity in the American concept of equality. Foreign travelers in that period are unanimous in reporting that they found in city after city, among the more substantial citizens, a wistful aspiration for some form of American aristocracy; most of them describe a sort of pathetic longing for an "elite"—just what kind of elite, these troubled spirits do not seem to know, but something that will deliver them from the vulgarity which seemed to be the most tangible consequence, fifty years later, of the Revolutionary equality. Captain Basil Hall, in 1829, incurred the wrath of good Jacksonians, but was covertly welcomed by numerous Whigs, when he explained that America was a chaos because it lacked any principle of "loyalty." In England, he argued, the operation of this quality preserves the distinction of ranks, but in America, the weakness of this natural law means only that the public "chop and change," and no man has or can have any character.

Our greatest novelist of the era, James Fenimore Cooper who was hailed as "our National Novelist," resented the criticisms of English aristocrats like Hall, and in Europe lectured the older societies on the virtues of democracy; but when he returned to

Jacksonian America he was aghast at what he beheld. "Equality of condition," he declared, "is incompatible with civilization." There may be less inequality in America than in Europe; but "Equality is nowhere laid down as a governing principle of the institutions of the United States, neither the word, nor any inference that can be fairly deduced from its meaning, occurring in the constitution." Despite the popularity of his *Leatherstocking Tales*, the national novelist, in the later 1830s, almost lost his public by this blunt speaking, but many were delighted to hear him.

Out of all this long story, one persistent factor emerges: in any thinking, from the seventeenth to the nineteenth century, there is an enforced alliance between the concept of equality and that of nature. Cooper was a man at war with himself because he had started as the prose-poet of the forest. Nature may be, as a result of the sin of man, vile; or nature may be, as compared with the positive and the artificial, admirable—although again because the sin of man prompts him to abuse the positive. In either case, or in every curious combination of partial viewpoints (as in the case of Cooper), there had from the beginning been an assumption so deeply hidden below the layers of consciousness that only in the perspective of time can we see that it was there: which is to say, that in either or any formulation, equality is equated with innocence. If the equality of nature was denied in the name of the positive or of the civilized, it was not because equality in its essential character was sinful, but because sinful man would abuse it. If equality was exalted as a virtue against the positive impositions of Britain, it was because good Christians might retain, in the midst of their own sins, enough comprehension of the innocence of the divine image in which man had been created to recognize the greater sinfulness of the abuse of power.

So the question, in terms of American experience, would inevitably arise, if only to a few sensitivities. In Jacksonian America, somebody, somewhere, had to ask himself whether this nation could not finally assert the equality of the human species without at the same time claiming for them in the post-Adamic period those excellences which had made equality feasible in, and only in, the Garden of Eden.

In the 1850s, two great writers did arise in America to venture upon this blasphemy. Herman Melville went out of his way to portray the crew of the Pequod in *Moby Dick* as a collection of "castaways and renegades," including Ishmael, his own alter ego. So this Ishmael could accept the ultimate challenge of democracy, and equate himself with the crew. Defiantly he prayed that, if he should ascribe high and noble deeds to these ordinary men, the great "democratic God" should bear him out:

> Thou who didst pick up Andrew Jackson from the pebbles; who didst hurl him upon a war-horse; who didst thunder him higher than a throne! Thou who, in all Thy mighty, earthly marchings, ever cullest Thy selectest champions from the kingly commons; bear me out in it, O God!

But the great point struggling for utterance in Melville's rhetoric is that the democratic God is a synonym for "thou just Spirit of Equality," and that this absolute is the center and circumference of democracy: "His omnipresence, our divine equality!"

The other American writer who in this same decade dared to move from the notion of equality as a check upon sinful misuse of power to the affirmative assertion of a positive ideal, taking all the sins of mankind with it, was, of course, Whitman. By this time—1855, a century behind this year—words begin to play tricks upon us; and so we say that, as opposed to the negativism of Mason, Jefferson, and the Revolutionary liberals, here at last is a "positive" content poured into the ideal of equality. They were possessed of a vision, but not by Walt Whitman's: they would revolt in the name of the American farmer, but not in the name of "the common prostitute." Whitman would reject nobody, would sing physiology from top to toe, and chant the divine average. He was familiar with the older conception, as when he warned the democracy to be on guard against the never-ending audacity of elected persons; but what he asserts is a democracy—she is intensely feminine—who has become one with nature, with all nature, and apologizes for nothing natural. She puts off the last vestiges of positive law, not only in social relations but in every area of being or of speech:

> The gross and soil'd she moves among do not make her gross
> and soil'd,
> She knows the thoughts as she passes, nothing is conceal'd
> from her,
> She is none the less considerate or friendly therefor,

She is the best belov'd, it is without exception, She has no reason to fear and she does not fear,
Oaths, quarrels, hiccupp'd songs, smutty expressions, are idle to her as she passes,
She is silent, she is possess'd of herself, they do not offend her,
She receives them as the laws of Nature receive them, she is strong,
She too is a law of Nature—there is no law stronger than she is.[1]

Through all the shifts in cosmology and theology between Winthrop and Whitman, in some curious way the case for equality was linked with the cause of nature. Whitman sometimes could put the social issue on what seems like a merely empirical basis:

Of Equality—as if it harm'd me, giving others the same chances and rights as myself—as if it were not indispensable to my own rights that others possess the same.[2]

However, the real sanction for the vision of *Leaves of Grass* is nature, the nature which is both the grass and the teeming river seen from a Brooklyn ferry. The president who fails to measure up to this natural dignity is dangling mirages before the republic:

You have not learn'd of Nature—of the politics of Nature you have not learn'd the great amplitude, rectitude, impartiality,
You have not seen that only such as they are for these States.[3]

But after this unnatural Buchanan, there did arise a president who, as Whitman was among the first to appreciate, had acquired the amplitude, the rectitude, the impartiality of the politics of nature; and then Whitman had to face the ultimate challenge to all philosophies of equality derived solely out of nature. Abraham Lincoln would, in the course of nature, have died; but death came forward to meet him so dramatically that the problem could not be disposed of in a passing sentence, as Mason had done: "And

[1]Walt Whitman, *Leaves of Grass*, "Song of the Broad-Axe" (D. Appleton and Company, New York), 1910, p. 157. Copyright 1924 by Doubleday & Company, Inc.
[2]Ibid., "Thought," p. 219.
[3]Ibid., "To a President," p. 215.

equals shall we go out of it." Thus Whitman followed the logic to the end; if for the Puritan, equality in a state of nature had been lost by the perversity of man, which brought death into the world, then Whitman would find the equilibrium restored in the equality of death:

Come lovely and soothing death,
Undulate round the world, serenely arriving, arriving,
In the day, in the night, to all, to each,
Sooner or later delicate death.[4]

The American people forgot Melville and let him die in bleak obscurity; the masses of them have never accepted Whitman, and both these militant champions of the kingly commons are prized today, if they are prized, mainly by students of literature, who by that very fact are apt to erect around themselves a wall of separation from the democracy. Of course, there have been further crises in the philosophy of nature—most notably the shock of Darwinism and what seemed to be its social implications. These crises have forced further rethinkings of the problem of equality, raised new doubts, resurrected old anxieties in barely altered forms. But the immense assertions of Melville and Whitman do stand there, to challenge all doubters. Perhaps, as I take it McKeon suggests, the time has come to dissociate entirely the definition of equality from any monolithic concept of nature, whether Christian or scientific. Still, Melville and Whitman remain, to remind this nation that until it can learn, and abide with, the full lesson of democracy, it is not yet worthy of the role in history their genius assigned it. And as Whitman made clear, fully to learn the lesson of human equality is to accept at last the supremely equalizing fact of all human life:

. . . O sane and sacred death.[5]

[4]Ibid., "Memories of President Lincoln," p. 260.
[5]Ibid., p. 257.

Nineteenth-Century New England and Its Descendants

I THINK that had anyone a generation ago, or say at the turn of the century, undertaken to speak about the heritage left by nineteenth-century New England to the whole nation, he would have commenced by instancing the landscape. In all the schoolhouses of the North and the West youngsters were getting whatever notions they ever were to get about responding poetically to scenery from "Monument Mountain," "To the Fringed Gentian," "The Village Blacksmith," "Snow-Bound," or "The Chambered Nautilus." Everybody paid homage, if only in the classrooms, to the classic spokesmen for New England, those bearded gentlemen who were bound in uniform volumes subtitled the "Household Poets."

It is a minor irony in the cultural history of America that these poets—Bryant, Longfellow, Lowell, Whittier, Holmes—believed with all their hearts that the great achievement of their generation had been their actually naming, in their verses, American places, American flowers, American birds—especially birds. They stopped addressing the skylark, they hymned the bobolink. And then, just as they banished English meteorological and ornithological presuppositions, they imposed on the American imagination those of New England. I have been told that even in the South well-educated

An address delivered as part of the Martin G. Brumbaugh Lectures in Education for the Summer of 1957 at the University of Pennsylvania. The theme of the series was the cultural inheritance of the modern mind.

young ladies used to think it vulgar to admire Spanish moss because it doesn't appear in the lyrics of Mr. Longfellow. That may be an exaggeration, but I know for myself that though I lived in Illinois, and saw the summer and winter there for myself, still whenever I thought of treating such phenomena poetically, I thought in terms of the imagery imparted by my grammar-school teacher's readings from the New England poets. We all saw the prairie seasons through Yankee eyes, until suddenly the Middle West found its own voice; Edgar Lee Masters, Vachel Lindsay, Carl Sandburg, made Spoon River, Springfield, and the hog-butcher to the world as honorable themes for poetry as the churchyard at Cambridge. A great part of the supposedly revolutionary impact of those Chicago writers in the 1920s was simply that they did mention what was around them. Because that much now seems obvious—we do not expect a poet in Carmel to use the backdrop of Haverhill, Massachusetts—it is difficult to appreciate the violence of the jolt they administered to the dominant orthodoxy. Hence it may seem that those once-insurgent geniuses have worn a little thin; we even find in contemporary criticism certain slight, judicious efforts to rehabilitate the once-spreading reputation of Henry Wadsworth Longfellow.

Of course, this uprising against domination by the New England Household Poets (Bryant, even though he lived most of his life in New York was counted one of them, because his nature scenes were the Berkshires) was part of a multifold rejection in American culture around 1920 of the hegemony of New England. This strain in the revolt of that irreverent decade—a period often nowadays as falsely glamorized as to us in the actual 1920s was the "mauve decade" of the '90s—is too large a subject to be more than mentioned here, but the fact that such a protest was made, and made emphatically, is a major reason why today there should be any interest at all in my topic. In the ubiquitous denunciations of the "Puritan" which enlivened that joyous—well, not too joyous—time, and which still echo in occasional growls, the real target was never the historical Puritan of the seventeenth century—about him the young rebels knew little and cared less—but the image of culture, of control of emotion, monogamy, temperance (or worse), which nineteenth-century New England had supposedly foisted on the country. Years ago George Santayana gave it a more accurate name, "The Genteel Tradition," yet he also—as in his tract disguised as a novel, *The Last Puritan*—argued that the sterile genteelism of New England was a Puritanism gone to seed. So, voices arose all over the land—from the South Side of Chicago; from St. Paul, Minnesota; from Charleston, South Carolina; from the Barbary Coast of San Francisco; from Greenwich Village; and then for a while a whole chorus from the Left Bank of Paris—all proclaiming the independence of the American mind from Puritanism and from prohibition. What was meant in effect was that the other regions were throwing off the yoke of New England. Indeed, hundreds of young New Englanders enthusiastically joined the wrecking crews.

All this, as I say, had nothing really to do with the Puritan heritage which the New England colonists had built into the foundations of the nation. Through successive modifications, divisions, transformations, Puritan theology has had a continuous history in America, and this never entered seriously into any of 1920s revolts against New England. If in the cold-water flats around Washington Square among bands of fugitives from Gopher Prairie, meeting over a bathtub full of gin to tell each other the inner mystery of this strange new apparition (smuggled through the customs) called *Ulysses*, the rebellion was sometimes proclaimed against Protestant doctrine as well as against the school marm's Mr. Longfellow, that aspect of their discourse was purely rhetorical and is of little worth to the historian. After all, the neo-Orthodoxy, so-called, of Reinhold and Richard Niebuhr is as much a product of the 1920s as the novels of F. Scott Fitzgerald. We can see that continuity in the development of American religious experience was not rudely broken by the emotional upheavals of post-World War I, though it was, in more fundamental ways, affected. But in the realms of literary taste and in the popular conception of artistic purpose, a real and permanent revolution was indeed enacted. The simplest way to describe it, or to designate what it did, is to say that it dethroned the cultural supremacy of New England.

I for one believe that it was high time this *sans-culottism* appeared. Possibly some of you know the book published in 1900 by my distinguished predecessor at Harvard, Barrett Wendell, *A Literary History of America*. It is a pioneer work, and does not always merit the contempt which now is automatically poured upon it. Still, the amusing fact about it is undeniable: after a cursory survey of the colonial and revolutionary periods (giving special attention and space to Cotton Mather), and brief glances at Irving, Cooper, and Poe, the substance of the book is two long portions called, "The Renaissance of New England," after which comes a very brief section, almost an appendix, arrogantly entitled, "The Rest of the Story." It has a fifteen-page piece on Whitman, which is mainly a demonstration that Whitman's notion of absolute equality is altogether foreign to the facts of American life and thought (as had been evidenced, according to Wendell, throughout the literature of New England, wherein not even Emerson entirely succumbed to the absurdity), but which is chiefly known to derisive fame because it characterizes "Crossing Brooklyn Ferry" as confused, inarticulate, and "surging in a mad kind of rhythm which sounds as if hexameters were trying to bubble through sewage."

Barrett Wendell was entirely a product of that late nineteenth-century culture of New England against which the attacks of the 1920s were levelled. After the battle was over and the insurgents had won their victory, Mr. Van Wyck Brooks endeavored to be gracious to this era by calling his book about it *New England: Indian Summer*. Probably many people read it—as a great many at least purchased it—because they really have a nostalgia for the serenity, the security, the courtesy which that age seemed to offer—certainly these it appeared to offer in ample measure as Mr. Brooks presented it. But actually that New England is an imaginary home to which none of us can go back any more—even supposing for a moment, what I am sure is untrue, that it ever was such an idyllic paradise. While critics, or such bludgeoners as H. L. Mencken, were demolishing its pretensions, a new historian of American thought and letters emerged in 1926. He came from the West, from the state of Washington; after Vernon Louis Parrington's *Main Currents in American Thought* nobody—not even the most inbred Harvard-Bostonian scholar—could ever dare again to survey the scene from the point of view of a Barrett Wendell.

I suppose that almost every chapter Parrington wrote has been superseded by the rush of later research; the truth seems to be that even then he worked out of very limited sources. Still, the book, even though tragically uncompleted, is a monument of scholarship in the whole field of what we now call "American Civilization" or, less boastfully, "American Studies." Anyone alive in 1926 who ws responding to the fresh interest in things American which blew like a gale across the country will remember the excitement of Parrington. There were a hundred illuminations in it—the seemingly comprehensive sweep of the South and the West, for instance —but one of the more vibrant was his resolute cutting down to size of Harvard University and the orthodox New England poets. He did not orate, he was no barbarian from without the walls, but in quiet, measured tones he ticked off the mentality of Back Bay:

> The immediate consequence of this concern for defensive breastwork was the reign of the genteel in life and letters, a reign that set up a court of critical jurisdiction over the domain of American letters. The essence of the genteel was a refined ethicism, that professed to discover the highest virtue in shutting one's eyes to disagreeable fact, and the highest law in the law of convention. . . . The first of literary commandments was the commandment of reticence.

In the general joy that this at last was publicly said, and said in such a way that it could never be forgotten, many neglected to notice that Barrett Wendell had just barely managed to end his chapter of Whitman with a quotation (I think from his colleague Charles Eliot Norton) to the effect that a man who could idealize the East River "is the only one who points out the stuff of which perhaps the new American literature of the future may in time be made." But then, though this is said, it is weakly said; so Barrett Wendell gets no great credit for it, any more than he gets credit for having mentioned Melville, on page 229, because it is obvious he had never read Melville, knew of him only from Robert Louis Stevenson's admiration for Melville's South Sea travels, and managed to spell Melville's first name with two "n's"!

Remaining a moment longer with the contrast of Wendell and Parrington—if I may do so without becoming tedious, for I know no better way of getting some historical perspectives on our problem—it is worth noting that Parrington entertained no hostility to New England as such. On the contrary, he adored its militant reforming zeal, its Puritan conscience when enlisted on the side of social justice instead of when sublimated into genteel reticence. His heroes out of nineteenth-century New England were William Lloyd Garrison, John G. Whittier, Harriet Beecher Stowe, Theodore Parker, Edmund Quincy, Wendell Phillips. The head and front of the Brahmins' offence, as Parrington saw it, was that they "took it ill when those barriers were assaulted by rude militants, and when indisputable Brahmins—men like Edmund Quincy and Wendell Phillips—took part in the assault, the Back Bay regarded them as more than a little queer."

Here the contrast with Barrett Wendell could not possibly be more extreme. Wendell had to write a chapter on "The Antislavery Movement," which he did with obvious loathing. In palliation of Theodore Parker's extremely bad manners, Wendell wrote, "there might be pleaded the excuse that [he], like Garrison, sprang from the lower class of New England which never intimately understood its social superiors." The self-made man, he moralized, can rarely quite outgrow all the limitations of his origin—thus paraphrasing Dr. Holmes's eminently Bostonian quip that the self-made man is necessarily an ill-made one. But, Wendell continued, his enmity becoming a screech, "No such excuse may be pleaded for the two other antislavery orators who are best remembered—Wendell Phillips and Charles Sumner." For Wendell Phillips, Barrett Wendell's only comment was that at the end of his life he did nothing but "exhibit the somewhat senile vagaries of a character whose leading passion seems to have become an ardour for disagreement with mankind." As for the whole movement, though of course slavery was an evil, Barrett Wendell sees in it a Yankee carry-over of a hypocritical trait of the English: "For no peculiarity has been more characteristic of the native English than a passion to reform other people than themselves, trusting meantime that God will help those who forcibly help somebody else."

One of the points Parrington heavily underscored in expressing his admiration for Wendell Phillips was that Phillips did not concentrate all his reforming zeal on abolition, that he did not give over being an agitator after Appomattox, but that he continued to fight for all liberal reforms, even for the rights of labor. For Barrett Wendell, these were senile crotchets. Here then we have two opposite poles from which to evaluate our own thinking, once we attempt to appraise our inheritance from nineteenth-century

New England, especially when we meditate upon that ferment of reform which was so cataclysmic a part of its spiritual expression. And we have to take account of the whole tremendous impulse, not just of abolitionism. In education, economics, sexual relations, religion, it was equally disruptive, equally extravagant, equally vociferous, equally noble and absurd.

Whereupon we run smack against an interesting phenomenon: the liberal mentality which came of age and so to free expression of the 1920s—of which Parrington was the perfect representative—took delight at one and the same time in denigrating the Brahmins of New England and in exalting its militant radicals. This seemed in 1926 eminently logical. After all, slavery was an evil, it did have to be abolished, at a terrible cost; did this not make the abolitionists prophets and heroes? And the other reforms—in how many of them had not the New England cranks also proved to be prophets —Horace Mann, Margaret Fuller, the enthusiasts of Brook Farm? Suppose they were sometimes comic in their eagerness, innocent in their dreams of how easy it would be to improve mankind? Have they not all been vindicated? Henry James thought he was treating Elizabeth Peabody with loving though amused consideration when he presented her as "Miss Birdseye" in *The Bostonians* of 1880, but he had to learn even then that in America these warriors of the once ridiculed newnesses had survived into a veneration which could no longer be treated with even a taint of derision.

The result has been that over what I may summarily call the liberal mentality—meaning that which inspired Parrington and which still informs upright citizens of this republic—New England continued to exercise a conceptual hegemony. Only now, it was a moral superiority rather than a literary one. If Longfellow appeared more and more tepid, and Dr. Holmes emerged as a parochial snob, still John Brown was a veritable martyr. There was no reason not to repeat with approval Emerson's statement that Brown "made the gallows glorious as the cross." Yes, by the civil code he had to be hanged, but did not the boys in blue march to bloody victory singing that while his body lay a-mouldering in the grave, his soul went marching on? And John Brown was the very essence of New England's reforming passion.

I need hardly point out that in the climate of today none of these positions seems quite so clear as it did to men of Parrington's generation and persuasion. In this day of the FBI, what sort of shrift would a creature get who organizes a plot to overthrow by force and violence anything in the social structure of which he disapproves on ideological grounds? How much tolerance would a reformer receive who calls the Constitution of the United States (as William Lloyd Garrison actually did) "A Covenant with Death and an Agreement with Hell"? And, when the historian comes, critically and detachedly to study the period, he is obliged to ask whether abolitionists actually did have any effect on the ultimate emancipation other than to exacerbate the discussion so that war, protracted war, became inevitable? And then, how many of them, once they took unto themselves the smug credit for having launched the crusade, thereafter basked in the glory, thereafter showed no concern whatsoever for the thickening crowd of evils that came in the wake of the Civil War?

I do not take seriously the literature which recently enjoyed a vogue under the catch-phrase, "The New Conservatism." But it is no doubt a symptom of our times; certainly there is much talk about the "conformism" of our age. Even if that be exaggerated, I think this much is indisputable: the reforming spirit of nineteenth-century New England gloried in chanting that Wrong was always on the throne and Right enchained at its feet; from this persuasion it derived the energy to go forth and do battle for the Lord. This "Hebraic zeal"—as it is sometimes called—transmitted itself from New England to the various protest movements of later decades. Populism and the Progressive Party included many latter-day New Englanders in their leadership; at Chicago in 1912 the rally cry was, "We stand at Armageddon." All this seemed to be entirely in the grand manner of Garrison and Theodore Parker.

Historians of a larger sophistication, with more subtle tools for sociological dissection, are now giving us rather different accounts of these idealistic uprisings. They note, for instance, that nothing much came of them, that they petered out as soon as the protestants got from government a few slices of the augmenting prosperity. The New England style of moral exhortation begins to seem at best an ethical rationalization for highly mundane strategies, at worst a form of propagandistic demagoguery. And so a suspicion has been suggested: was the reformist surge in pure New England of the 1840s entirely so selfless? Even though Back Bay found reformism vulgar, still New England, with its burgeoning factories, did need to strike down the South, to wreck the plantation economy, and to persuade what was left of the country to indulge it with a protective tariff. And as for the other reformers—when you study some of them closely, are they not unlovely egotists of whom Nathaniel Hawthorne gave the prototype in his Hollingsworth of *The Blithedale Romance*?

Just as soon as you raise queries of these sorts—which, as I say, are uncomfortable—you find yourself realizing (as too few students of literature and religion do) that after 1815 New England was gaining an ascendency over the mind of America not only by flooding it with the irresistibly popular verses of its Household Poets or by calling it sternly to task in the name of moral idealism, but less spectacularly though more remorselessly it was leading American society into the Industrial Revolution. This is hardly the place to insert a survey of American economic development. But the rough outlines are familiar. It all begins with the supremely ironic joke of American history: agrarian Mr. Jefferson, believing that the preservation of this rural economy depended on keeping it unentangled with Europe, imposed on the Atlantic ports the embargo of 1807, and so turned New Englanders from the ocean to the rivers. Then the story jumps ahead, as a result of a Yankee trick: Francis Lowell, visiting England from 1810 to 1812, spent more weeks walking the aisles of cotton factories than of cathedrals, and stored his clever head with plans for the machines of which the British, striving to protect their monopoly, would not tell the secrets. By 1814 his loom was functioning in Waltham, Massachusetts.

One has always to remember that in New England there were other forms of aesthetic indulgence than the sweetly melancholy lyrics of Longfellow. When Francis Lowell exhibited his loom to Nathan Appleton (who had been so sceptical that he would advance Lowell only five of the ten thousand dollars Lowell needed), Appleton saw the portent: "I well recollect the state of admiration and satisfaction with which we sat by the hour, watching the beautiful movement of this new and wonderful machine, destined as it evidently was, to change the character of all textile industry."

It not only changed the character, it introduced acceleration. Any good textbook, of which there are several, will quickly show the imbalance between the mechanical facilities of New England as against the rest of the country combined: in 1860, sixty-nine per cent of the cotton manufacturing was concentrated in the region; at that date it was the center for the manufacture of smaller metal products. With the canals and railroads, the revolution spread rapidly westward across the northern tier of states, but it expanded out of New England.

Historians point out "reasons" for this rapid transformation of New England's economy. The availability of water power is clearly central, as is the existence of an intelligent populace which could quickly master skilled manual operations. As the hard soil was becoming harder, hundreds who would not go to Ohio went to Lowell and Pawtucket. Yet I am strongly of the feeling that the amazing extent and speed of the process cannot wholly be explained by purely economic factors. It is not enough to account for these by phrases like "Yankee ingenuity," "the land of steady habits," or a high concentration of what Max Weber taught us to call "the Protestant ethic." Finally, abandoning historical causality altogether, you permit yourself the purely intuitive divination that here, at the beginning of the dramatic century, was a culture with a highly developed personality, amazingly homogeneous despite its many divisions and its inner animosities. We may then hazard a guess that we get some sense of what was really the configuration of this culture when we see that it was, at one and the same time, expressed in the genteel elegance of the Brahmins, in the fiery energies of the reformers, and in Nathan Appleton's ecstatic encounter with beauty in a power loom.

There is always the danger, in trying to describe a complex business in a short time, of oversimplification; I assure you that the pattern of nineteenth-century New England is a bit more incoherent than I am making it seem. Still, to repeat, at the beginning of the century, it was remarkably homogeneous. And if these three elements seem at first sight to have little in common, on second thought, we can see that they join hands to form, so to speak, three sides of a quadrilateral. The mind of Brahmin gentility is obviously related on one side to the success of the Industrial Revolution. James Russell Lowell was, after all, a Lowell, and Longfellow married Nathan Appleton's daughter, and Nathan bought Craigie House on Brattle Street as a wedding present for them. Dr. Holmes, in his peculiar manner, says some of the most brutally realistic things about the value of money, the importance of a social position backed by wealth, that cynicism could achieve. Yet on the other side, while Brahmin gentility disliked the uproar of reform, it is allied to that phenomenon by its high ethical devotion. Back Bay would take care not to become abolitionist, but it would never accept the Southern thesis that slavery was ethically justifiable; when the fight had to come, young Brahmins fought gallantly, ferociously, even though it seemed shocking to men like Garrison that they should fight without sharing his conviction. And across from each other, the reforming spirit and the business spirit of New England, which contended on the surface against each other, are united underneath that surface by their derivation from the tremendous earnestness of the Puritan heritage. Whatever they did, they did hard.

If the three may thus be said to link at the corners, at least enough to give us a discussable outline of coherence, we should then need a fourth side to complete my rhetorical design. We have an east, with a northern and southern flank reaching out from it, but have we west? And if such there be, does it join the dance?

Emerson artfully concluded the second series of his *Essays* with one called "New England Reformers." It is probably little read today; I have difficulty explaining to students why, along with such lofty topics as Love, Friendship, Experience, The Poet, Emerson should have been obliged to descend to this hubbub. But the reason we today are puzzled is that we forget with what importunity the reforming spirit pressed upon the spirit of sensitive, intelligent youth. It threatened to gobble up the mind, it was an invasion of privacy, it had to be resisted. Emerson's essay was truly an appropriate rear guard for his two series; it stands in the gap, holding off the most dangerous or insidious enemy, while his free thoughts make good their escape, while they can run wild.

When taken in the context of the 1840s, Emerson's inventory of the causes advocated by the New England reformers is one of the few funny passages he ever wrote; he starts off with the more serious issues, then develops his list into slapstick:

> Even the insect world was to be defended,—that had been too long neglected, and a society for the protection of groundworms, slugs, and mosquitoes was to be incorporated without

> delay. With these appeared the adepts of homeopathy, of hydropathy, of mesmerism, of phrenology, and their wonderful theories of the Christian miracles. Others assailed particular vocations, as that of the lawyer, that of the merchant, of the manufacturer, of the clergyman, of the scholar. Others attacked the institution of marriage, as the fountain of social evils. Others devoted themselves to the worrying of churches and meetings for public worship; and the fertile forms of antinomianism among the elder puritans seemed to have their match in the plenty of the new harvest of reform.

As was his habit, Emerson was considerably fair to these fanatics; he saw their mood as a sign of the times, and he could pay tribute to disinterestedness. But in the end, he condemns them for being "mechanical." Though the reformers always thought he should become one of them, just as George Ripley assumed that he would join Brook Farm, Emerson all his life fought not to let himself be distracted from the siege of his hen coop to march off to a pretended siege of Babylon. When they realized this, the reformers came to hate him worse than they hated the conservatives of Back Bay; to them he became the archtraitor. But in his essay about them, quietly but devastatingly showing wherein they had narrowed their minds and given up to reform what was meant for the Over-Soul, he insisted that the true advance of the age was a casting off of material aids and "the indication of growing trust in the private, self-supplied powers of the individual."

Remember that when he wrote these lines Emerson was still considered by conservative Boston and by Harvard College the radical of "The Divinity School Address." And remember also that as he watched the industrialization of New England he saw nothing beautiful in power looms; he lamented that things were in the saddle and were riding mankind. I agree, at once, that over the years Emerson did not hold in strict consistency this individualistic stance. Eventually, by the marriage of his daughter to a Forbes, he too was incorporated into the web of wealth, and in his last days was supported, as were Lowell and Longfellow, by the proceeds of the Industrial Revolution. In the course of time, his preaching of individualism, especially "self-reliance," came to seem not at all dangerous, but rather the proper code for a young businessman with get-up and go. It was discovered that Emersom could be admitted to the placid manners of the Saturday Club, which met in the Parker House. And after the Fugitive Slave Act he did speak out against slavery so that, once the Civil War was finished, he could not be accused of having failed to do his part in the supreme among the New England crusades.

But these are pieces of Emerson's biography, not of the doctrine he promulgated, which in historical textbooks we call "Transcendentalism." As you know, the problem for the historian of defining Transcendentalism is virtually insurmountable because nobody at the time could define it, or rather no two Transcendentalists could agree on the same definition. Yet that it is there, and that it was an element in the intellectual configuration of the culture, this cannot be denied. And its importance is by no means diminished by the fact that the band of Transcendentalists was numerically very small, or that for years they were universally ridiculed by the Brahmin gentlemen, by the grubby reformers, and by the captains of New England industry. James Russell Lowell, William Lloyd Garrison, Nathan Appleton—to take these as symbolic figures—had one thing in common: they could despise Henry Thoreau.

For as we can see now, what was hard to see then, Thoreau made none of the concessions or compromises Emerson did. When Emerson once tried to get him to come a little way toward healing the breach with gentility, to attend a meeting of the Saturday Club, Thoreau replied that he went to Boston as little as possible, that when there, as soon as his business was done, the only room in all the city he wanted to visit was the men's room of the Fitchburg Station where he could wait for the train back to Concord. Nor do I need to read any of his by now famous indictments of the American absorption in business. If his target was not so clearly the factories and mills as it was the agricultural economy of his town, still it is clear that what he was orating against was the whole spirit of money-making. When he did for a moment turn his attention to those looms which Nathan Appleton had found beautiful, he perceived a beauty which might go far to explain Appleton's sense of the aesthetic:

> Where is this division of labor to end? and what object does it serve? I cannot believe that our factory system is the best model by which men may get clothing. The condition of the operatives is becoming every day more and more like that of

> the English; and it cannot be wondered at, since, as far as I have heard or observed, the principal object is, not that mankind may be well and honestly clad, but, unquestionably, that corporations may be enriched.

And as for reform, for doing good, for bettering the lot of his fellows, when he was told that his way of life was selfish, he could reply that he had no genius for charity, and that, "As for Doing-good, that is one of the professions which are full." In 1853 his mother's boardinghouse was suddenly infested with "three ultra-reformers," and Thoreau's pages on them are among his most vitriolic; he is disgusted with "the greasy cheeks of their kindness"; "They would not keep their distance, but cuddle up and lie spoon-fashion with you, no matter how hot the weather nor how narrow the bed." One of them so sought to convert Henry as though to take him into his bowels—"Men's bowels are far more slimy than their brains." This is about the nearest to a string of profanity Henry Thoreau ever came in his *Journal*, and here he did show the inveterate hostility of the true spirit of Transcendentalism to organized reform.

Again, all this is not a complete story. I am leaving out, for instance, Emily Dickinson: she makes another and a longer lecture. And it is true that some Transcendentalists have links with Brahmin Boston: Dr. Holmes would write a life of Emerson. And many authentic Transcendentalists, like Parker and Ripley, got involved with some or another of the reforms. But, for the sake of clarifying our terms, Henry Thoreau is invaluable: Transcendentalism, he lets us see, was in essence a protest against the internal linkage of our other three actors. The fourth side of our parallelogram does not join at the corners, it breaks away. And yet it is as authentically of New England as the others, and because it was articulate it comes down as a principal, maybe *the* principal, heritage of nineteenth-century New England.

I think it evident on all sides as times goes on, as our perspective of the New England terrain gains distance, that critical estimate of Thoreau proves him more and more the major writer of the Transcendental group, indeed of the period. This occasionally causes discomfort to those who admire him no less than to the many who still dislike him and always will. If you toy with the question of what modern society might do with a reformer who denounces the

Constitution as a covenant with Hell, or with an ideologue who seizes a United States arsenal and starts shooting, what, you must ask, would it do with the author of "Civil Disobedience" and "'Life without Principle"? There really isn't anything you can say about him except that he is ultimate in subversion, because he would subvert even the reformers, let alone the conservatives. It is New England's Thoreau who still exhorts us: "If the law is of such a nature that it requires you to be an agent of injustice to another, then, I say, break the law. Let your life be a counter friction to stop the machine."

I leave you to settle with yourself how you shall take Henry Thoreau. To go back to our starting points, Barrett Wendell recognized Thoreau's craftsmanship in prose, but concluded that the constant obtrusion of his personality, his unflagging self-consciousness, make him an inferior writer; the best Wendell could say for *Walden* was that "it remains a vital bit of literature for any one who loves to read about Nature." Twenty-six years later, Parrington plays down the poet-naturalist, hails the social philosopher precisely for the extremes of individualism, calls his "one of the great names in American literature," and predicts (in 1926) that he is only beginning to come into his own.

This story would surely puzzle Thoreau's fellow-townsmen and his contemporaries. What of "his own" does a man have to come into who, upon getting a Harvard degree, does absolutely nothing with it—nothing, that is, that Concord village or Nathan Appleton could see? Assuredly we can say this much: New England made him, and New England gives him to us. Ghandi might admire him, but he is inconceivable outside New England. In the long run it may possibly be that if you want to enumerate what has descended to us from nineteenth-century New England, and you find it difficult to put a finger on any specific idea or literary influence, when you perceive that the Household Poets no longer inspire our poets, that the reforming spirit has evaporated, and that the Industrial Revolution has gone so far beyond its Yankee origins as to render any study of them a work of archaeology—it just may be that the one thing which you will find has most emphatically descended from that age, which is effectively present with us today, is the growing reputation of, and the inescapable challenge of, Henry Thoreau.

The New England Conscience

IN 1891 Henry Adams took what subsequently became a famous trip to the South Seas with John La Farge. Tahiti was still as unspoiled, as lush, as sensuous, as when Melville advertised the region through *Typee* in 1846. La Farge, being an artist, gave himself up entirely to the warmth, the color, the fragrance; but Adams went on dissecting his mind, analyzing his impressions into abstractions, and commenting at length on his inability to surrender himself. "Adams," at last exclaimed the irritated La Farge, "you reason too much." La Farge should, the author later observed, "have blamed Adams for being born in Boston."

Take any odd lot of New Englanders coming from the Puritan stock—Winthrop, Roger Williams, Cotton Mather, all the Adamses, Harriet Beecher Stowe, Henry Thoreau, Senator Leverett Saltonstall—and what do they have in common, despite differing philosophies or the contrasts among their centuries? The answer follows quickly: they are possessed by what has come to be stereotyped, both in New England and in more pagan areas, as the "New England Conscience." Other sections of the country and other cultures of the world exhibit, I have no doubt, scores of conscientious men and women; only in New England is there a Conscience so standardized that it must be capitalized. As John Quincy Adams succinctly put it, "New England was the colony of Conscience."

The conventional observation is that this habit of obeying with slavish fidelity—some term it a morbid curiosity—the inner promptings of rectitude goes back to the Puritan migration of the seventeenth century. However, other Calvinist peoples came to other colonies, and the great Scotch-Irish clans who marched to the Pennsylvania frontier and down the valleys into Georgia carried with them a respect for conscience as militant as any cherished in New England. If one puts John C. Calhoun, who was born of these pioneers, beside Daniel Webster, the "glorious" keeper of the New England political conscience, one would hesitate a long while before arguing that Webster was more in the clutch of moral principle than the gaunt Carolinian. In fact, there were many, including some New Englanders, who would swear that when he came to his personal finances, Webster simply had no conscience whatsoever!

The first remark to be made, therefore, is that the New Englanders so early and persistently advertised their unique devotion to the faculty, and so ordered their society as to enforce its obligations upon every department of life, that in effect they persuaded themselves (and so others) that they had a monopoly of the article. Having thus convinced themselves, they were obliged to display the habit long after they had abandoned the Calvinism of the founders. Indeed, if today one wishes to study the configurations of New England's Conscience, one is more apt to find prime specimens among "liberal" Unitarians, or even among those professing to have outgrown religion altogether, than among the "orthodox" communions.

The primitive order of New England was an ingenious method for institutionalizing what had been known in medieval England as "the Agenbite of Inwyt." This can legitimately be translated merely as "remorse of conscience"; but in the language of the people it had a more savage connotation: the gnawing bite of that wit which festers within a man and which he cannot control. The Puritans set up churches in the form we call "Congregational." The primary requirement was that a candidate could not become a member of a church until he had relentlessly examined his soul and discovered therein fairly certain evidence of his regeneration; then he had to submit to examination by the church or at least by the elders, experts in this probing of the psyche, until they could attest that he was at least a "visible saint." (They never permitted themselves to say of anybody that he positively *was* a saint before his funeral sermon had been pronounced.) Since all those concerned worked every minute of their lives in the Great Taskmaster's eyes, the inspection was conducted through His and not through their own eyes.

These settlers brought in large quantities copies of a handbook that for two centuries was to guide them and their posterity through the labyrinth of "inwyt"—*Conscience with the Power and Cases thereof*, by William Ames (it was published originally in Latin around 1620, but an immensely popular English translation appeared in 1643). He had been the teacher, the revered mentor, of many of the first generation of divines, and for years, from his professorship in Franeker, had educated Protestant Europe in the English version of the religious conscience. He died just as he was about to embark for Boston in 1633; had he come and been able to work there, his would be the great name we remember as originating the Puritan intellect in America, and Mather, Cotton, Hooker, and Shepard would figure as his satellites. But although his body did not migrate, his book did. It was the standard text at Harvard and Yale; it was in every minister's study; and thousands of unmetaphysical yeomen had their perplexities resolved or the precise character of their trespass defined according to the minute regulations of Ames's casuistry.

Ames put his central thesis, around which the massive tome revolves, with terrifying simplicity: the individual conscience "is man's judgment of himself according to the judgment of God of him." This is to say that it would do the visible saint no good to plead extenuating circumstances, the frailty of his flesh, ignorance or stupidity, or to try to even the balance by citing his manifold good deeds against just one mistake. His was the task of judging himself remorselessly by the divine rule. Moreover, he was to submit himself to such a moral autopsy not only *after* he had done or not done something, but also *before* it. For conscience, as Ames unflinchingly asserted, is not a contemplative exercise but a practical engine "whereby man applies to himself, to direct his will, to that which is either good or evil to him."

There were critics at the time, as there have been many more in later centuries, who argued that an ecclesiastical system embodying this sort of ethical imperative would succeed only in putting conscience to sleep. Once the trembling candidate was accepted by the church, would he not calculate that he was safe and cease to tremble? Indeed, the great revivals, that of Jonathan Edwards in 1740 and that in Connecticut around 1800, arose out of deep conviction that the churches had indeed become complacent. In New England, revivalists always endeavored to distress the historic conscience so that it would once more go to work.

Yet despite these intermittent periods of "deadness," there was always a maggot in the New England brain that gnawed at security, for nobody, not even Cotton Mather himself, was allowed to be absolutely assured of his election. Indeed, the immense diary that Cotton Mather kept every day of his adult existence is a search of his own condition that a modern reader finds extravagant to the point of becoming wildly ludicrous. "Many, many Things I have to do," runs a typical entry, "Many Things of the greatest Consequence. I shall either leave them undone, or do them not well, or miss the Time of doing them, if I do not with much Resignation unto it, obtain the heavenly Conduct." A man thus perpetually driven might develop, as Cotton Mather conspicuously did, disagreeable manners of self-righteousness and censoriousness, but he would live without inward peace. What is more, Mather did not want such peace. He would have despised it.

For in the New England doctrine, as developed from Ames, that was an elaboration of the central position that seemed to those outside the Puritan pale, whether in England or Virginia, to put the seal of approval upon cultivated hypocrisy, but made the search of soul an unending torment to the Puritans. The true goodness or sinfulness of a deed was not a matter of external conditions—giving to charities, rescuing a drowning boy, conducting a profitable voyage, accepting a token from one who had been aided—but consisted wholly in the intention. "Outward action without the inward," said Ames, "is not properly good or evil," because the merit of an act, whatever the circumstances, "depends first and foremost upon the will, which is often accepted with God, though outward work itself be absent." So it might be legitimate in a thousand situations to employ some form of deceit; the Old Testament tells of many cases in which the elect admirably hoodwinked the enemies of Jehovah. But Ames and his Puritan disciples, into the twentieth century, always contended that they never tolerated a double standard in morality—never permitted a distinction to be made between the code for politics or business and the one for private behavior. Therefore, they were bound to be all the more racked by the question of whether their motive was good when they closed a deal, sold an article, fired a workman or foreclosed a mortgage. If the motive is good, the rest does not matter, for as Ames had sagely instructed them, "A lie is properly a testimony whereby one pronounces otherwise than is in his heart." As John Cotton explained to Roger Williams, he was exiled from Massachusetts Bay not for obeying his conscience but for going against what Cotton and the authorities really knew was his conscience. If there be an element of cynicism in this program, then it is there due to deliberate calculation. As a modern child of the Puritans, a man much in the public view, recently expounded it, the crime is not that one steals but rather the enjoying what one has stolen.

So, because the saint or the would-be saint had constantly to maintain the closest scrutiny of himself, New Englanders became the most prolific keepers of diaries in all history. Here again the habit persisted after the theological incentives weakened. Every Adams, we know, kept a diary, and a great scholarly enterprise is now under way to present the public eventually with every last bit of their pertinacious self-criticism. The journals of Emerson and Thoreau are simply the greatest masterpieces of this vast array of New England introspection. *The Education of Henry Adams* is another of these Puritan introversions, written under the compulsion of a conscience that can never rest until it exhausts its victim. If, as an unsympathetic reader once suggested, the title of the book ought to be *The Unfortunate Relationship of the Universe to Me*, then the joke is applicable to all these manifestations of the New England Conscience. As Henry Thoreau summarized the issue, "We do not attend to larks and bluebirds so leisurely but that conscience is as erect as the attitude of the listener. The man of principle gets never a holiday."

Among the most monumental of Puritan diaries is that of a contemporary of Cotton Mather, sometimes his friend and often his opponent, Samuel Sewall. He was a less hysterical being than Mather, so that his self-portraiture is more ingratiating. Although he never received any formal legal training, he ended his days as Chief Justice of Massachusetts and, from all accounts, a good one. Yet when he was younger and less skilled in the law, he had the misfortune to be appointed to the improvised court that in 1692 condemned the Salem "witches." The legend goes that the presiding judge, William Stoughton, never repented his part in the judicial massacre. One of the most charming dormitories in the Harvard Yard is named for him; I know not what effect, if any, a year's residence therein has on the consciences of modern freshmen. But within five years of this colossal blunder, Sewall realized how ghastly it was. He gave a statement to his minister, Samuel Willard, asking that it be read from the pulpit of the Old South Church while Sewall stood in shame before the congregation. Openly Sewall took the blame of it upon himself and asked for the prayers of men, that God would pardon his crime and not visit deserved punishment for his stupidity "upon the Land."

Assuredly, the New England Conscience has its angular, stifling, inhuman aspects, as well as its uncanny refuges, and frequently it seems no more than a neurotic tic. Hundreds of generous, gay-spirited children of the Puritans have, like Shaw's Devil's Disciple, so reacted against it as to go over to the enemy. But if there is a nobility, a dignity in it, the tableau of Samuel Sewall, substantial citizen, standing in humiliation before his church while his accusation against himself is made public, symbolizes its majesty. Also, in its deliberateness and stateliness, it points up the difference between the workings of the New England Conscience in its purity from those perfervid confessions of wrongdoing excited by nineteenth-century revivalists in Kentucky or in Chicago. What then must particularly be noted is that Sewall makes no attempt to gloss over anything, to plead the excitement of the moment or his loyalty to Stoughton. He is thinking hard of others, of what his guilt may bring upon his country in the way of retribution. But above all, he is passing upon himself such a judgment as no earthly tribunal could phrase.

In the same year of his confession, 1697, Sewall also published an esoteric tract on the fulfillment of prophecies. Midway into it, he chanced to mention Plum Island, where he had played as a boy and where he still visited in meditative solitude. At the sound of the name, he lost track of his sterile logic for a moment and launched into a paean to the sensual beauties of the place: it is a chant upon the sweetness, the salmon and sturgeon in "the streams of Merrimack," the sea fowl that annually visit the places of their acquaintance, the cattle fed "with the Grass growing in the Medows, which do humbly bow down themselves before Turkie-Hill." So perhaps we get somewhat nearer the essence of the New England Conscience as we realize that the unsparing lash of judging according to God's judgment developed from intensity to intensity along with the New Englander's discipline in learning love for his land.

The conscience of Henry Thoreau burst into flame upon the news of John Brown's raid on Harper's Ferry. Nothing in the sheer recklessness of the adventure, nothing of its brutality or lawlessness, inhibited Thoreau's exultation. Rather, for Thoreau all the considerations that would persuade reasonable men of its utter folly proved only the more conclusively that Brown acted solely from the dictate of conscience. Yet the secret cry of the Puritan conscientiousness, as it had become adapted to New England, came out in Thoreau's indictment of his compatriots: "Our foes are in our midst and all about us. There is hardly a house but is divided against itself, for our foe is the all but universal woodenness of both head and heart, the want of vitality in man, which is the effect of our vice."

However, what most puzzles the outside world is not the moment when an exacerbated Edwards or an infuriated Thoreau let the violence of New England's Conscience erupt, but the steady way in which, day after day, it regulates ordinary transactions. In 1936 George Santayana unexpectedly became a best seller with a novel called *The Last Puritan*. It was read as a caustic attack on the New England Conscience, and its popularity must be taken as evidence that a great part of the public, including some in New England, welcomed this surgical operation upon the incubus. In the person of his "hero," Oliver Alden, Santayana incarnated those fears of life and love, the emotional sterility, the doctrinaire joylessness, that for all the years of his enforced sojourn at Harvard had disgusted him, until at last in 1912 he was able to escape permanently to Europe and to end his days in Rome where, as he told me and others, he was never troubled by the slightest twinges of the virus. Yet in his preface, Santayana constructed a dialogue with his young Italian friend, who in everything is the opposite of the Bostonian, in which even they find a perverse sublimity in Alden's conscientiousness. He was a millionaire, says Santayana, and yet scrupulously simple and silently heroic; Mediterranean types "can't help admiring people purer than ourselves, more willing to pluck out the eye that offends them, even if it is the eye of beauty, and to enter halt and lame into the kingdom of singlemindedness." This is a tribute, the more eloquent for being a reluctant one, to the persistence of a mentality from the time of Cotton Mather into the twentieth century.

What often amuses the Yankee in such external appraisals as Santayana's—and for all the years Santayana lived in the neighborhood of Boston, he remained an outsider—is his inability to cope with another dimension of this localized conscience that was present at the beginning, but that expanded with the centuries of adaptation to the soil: that is, its fondness for being amused with itself. Samuel Sewall in narrating his courtship of the Widow Winthrop, bringing her his ridiculous "Sugar Almonds" that cost three shillings the pound and attempting his elephantine gallantries, is quite aware of the comic figure he cuts. In our own time, two highly conscientious poets have demonstrated both in their techniques and subject matter a concern about inward judgments combined with a love of the land, and yet they have taken care to relieve the tension with humor. Robert Frost's admonition about the need of being versed in country things before one supposes that phoebes weep is a warning against allowing the conscience to be contaminated by sentimentality. Edwin Arlington Robinson rang many changes on and within the paradox, and summed it up succinctly in a sonnet boldly called "New England." Here "the wind is always north-north-east," "children learn to walk on frozen toes" and to envy those who elsewhere shamelessly enjoy a lyric feast:

> Joy shivers in the corner where she knits
> And Conscience always has the rocking-chair,
> Cheerful as when she tortured into fits
> The first cat that was ever killed by Care.

Younger poets in the New England heritage have even more radically than Frost and Robinson resented the tyranny of rocking-chair conscience, and so have succeeded primarily in torturing cats with more exquisite care. One thinks especially of E. E. Cummings and Robert Lowell.

One may interject at this point that it is plausible that writers would retain a sense of the Puritan heritage and make literary capital out of its patterns of conscience. The serious question, sociologically speaking, is whether, as New England has moved into modern prosperity and materiality, as it has become only one region within a vast industrial complex, as it has also become populated by supermarkets, there is any reason for the casual citizen to give thought to an ethic of abstinence, self-denial, and worry about internal motives.

Assuredly, the hordes of foreign tourists who come every summer get little chance to perceive the New England Conscience in action. The one hint they are likely to receive is the latent hostility of small-town tradesmen against the "summer folk," which, the tourist notes, is perfectly combined with the natives' determination to get as much profit as possible out of the season. And, as all the world knows, the old Yankee stock does not control the political life of the area, only a part of its business life, and by no means all of its social parade. As a result, it has been argued that the New England Conscience must be a thing of the past, obliterated by the automobile and rooted out by Freud.

Yet, let us think again of Sewall standing in the Old South Church. There is a proud assumption implicit in his self-abasement: he has this duty to perform for the sake both of the community and his own judgment of himself. Pre-eminence spells responsibility. In 1842 Charles Dickens recorded his amazed delight with the public institutions of Boston, finding them "as nearly perfect, as the most considerate wisdom, benevolence, and humanity, can make them." The one thing in all America upon which he could heap unqualified praise was the Perkins School for the Blind. Without making invidious comparisons, I think it may be suggested that in Boston today charity is a major industry. And as for business, the department that has most consistently remained in the hands of descendants of the New England Conscience is the trust funds—the handling of other people's money by those who, from a long accumulation of wisdom and anguish, have the skill and the dedication.

It is a matter of history that New England did produce out of its Puritan ranks a considerable number of rascals. Many of them, like the proverbial sellers of wooden nutmegs, wrapped themselves in the toga of a special conscience and argued that their frauds were not evil because their hearts were pure. Until fairly recently, the sale of votes in rural elections was conducted with so open and callous a disregard of rudimentary decency as to bring the blush of shame to any leader of the toughest ward in one of our cities. Yet even this bribery was attended with a scrupulous regard for conscience, and once a farmer sold his vote, he stayed bought.

However, as for the New England Conscience still persisting with enough vitality to stand up against a sinful world, as for its not being intimidated by the rapaciousness of our century, we have constantly fresh examples. I might, for instance, cite the conduct of Senator Warren Austin at the United Nations, and Mr. Austin comes from Vermont, where the New England Conscience is reputed to survive in all its pristine severity. But also I might mention another exemplification that recently put on view for the whole nation to marvel at: the bearing of Mr. Joseph Welch at the Army-McCarthy hearings.* Mr. Welch practices law in Boston; it is to be remembered, however, that he was born in Iowa. That particular conscience created in New England by the geographical isolation of the region and solidified under the pressure of the climate eventually proved to be an exportable commodity.

*Born in Highgate, Vermont, Warren R. Austin was United States ambassador to the United Nations from 1947 to 1953. Both as ambassador and as U.S. senator (1931–1946), he was an advocate for active American participation in world affairs. Joseph N. Welch, born in Iowa and educated at Grinnell College and Harvard Law School, was special counsel for the army between April and June 1954, in the dispute between Senator Joseph R. McCarthy of Wisconsin and Secretary of the Army, Robert T. Stevens. During the hearings, reporters commented about his irony, fluency, calmness, and humor.

Liberty and Conformity

WITH A GREAT SENSE of relief in my heart—indeed, with a positive exultation—I take this chance to deliver a "commencement oration" to a group composed exclusively of graduate students. First of all, I am allowed to be brief, for you are now entering into that fraternity of satiety wherein, henceforth, you will never willingly listen to any lecture you do not yourself deliver. Second, I am excused from having to ring some tedious change upon the traditional elegy over your loss of innocence. I do not have to lament your being cast out of the academic shelter to seek your fortunes in a cold, vile, dirty world. For you, by virtue of the degrees conferred upon you this day, have taken the vow of intellectual celibacy. You are not going to have anything to do with the sinful, voluptuous society. You are hereby ordained brethren of the academic monastery. You like it here. For you, there shall be no question of someday passing a point of no return: you have returned before you started. Nobody will need to tell you that you can't go home again: you are staying home.

Of course, I know that several of you who today become certified physicists, chemists, biologists, will take positions in industry rather than in the scholastic enclosure. Possibly two or three of you, starting in the laboratory of some electronics firm, may even-

An address delivered at the Graduate Convocation, Brown University, June 2, 1958.

tually find your way to the executive suite, and devote your last years, while your feet bask angle-deep in lush wall-to-wall carpeting, to clipping coupons. There is also the possibility that two or three others of you who do not go into business and who set out as of today to be simply teachers and scholars will wind up as college presidents, sitting behind a gleaming desk but not so much clipping coupons as begging for a portion of those the first sort garner. I fervently hope that the numbers of either type in this assembly will prove small. If there turn out to be such, I pray that in the midst of their sordid prosperity they will experience a few uncomfortable moments when they recollect how on this occasion I denounced them in advance as traitors to the guild. "Vengeance shall be mine," saith the Commencement Day Orator. Could I actually foresee which of you, if any, are predestined to this act of betrayal, I would here and now move to Brown University that your degree be withheld, no matter how distinguished has been your academic record, on the ground that you are fated to indulge in conduct unbecoming a scholar and a gentleman.

However, there is no point in my spending our precious time castigating those who are doomed to success. Nobody remembers what is said in a commencement talk anyway; and those who will turn aside for mere wealth or prestige are not the sort who will be deterred by moral admonition. That the scientists among you will straight off get better jobs than the Ph.D.'s in English or Romance Languages goes without saying: but as long as you retain a vital connection with a laboratory, a library, a classroom—as long as you are investigating, endeavoring to discover something new, something hitherto unknown, about finance, fission, fish, or *Finnegan's Wake*—you have taken, in relation to the dominant pattern of this society, the vow not only of poverty but of failure. Already you are square pegs in the round American hole. You do not conform to the code. In short, you publicly, blatantly, unrepentantly own up to having minds.

That once-eloquent sage, President Calvin Coolidge, is reputed to have summed up his monumental wisdom in a sentence unequalled by Confucius: "The business of America," he declared, "is business." However, unless you get lured, by some weakness of character such as I have deplored, into business or administration (which is only a more genteel form of business), it will not be for you to devise the slogans which hustle the American people to purchase gadgets they do not need and really do not want. Not for you to propel them into buying—buying just *anything*—and so receiving the plaudits of a patriotic nation or swimming pools in Bucks County donated by grateful sponsors. Nor, in all likelihood, will ever be given to you the gratitude, and the checks, of the motorcar industry by hitting upon the brilliant pun which has lately identified the shortened word for its product with the imperative of the verb *ought*. You, doubly educated, restrained by both an undergraduate and a graduate degree, are condemned to respecting the decencies of language. You are prohibited, by your now built-in monitor, from calling colossal that which is not stupendously big. Indeed, you can term nothing stupendous which does not in actual fact do what the Latin root of the word—*stupere*—requires that it should do, namely to astonish.

The catalogue of nicknacks which the massive industrial plant of the United States produces—and distributes—is so long that the tongue of no man can recite it. Those countries which most accuse us of materialism eat out their hearts in envy of it. Hundreds of these artifacts, from automobiles to aspirin tablets, from lipsticks to airplanes, add to the comfort, efficiency, even the beauty of existence in this century. Yet the dismaying fact about our civilization, with its plethora of conveniences, is the speed with which every new device, the product presumably of solemn research, of intellectual endeavor, is taken for granted by a populace utterly ignorant of, completely indifferent to, the principles by which it has been developed. Hence the people quickly cease to be astonished, and merely complain if the incomprehensible television set fails to show the evening's western. But who among us can ever leave off being astonished at the table of atomic weights, Mendel's law of inheritance, the structure of *Hamlet*, or the never-ending sequence of reinterpretations of the American Revolution?

I do not, as I trust you understand, intend to imply that American businessmen are necessarily brainless. Some of my best friends are businessmen. And hundreds of them have a wider-ranging curiosity, a larger appetite for ideas, than the average professor of an erudite specialty. Nor can there be any doubt that the learned professions—law, medicine, the ministry, the armed services—make demands upon the intellect. Even so, the businessman, the professional man, and to a great extent the general and admiral, conform to the compulsive ethic of this society: they have duties to perform, but the basic problem of their careers is that of earning a living. We who have perversely dedicated ourselves to failure may indeed pine for as much money as we can get, and assuredly we do not relish being, in relation to the others, poor. But we have cast the die of our lives into a dedication to some aspect of the multiform life of the mind. We have said, "This is what we are primarily interested in; this is our business; we'll worry about other matters later." Naturally, we hope that the business community, which pays the bills for higher education, will see to it that we can afford a crust of bread while we pursue our interest. Yet, what we arrogantly throw in the face of community is our declaration that even though it starve us of the crust, we shall strive to do just what we have chosen to do. We refuse to conform. We are not to be bought. We wear no price-tag. Within the schools we may compete for promotions or raises, but that is incidental to our real purpose: that purpose is to compete not with rivals but with ourselves. What we are worth is much more than even this luxurious America can afford to pay us, so that it shamefacedly reacts by underpaying us. This it does, I hasten to say, by its standards, not by ours.

In this sense, it is correct to insist that anybody within the American economy who deliberately decides to spend time in a graduate school—rather than in an office, factory, or in professional training—stands convicted, by the nature of his act, of being un-American. By every implication, he is a subversive. The hundred-percenters, who periodically accuse the colleges of spawning radicals, are, by their lights, correct. Or rather, I should except the colleges. The colleges may be conservative, and so teach good manners. Good manners are inevitably conservative. But a graduate school, confine it as one will, is an unsettling school: you do not get good manners out of it.

Lately we have been enabled to study the manners of the prosecutors of intellect. There can be no doubt about them: they are driven by a pitiable sense of insecurity. The human mind is the most unsettling force, and the most uncontrollable, that afflicts humanity. One needs no extraordinary insight into the psychology of mortals to comprehend why, once anxieties spread like a plague through that external world in which you have declined to participate, the creatures of that world turn upon you for not being like unto themselves.

Anybody seriously concerned with the life of the mind in modern America must have been at least amused over the hysteria of breast-beating (should I say brain-beating?) and tearing of hair which overcame the country immediately upon the Russians' launching of their memorable Sputnik. Overnight, the tenor of the voices of accusation altered. Those which had been denouncing learning for unorthodox propositions in economics dropped their tedious refrain; they commenced to wail that we had failed to pound into the heads of children the stern tabulation of mathematics, the unpalatable rudiments of elementary physics. Those of us who have long been resisting, with all our strength but without much success, the watering down of instruction induced by the professional educators, now find these earnest souls branded as betrayers of the citadel, and are almost—though not quite—moved to pity them. Meanwhile, we remember that the arraignment comes from parents who for years have complacently allowed the secondary schools to accommodate the curriculum to the mental torpor of their own children. Suddenly, these champions exclaim, we must get tough with their babies, and drill them through the harsh realities of the multiplication table. Otherwise, the nation will be undone. Otherwise, the Russians will produce more engineers than we do. The schools and universities will then be to blame.

Yes, this spectacle is comic. How widely do we now read, even in the most popular magazines, portentous assertions about the need for basic research? It was only a few months before Sputnik that the then-Secretary for Defense was approvingly quoted throughout the country for sneering that basic research is that futility occupied with the metaphysical question of why grass is green. Assuredly such an episode in the official history of intellect in this country is good for a laugh. But for not much more. Operating behind the latest outcry is clearly discernible a more sinister thrust than has yet manifested itself in the various attacks upon academic independence. The powers of repression, thrown into an aggravated panic, respond by demanding under a new authoritarianism that the mind of the scholar and scientist be conformed to a rule of their devising —and of their imposition.

Ralph Waldo Emerson continued all his life to be a loyal son of Harvard College, even though it treated him shabbily. When young Henry Thoreau first became an intimate of the Emerson household, around 1838 or 1839, he sat quietly in a corner while Emerson expounded to English visitors, "At Harvard College they teach all the branches of learning." Henry then embarrassed his patron by blurting out, "Yes, but none of the roots." About this time Emerson had to learn, to his deep distress, just how savagely an American institution will defend its branches at the expense of the roots when Harvard University turned on him for delivering *The Divinity School Address*, and thereafter for thirty years officially banished him from the Yard. The Reverend Andrews Norton termed Emerson "the Latest Form of Infidelity." Smarting under this censure, Emerson would secretly pen such scathing remarks as his phrase, "The corpse-cold Unitarianism of Brattle Street and Harvard College." As is well known, when Charles William Eliot led Harvard out of the corpse-cold refrigerator, one of his first acts was to offer Emerson a formal apology by having him elected to the Board of Overseers.

However, more telling is the fact that in 1905 was dedicated within the Harvard Yard a building for philosophy: it is named for Emerson, and in the vestibule sits a sculptured figure of the heretic, done by Daniel French, which by slightly accentuating the contradictions between his profiles, sheds an ironic benignity upon the hordes of students, male and female, who daily pass before him—most of them, I must say, wearing faces of appalling symmetry. I hope, as would Emerson, that they are receiving instructions in something beyond corpse-cold liberalism, that they at least smell the thrust from the roots. Whether they do or not, the existence of Emerson Hall is a standing rebuke to Harvard University, and so by inference a rebuke to all American universities. It demonstrates the folly of attempting to ostracize an intellect, even when the governing boards rightly and honestly consider his thinking dangerous, infidel, or immoral.

I admit, Emerson is a somewhat special case. But then—so are all disturbers of the academic truce. Still, while he did resonantly assert, "Whosoever would be a man, must be a nonconformist," he never in his own life and conduct showed himself other than exemplary. By the time President Eliot restored him to Harvard officialdom, it was evident that nothing was to be feared from him—that he was in fact a saint. Furthermore, by that time Henry Thoreau was safely dead. To put the story another way: by 1869

Emerson proved to be not half so much the radical he was supposed to be in 1838. Yet the account of his dealings with proprieties endorsed by the Harvard Corporation stands as the archetypal enactment in the history of American higher education. Emerson may have been taken aback when Thoreau crudely interjected, but Thoreau rather than Emerson was warning the university that from the roots of learning more grow than little acorns. Out of them, not out of the branches, emerge formulae for nuclear fission and for a total revision of Homeric studies. Even more destructively, from the roots, despite administrative endeavors to smooth over the lawn of conformity, come the ugly, uncouth stalks of ideas, hypotheses, conjectures. Those who already are corpse-cold are bound to regard these sprouts as poisonous, to try to cut them down. These have a way of persisting, in defiance of such gardening, and frequently of taking over the parent-plant.

I retell the familiar story of Emerson and Harvard because it is, as far as I can review the academic history of America, truly prophetic. The controversy raised, even though in what must seem to us comparatively pastoral circumstances, the issue which has subsequently been contested with vehemence, fury, exasperation. It is not a matter of our having, necessarily, the slightest sympathy with the "transcendental" notions that Emerson blandly propounded in 1838 to a scandalized faculty of the Divinity School. We may even term these a fanforonade of romantic nonsense, which nobody post-Darwin need take seriously for a moment. The incontrovertible fact is that Emerson somehow acquired—we must suppose that he did so even in that somnolent college—an inclination for both rhetoric and boldness. He brought back to the college, like a cat bringing home to the feet of his mistress a dead field mouse, the results of his investigations. He was never trained in a formal graduate school, so that in his days the method of disposing of these carcasses was less defined. He had to take his chances, which proved to be precarious. Yes, we must have learned something! Among the aid and comforts which our business civilization has devised we include the various organizations for advanced study. We can drop our prey on some doorstep. These did not exist in Emerson's day. Now we have them: would he have been any better had he known them? Yet the essential concern is that while they have not been created out of the payments of the graduate students, they are mainly demons summoned from the vasty deep by a commercial culture. The paradox we then have to deal with is that the very being of a graduate school is inevitably a challenge to that policy which brings it into being and which manfully supports it.

A graduate school, however it be, is in this country a place in which the individual makes a separate peace with the plenipotentiaries of business, and resigns from the war. It downs tools in the trenches, and withdraws to prepared positions. At this point, the mind decides to devote itself solely to the business of the mind, which is to say, to its own exercise. As with the training of colts in a racing stable, we want all runners to be winners, but the crucial problem is whether they will try to run at all.

I do not contend that all who have been exposed to graduate instruction should thereupon become Emersons or Thoreaus. I do not complain if a majority of graduate students in arts and sciences regard their sojourn therein as preparation for securing a moderately decent job. Nevertheless, while you have been in the course of study, you have somehow been required to subject supposedly eternal verities to a bit of re-examination. I think it fair to say that on this level (leaving aside for the moment the number of brilliant undergraduates who have disturbed our serenity), all of us, faculty and students together, are less occupied with imparting or securing information than with criticism—with moving beyond the established, beyond the accepted, into the unexplored space of the disturbing.

In the career of such adventuring, both the instructor and the student are perpetually reminded of their invincible ignorance. The beauty and terror of our study is precisely that we constantly face this admission, but that somehow we persist, even though upon confronting it we ought to cut each other's throat.

So, I see not how anyone can give himself to advanced study, beyond the conventional four years of the unperturbed American college, without becoming conscious of the exciting insecurity, the inspiriting inconclusiveness, of the modern intellect. An undergraduate may be given some sense of the turmoil, and may even thereby become invigorated to go forth as a success-boy. In the graduate school, the student foregoes such adventitious gains. He gives up all fringe benefits.

He has to face the labor of learning for its own sake—bare,

stark, tedious though it be. How otherwise dare he look out from these ivy-cloaked walls upon the panorama of manufacturing and huckstering, and still keep in his eye the glint of disapproval?

By his deed of choice, whether he was fully conscious of it or not at the beginning, he has eliminated himself from the herd. He has perforce, wittingly or unwittingly, become a nonconformist. No amount of church-going or payment of income taxes (assuming that he will have enough income to be taxable) can ever restore him to respectability. He will never be at ease among the men of business. There is a law of the pack in this republic which sounds like Kipling, but owes nothing to him: he who hunts outside the pack, hunts alone.

What I say may be unwelcome news to the masters of this society, and even to the deans of graduate schools. Most of the students, I am sure, know what I am trying to say even before I have said it. We all have to work toward the engendering of dissimilarity, work for the opportunity to examine, question, and if need be to dissever the nerves of solidarity, rather than to rest in precommitment to their preservation. For this purpose graduate schools exist.

The Responsibility of Mind in a Civilization of Machines

EVER SINCE 1840, when Alexis de Tocqueville published the second volume of *Democracy in America*, which was quickly translated and avidly studied in the United States, anyone speaking formally about the role of intellect in our civilization is virtually forced to invoke chapters 9 and 10 of his first book to explain why, to repeat his own chapter heading, "the Americans are more addicted to practical than to theoretical science."

We must be meticulous, therefore, to observe sanctified ritual by reciting, as though an incantation to the gods, at least a few of Tocqueville's venerable pronouncements. Certain of these are worth repeating when we recollect how immensely helpful they were to pioneer champions of the "theoretical" in the early struggles of American scientific ambition. In the long and bitter fight over the structure of the Smithsonian Institution, for instance—a battle which, by the ironic comedy of Smithson's leaving his bequest "to the United States of America," had to be fought, of all unlikely places, on the floors of Congress—Tocqueville proved a powerful aid to Joseph Henry, Alexander Bache, and John Quincy Adams in their resistance to the congressional attempts to furnish only a menial trade school. The victory, in 1846, of these eastern "theore-

Perry Miller adapted this essay from his address to the conference, "Toward a Community of Learning," held at New York University in April 1961.

ticians" over the grim-faced "utilitarians" from Ohio and Indiana is customarily saluted in chronicles of the American mind as a vindication of Tocqueville's bold surmise that the then observable state of American culture was not to be taken, considering the nation's youth and immaturity, as precluding in some distant future an appreciation of abstract or pure science among a democratic people.

Because I am convinced, after years of being bored with the Tocqueville myth, that long citations from him are the handiest means by which social historians, when expounding American manners, evade intellectual responsibility, I am the more prepared to put before you these hoary articles as proceeding from faulty observation and naïvely a priori notions, and as being correct only in a limited range of matters, largely by accident. In this sense Tocqueville is a help to us, much more than if he had always been right. His confusions illuminate ours, as we here move in unorganized bands in the midst of a darkling plain, often striking at friends whom we do not recognize and at foes who in reality are our friends.

On the surface Tocqueville is highly persuasive. Let us suppose, he wrote, that the Americans, coming to the wilderness with all the knowledge they actually did import, had then been left alone in the world, with no further importations from intellectual Europe. In that case, he asserted, "they would not have been slow to discover that progress cannot long be made in the application of the sciences without cultivating the theory of them." However absorbed they might have been with applications, Tocqueville strove to assure himself—if only because he was dismayed by their apparent fanaticism for the practical—that Americans would speedily admit the necessity of "theory," because, being a shrewd people, they would see in it a means of attaining the effectual end.

Or in other words—if I may venture to paraphrase Tocqueville—Americans were at that stage of their development exclusively preoccupied with the useful arts and with the comforts of living. This was not too reprehensible when one reflected, as did Tocqueville, that "learned and literary Europe" was also striving to improve those means that ministered to the pleasures of mankind. But at the same time Europe was vigorously "exploring the common sources of truth." By contrast, in America all the incentives were toward utility. Whereupon Tocqueville came to the happily ambiguous conclusion that, while men in a democratic society are not inherently indifferent to the sciences and to the arts, they are obliged to cultivate them "after their own fashion and bring to the task their own peculiar qualifications and deficiencies."

Thus Tocqueville did not quite despair of the scientific mind in a democracy, yet neither was he overconfident about its future. During the short period of his visit—less than a year—he spent a large part of his precious time with Whig lawyers in New York and Boston, especially with Mr. Justice Story, and with such pundits as Jared Sparks; by them he was supplied with several low estimates of the average American intelligence. These informants were so eager to explain to him the ignorance and barbarity of Andrew Jackson that they quite forgot to call his attention to the then-mounting surge into technology.

Left to himself, this highly logical Frenchman was wondrously unqualified to comprehend what he saw. Hence, while he was generous enough to allow that a democracy, when it found the leisure to direct a particle of its energies to theory, might prove to have some qualifications for abstraction, he had also to stress its probable "deficiencies." Tocqueville was incapable of grasping how, in a democracy, traits that he termed deficiencies would not be admitted by the democratic scientist to be serious defects. Joseph Henry did contend at times during the contest over the Smithsonian, "He who loves truth for its own sake, feels that its highest claims are lowered and its moral influence marred by being continually summoned to the bar of immediate and palpable utility." Yet Henry himself was not averse to the useful; his experiments on electromagnetism and what he called "electrodynamic induction" were eminently addressed to the use of mankind. His campaign for the Smithsonian did not mean that he would not participate in the national exultation over the steamboat, the railroad, the telegraph (which he almost invented), the Hoe Press. Henry and his ilk did not feel they were demeaning themselves when they pleaded that their concern with a science not aimed at immediate application was really a strategic maneuver to gain, in the long run, still more efficient machines.

As the gadgets multiplied—steamboats, railroads, the telegraph—the intellect of the Republic was more and more bemused by the glory, the thrill of the technological transformation. I suppose one may say that we are still hypnotized by the glitter of supermarkets, television, turnpikes, frozen foods, bras and girdles, and—especially when vacationing in Europe—by the sublimities of our plumbing. Yet we become sadly unhistorical when we assume, as several of our polemicists do, that the early Americans were a simple, ascetic, and pious rural people who suddenly had their idyllic way of life shattered by a barrage of mechanical contrivances. The truth is, the national mentality was not caught unawares, not at all so rudely jolted as is generally supposed. There were of course, as there still are, rural backwaters where the people clung to the simpler economy and there was a certain amount of folk resistance to the temptations of the machine. But on the whole, the story is that the mind of the nation flung itself into the mighty prospect, dreamed for decades of comforts that we now take for granted, and positively lusted for the chance to yield itself to the gratifications of technology. The machine has not conquered us in some imperial manner against our will. On the contrary, we have wantonly prostrated ourselves before the engine. Juggernaut seems by contrast an amateur contrivance; we have invented the superhighway, an impressively professional mechanism for mass slaughter.

In order to comprehend the mentality that still prevails in the America of the 1960s, we must rediscover that of a century or more ago, from which our own is directly descended. The code was even then in process of formulation. The economy was agricultural and a frontier still beckoned masses away from the cities, but then the code appeared. Immigrants quickly learned the improvised game, and proved themselves adept at profiting from it, whereas older families often failed (but not always) to grasp it in time. The pioneers conquered the forest and plowed up the plains in the hope that they too would benefit by it. They were not fleeing the machine; they were opening the areas in which it could operate.

This is to say that when Tocqueville paid the democracy what he thought was the compliment of foretelling a day when it might redeem itself from its base standards of value, the democracy itself was identifying its innermost being with the vibration of this triumphant utility. It would dismiss with a sneer European pretensions to a theoretical superiority as just another sign of the incurable corruption of Europe; it would consider any addiction to this superstition within the native community an un-American activity. Tocqueville, supposing the basic problem to be a conceptual one, simply could not comprehend the passion with which these people flung themselves into the technological torrent, how they shouted with glee in the midst of the cataract, and cried to each other as they went headlong down the chute that here was their destiny, here was the tide that would sweep them toward unending vistas of prosperity.

We today are still bobbing like corks in the flood, unable to get our heads high enough above the waves to tell whether there are any longer solid banks on either side or whether we have been carried irretrievably into a pitiless sea, there to be swamped and drowned. Those who are worried enough to seek glimpses of the receding horizons are those most likely to acquiesce in the charges of vulgarity and materialism levied against America by outside observers, from Mrs. Trollope and Charles Dickens to Simone de Beauvoir. In recent years we are apt lamely to murmur that the situation is not so bad as it used to be: witness the increased attendance at opera, ballet and concerts, the huge sale of classical records, the throngs attending exhibitions of paintings and the guided tours of schoolchildren through art museums. In academic institutions those who administer courses that in modern terminology are called the "humanities," while out of one side of their mouths complaining that budget-makers and foundations and the federal government provide millions for laboratories but only a few pennies for languages, will out of the other side admit to having lately been encouraged by an augmentation in the number of their graduate students.

Our disposition to treasure these miscellaneous manifestations of a taste for culture, of a publicly advertised thirst for beauty not yet obliterated by the weight of technology, has been accentuated by a tendency among students of the American past to emphasize the minorities who have protested here and there against the majority's infatuation with the machine. By blowing them up to a size out of all numerical proportion to the mass, we perpetuate the notion that the way for mind to survive in the midst of the glare of blast furnaces and the shriek of jet planes is to construct tiny oases of gentility around the library, the art museum, the concert hall. We repeat to ourselves Emerson's lines about things being in the saddle and riding mankind in order to encourage ourselves to buck against the pricks of metallic spurs. Possibly the cult of Edgar Allan Poe is not quite so legion as it was in my youth, but anthologies reprint his sonnet, "To Science," and students still sigh with a sympathy, even though fleeting, for its denunciation of science for having mangled the imagination, for its rhetorical questioning of why the poet should be required to love this vulture,

> or how deem thee wise,
> Who wouldst not leave him in his wandering
> To seek for treasure in the jewelled skies,
> Albeit he soared with an undaunted wing?

Although we read this verse by the light of an electric lamp, warmed in the dead of winter by an oil-burning furnace, having dined on a dish of frozen peas and been gratefully assured with the latest reading on our electrocardiograph that we are in no immediate danger, while we plan a trip for the morrow in a scientific fabrication propelled by gasoline, we not only palpitate with pity for poor Poe, but by sharing his anguish we enjoy the illusion of being entirely independent of all these daily conveniences. Yet in point of brute fact we cannot do anything about their hold over us, any more than we can liberate ourselves from the indignities of commuter trains, not to mention the obscenities of subways. Still, as long as we can respond to Poe we are able to assure ourselves that we have not become wholly rigidified in what Henry Miller defined as the "air-conditioned nightmare" of the American way of life.

A more eloquent symptom of the dislocation between the sensitive mind and the confessedly insensitive environment in which the machines have corralled us is a steady enlargement of the popular regard for Henry Thoreau. To judge from the number of editions now in paperbacks and the volume of their sales, the vogue of Thoreau is a phenomenon that no modern Tocqueville should ignore. Yet, while these reprints are sold openly in drugstores, there is something clandestine about the transaction. By rights, while *Lady Chatterley's Lover* is patently a legitimate article of commerce, *Walden* ought to be bootlegged under the counter. It does seem clear that the appeal of Thoreau is not mainly to beatniks who have signed off from the reign of the machine, but to hundreds most abjectly enslaved by it. Thoreau appeals to those prisoners of megalopolis who from him gain at least a passing sight of blue sky. He keeps alive the flicker of an almost extinguished fire of the mind amidst piles of nonflammable steel and concrete—and chromium.

Most of us, I am sure, find something admirable, or at least moving, in this surreptitious adherence to Thoreau. I rejoice when told that in the lower echelons of Wall Street there are young executives who, once they have contrived through the rush hour to reach their ranch-type homes in Scarsdale, mix a bit of Thoreau with their martinis. Also I am uplifted when informed that even in the higher echelons there are several collectors of Thoreauviana. I hope that in the practice of their secret vice, although they shall never be manumitted, they will reach beyond *Walden* to Thoreau's lesser-known but gay review of an otherwise forgotten production by one J. A. Etzlar, which was entitled *Paradise Regained*, and which Thoreau lampooned by heading his discussion, "Paradise (to be) Regained." Etzlar was a German immigrant so wonderstruck (as were almost all of his sort) at the technological prospect offered by America that he extrapolated a future that is astonishingly similar to our present. He proposed to bring this paradise on earth within not a century but a decade: "If we have the requisite power for mechanical purposes, it is then but a matter of human contrivance to invent adapted tools or machines for application." Breathes there among us a man with soul so dead as not to feel a slight thrill of release upon hearing Henry's riposte: "Every machine, or particular application, seems a slight outrage against universal laws. How many fine inventions are there which do not clutter the ground?"

Yes, many of us will confess that our ground has become fearfully cluttered. But then we have to ask ourselves, with how many of the inventions would we willingly dispense? The telephone? Television? The airplane? Metrecal? In this interrogation consists the fundamental query for the mind of America. It is pressed upon us, on the one hand, by our Far Eastern friends, who find us sunk in materiality and incapable of understanding such an embodiment of spiritual power as Gandhi. On the other hand, the same question is forced upon us by those empires that have found their configuration in dogmatic materialism, and therefore ridicule us as hypocrites and sentimental evaders of reality. They accuse us of being mentally incapable of coping with the colossal mechanism we have devised. They make the issue terrifyingly clear: if the mind of this society is not competent to master the assembly line, the reactor, the computer, if we can endure these monsters only by snatching at impotent dreams of Walden Pond, then it is fitting that the machines take over; it is time that the mind abdicate. A recent authority—significantly remaining anonymous—has publicly asserted that with "perceptron" we shall shortly have a mechanical intelligence infinitely more advanced even than the computer, a true robot; then he adds, "But remember, all this was begun and devised by human brains, so humans—if they take care—will remain supreme." The nervous giggle that his cunning insertion, "if they take care," is designed to excite is all too evidently a momentary release of an anxiety steadily gnawing within us, the fear that possibly we shall not be able to take sufficient care. The essence of great tragedy, Eric Bentley says, is the realization by the self that it is totally unequipped to confront the universe. We might venture that even more tragic than any classical or Shakespearean drama is the crisis of illumination when man realizes, much too late for any last-minute panaceas, that he is unequal to the task of dealing with a universe of his own manufacture. Gloucester in *King Lear* blames the gods who kill us for their sport, as wanton boys do flies. Shakespeare was even then at liberty to accuse the "gods." But whom dare we blame for Gary, Indiana?

At this point it may be rewarding to consider more objectively than we have hitherto the mentality that in the period of Tocqueville's visit was welcoming the onrushing age of mechanization. In fact, "welcoming" is too pallid a verb: the age was grasping for the technological future, panting for it, crying for it. Such a reappraisal of the temper of the times becomes for us all the more urgent once we concede how seductively our fondness for Poe or for Thoreau distorts our image of the era. The critical historian must restrain his sympathies; in all candor he must report that the dissenters were at best minor voices and that they were sadly ineffectual. They provide us today with no usable programs of resistance. Whereupon we are compelled to pose the question we try to avoid. Is it, after all, the real issue that mind must stand in an attitude of intransigence against the machine? Is this opposition, celebrated by poets and encouraged by the heritage of romantic literature, this flattery of the private self—is this the one and only frame of reference in which the problem must be stated? Is it true that the mind in America is condemned always to be arrayed in unrelenting antagonism to the dynamo? If so, the outcome is inevitable: such a resistance movement is bound to be unavailing; if so, the mind is foredoomed to recurrent and increasingly disastrous defeat. From the commencement of the industrial transformation of the agrarian economy so dear to the heart of Thomas Jefferson, this doctrine of the mind, inherited from a thousand sources in Western history, from Christianity and also from John Locke, has collapsed. If this be all that the word "mind" can evoke in the modern situation, to what then have we to cling, as we find ourselves upon the wastes of matter, but the floating fragments of Poe's poetry, of Thoreau's individualism and odd bits and pieces of Henry Adams, Veblen, and Randolph Bourne?

Or else must we cultivate what Thoreau scorned as resignation? Whereupon we admit that human existence is incurably shabby, that it is merely another evidence of the operation of inherent depravity, that the terrors of the machine can be withstood only by a delicious few anchored in religion. There is abundant evidence that to many this option appears the only way out. These anchorites will resent my describing their clause as one of escape. They insist that by their reinvigoration of spiritual resources the mind will be fortified against the thrusts of the material, will subdue the inhuman to humanity. However, the most energetic of modern Protestant thinking—I have in mind Reinhold Niebuhr's—hardly lets us off the hook. Catholicism does indeed have the majestic order of the historic Church; yet, so far as I can follow them, individual Catholics are as perturbed as the rest of us. Without entering further into a highly complex area, let me simply assert that an overall examination of American history from about 1815 gives no support to any contention that the religious solution is workable for more than a few votaries of particular persuasions.

In the early nineteenth century the loud hosannas of the revivalists were as much swamped by the swelling chorus of praise for the machine as were the drawling sarcasms of Henry Thoreau. If we wish to locate where in the dominant theme of American culture the prospect of a healthy relation of mind to machine arose, and where it assumed the character that has subsequently ruled our society—disregarding the whimpers of humanists, religionists, agrarians and poets—we must pass over names of literary or ecclesiastical repute. We are obligated, for instance, to resurrect an address of Charles J. Ingersoll to the American Institute of Philadelphia in November 1835:

> Even in Europe . . . this is the era of utility. With us it is the age of navigation, plantation, habitation, and transportation, of steamboats, canals, and railroads, magnificent prisons, costly poor-houses, school-houses, custom-houses, court-houses, warehouses, factories, forges, laboratories, and all the contrivances of ingenuity.

If this does not adequately convey wherein the majority of Americans conceived their future to lie, let me further illustrate the lesson by repeating what Henry Meigs proclaimed upon the opening of the annual fair at Albany in 1850:

> All over our great domain we hear the ceaseless hum of human and machine labor. The latter has become in our time the object of wonder. We are almost as much astonished at modern inventions, as our Indians were at the ships and artillery of Columbus. By the constant habit of observation, and with entire self-reliance, and with a liberty which has no other boundaries than those which morality and religion impose, the freemen of our country will carry to the uttermost perfection all the arts that can be useful or agreeable to man.

Now, as I trust is clear, I am not arguing that in the record of creative intellect Henry Meigs is to be placed on a level with Henry Thoreau. Nevertheless, the fact remains: Meigs spoke for the community, and Thoreau did not. Thoreau spoke for himself, but not for Pittsburgh.

Further, men like Meigs were not uncultured. They were certain that when orating in this vein they were not becoming Philistine barbarians. They marvelled at the machine, but they took full responsibility. Never did any weird notion that the machine might someday dominate the men cross their minds. There was indeed some uneasiness throughout the country—not confined to "radical" circles—that the workers (or the "operatives" as was then the word) might be victimized. But this resulted in a determination that

American industry had no need to follow the course of the English, that it resolutely should not. Thoreau again spoke the extreme concern:

> The condition of the operatives is becoming every day more like that of the English; and it cannot be wondered at, since, as I have heard or observed, the principal object is, not that mankind may be well and honestly clad, but, unquestionably, that the corporations may be enriched.

Again, Thoreau alerts our attention, where Meigs merely bores us. But the Meigses of his time (I suppose plenty of them survive in today's chambers of commerce) would have seen in Thoreau's passage, had they ever noticed it, only further proof of Thoreau's irresponsibility. Emerson also had moments of asking whether the machines might not damage the workers; but he, unlike Thoreau, was so in tune with his times as to be able to banish such apprehensions and to say in resounding amplitude, "Machinery and Transcendentalism agree well. Stage-Coach and Railroad are bursting the old legislation like green withes." His essay "Napoleon" in *Representative Men*, although at the end it brings to bear the same pompous moral judgment on the man of action that finds Shakespeare guilty of frivolity, is in substance his love letter to the entrepreneurs, to the practical men who brushed aside the "old legislation" and were building railroads.

Likewise Theodore Parker, the professional reformer pitching into every cause that offered itself, was worried about the condition of the laboring classes; however, he even more than Thoreau was the Yankee handy with tools, and to him the machines in themselves were as much objects of sheer beauty as to Francis Cabot Lowell. Parker hailed the factory as a creation of intellect. The observer of a carpet manufactory, he said, departs "wondering, thinking what a head it must be which planned the mill, a tool by which the Merrimack transfigures wool and dye stuff into handsome carpets, serviceable for chamber, parlor, staircase, or meeting-house." Occasionally the Old Testament prophet strain in Parker would predict that just so soon as the machine threatened to afford workers the leisure for intellectual relaxation, the bosses would invent markets for useless luxuries in order to keep their employees tied to a fourteen-hour-a-day regime. Yet these utterances came easily when he was tongue-lashing the Boston industrialists, several of whom came to his meetings in the Melodeon and helped pay his salary in order to be lashed. When, by contrast, Parker wanted to array the strength and virtue of his region against what for him was the supremely monstrous evil of the century, Negro slavery, he had no hesitation in telling Southerners that they, hamstrung by this iniquity, could never develop the exquisite machines that made New England almost such a paradise as Etzlar had foretold:

> While South Carolina has taken men from Africa, and made them slaves, New England has taken possession of the Merrimack, the Connecticut, the Androscoggin, the Kennebeck, the Penobscot, and a hundred smaller streams. She has caught the lakes of New Hampshire, and holds them in thrall.

Thus inspired, Parker would promise that "the machinery" of the free states would outproduce the three million bondsmen of the South. Although he, dying of exhaustion in 1860, did not live to see the Civil War prove his thesis, hundreds of his admirers, those who did not perish in the demonstration, did so perceive it and pointedly included his sagacity in their encomiums. In those respects the reformer Parker was not at all out of step with what some historians term the "conservative" temper of his age. He would fully have applauded, as would have all except a few grumblers like Thoreau, a paragraph that another Meigs, this one J. Aitken Meigs, spoke in Philadelphia on July 13, 1854:

> Such is the general picture; examine it more carefully for a moment. See how true children of the sun, heat, light and electricity have been deliverd into the hands of man, as bondservants, obedient to his call. . . . With consummate skill the marriage of water and heat was effected. The child of that marriage has grown to be a herculean aid to onward-moving humanity. Certainly steam is a benefactor to the race. The printing press and the electric telegraph have become the handmaids of thought.

"Bondservants!" "Handmaids!" There we have it, the veritable American religion! Such assertions that machines had become creatures of the mind were customarily followed, as with Meigs, by the substantiating proposition that in turn they would obligingly prove to be assistants to the intellect. They would further the empire of "intellect," they would add trophies to its dominion, they would be dutiful and obedient. As early as 1817, for instance, when the industrial revolution in the northeastern states had barely commenced, a society was formed for the encouragement of domestic manufactures, not, according to its own profession, because of the assurance of profit (as Henry Thoreau would insinuate), but in the cause of intellectual fulfillment. "The exhaustless stores of mind and matter shall be this nation's treasury."

When therefore, we must ask ourselves, do glowing periods in this optimistic strain begin to excite in our breast only a languid pity for those simple decades, or else a bitter resentment at having been so cheaply betrayed? Why do I discover when addressing a classroom loaded with the heirs of industry and with future vice-presidents that the mordant aphorisms of Thoreau are greeted with an appreciative recognition, while the prognostications of industrial bliss are heard with an obvious subsiding of enthusiasm? Surely it is not that these youths are actively in revolt against the machine, like the rick-burners of Wellington's England. On the contrary, we all live by means of several hundred more apparatuses, of increasingly vaster scale, than either of the Meigses could have imagined. And nobody doubts that these instruments require intelligence to design, intelligence to construct, and even more intelligence to improve. The Massachusetts Institute of Technology is a citadel of the mind in America, if any bastion is. Whence, then, comes this insecurity, which my title assumes is everywhere recognizable? Where, when and above all how did the mind of this fabulously successful enterprise become darkened with a dread that its jinni—summoned not out of a magic bottle but from a supposedly rational conjunction of the test tube, the wind tunnel, the steam shovel and sweet Professor Einstein's equation—would become its mortal enemy?

The most obvious answer is that millions of Americans, more than enough to win an election, have only vague notions, barely restive worries, as to the existence of any such enmity. The less obvious but more terrible fact is that they have no slightest sense of responsibility for any bifurcation of which they cannot conceive. They dwell in a mental fog of perpetual neutralism. They remain there despite reports of children burned to death in what newspapers euphemistically call "tenements," despite the disintegration of urban transportation, despite the increase of murders and disfigurements on our highways, despite the criminal pollution of the very air we breathe. Yet after countless tirades on dangers such as these have left the public staring in blank incomprehension, we further have to confront, as have many frustrated scientists, the massive indifference of the populace, most of them supplied with a standard set of human emotions, to the ultimate meaning of a war conducted through the mysteries of nuclear physics.

Can it be that a father is incapable of grief for the daughter miserably crushed in an "accident" on Route 999? Do children in a burning tenement not suffer all the agonies of Joan of Arc? And we all have been told, by John Hersey and by the Bombing Survey, what an atomic blast does to our love-life, our libraries, our galleries, our universities, to our fragile oases as well as to military installations. Except that in this department we are reliably informed that Hiroshima was child's play; the next bomb will obliterate consciousness itself. We have no choice but to consent, and so go dumbly down the appointed runways as do cattle in the stockyards.

How did the disseverance come about? This question is widely debated among historians, sociologists, psychologists, and the more conscientious of physicists. In American historiography the fashion has become to regard *The Education of Henry Adams* as the tocsin of alarm, even though none heard any fire bell when the book was first printed in a private edition in 1907. When it was released to the public, in 1918, it surprisingly became a best-seller, possibly indicating that it by then found a partially disturbed audience. Yet the relation of the work to the current frame of the public mind is a baffling business. My late colleague, Thomas Reed Powell of the Harvard Law School, used to growl that the title of Adams's autobiography ought, in loyalty to its content, to be "The Unfortunate Relation of the Universe to Me." If this be so, and many equally exasperated with Adams's conceit and attitudinizing think it is so, the *Education* is the reverse of Mr. Bentley's definition of tragedy. Therefore it has upon the mind of the present, especially upon the minds of students for whom Adams is prescribed reading in college surveys, a dulling instead of an arousing effect.

Let us grant all this. It remains a fact that Adams endeavored to concentrate on the dynamo as the master engine—the archengine, shall we say?—of the twentieth century. But in the operation of a dynamo there remains a vestige of human responsibility: at least the engineer can, when it threatens to get out of hand, pull a switch. Yet Adams was sensitive enough, or neurotic enough, to read through the dynamo to the void beyond it: "In plain words, Chaos was the law of nature, Order was the dream of man."

I know some will object, and I heartily go along with their insistence, that a contemporary physicist so thoroughly trained in his métier as to be able still further to "improve" our bombs must be convinced that he manipulates not a chaos but some sort of order. This realm is so minuscule, so imperceptible by even the most powerful of microscopes, that it can be calculated only by a sign language that is a scandal to traditional norms of human reason; even so it has, according to these high priests, enough coherence of its own to enable their minds, if not ours, to produce tangible results in more and more lethal explosions.

This may be the insoluble conundrum of the epistemology with which we have to live—or perish. It would work extremely well if we were medieval serfs allowed an occasional glimpse of a Mass, the mysteries of which we were assured were beyond our comprehension. The odd circumstance is that in our case the hierophants have striven to divest themselves of the mystery, to account for themselves in the language of laymen, and have subsided into sorrow when obliged to confess that they cannot interpret physics to any but fellow technicians. Henry Adams was brought to the abyss by a sentence of Karl Pearson's: "In the chaos behind sensations, in the 'beyond' of sense-impressions, we cannot infer necessity, order or routine, for these are concepts formed by the mind of man on this side of sense-impressions." If at the beginning of our century—now seemingly as remote as the age of Voltaire—a responsible scientist warned the commonsense intelligence that it could not follow these lines of investigation past the barriers of sense impressions, and so would have to crouch outside the gates, hugging its cold and empty jars of order and law, how much more crushing is the exclusion when a J. Robert Oppenheimer says flatly that the working principles of modern physics cannot be translated into the discourse of logic, or when a C. P. Snow concludes that the scientists and the humanists can no longer speak a common language! If this has been the true, and the deceptive, course of history in our time, only one conclusion is left: the mind, as our Western culture has conceived it since the antiquity of Thales, is cut adrift. It is not even shut up, as Emerson feared Kantian idealism would confine it, in the splendid labyrinth of its subjective perceptions. It can behold splendors and colors to its heart's content; but that is an irrelevant game, less related to the actual universe than whist or baseball. There is no point in rigorously subjecting the self to the ascetic discipline of Walden Pond; nothing is to be gained that way any more than through an afternoon at the stadium. The mind, as men in general know it, and through which they have tried to manage their universe, is no longer responsible for anything, least of all for the destruction of its own species.

This attitude, somehow communicated to the least reflective of our population, shows itself repeatedly in our dealings with our machines. Everyone who starts a drive in his automobile assumes that the collision will not happen to him. Otherwise he would never take his car out of the garage. The commuter notes in the headlines of his morning papers the number of the dead in a tenement fire and turns hastily to the sports page, meekly grateful that he has so much as a train to ride in. Yet within these areas the assuring consolation persists that even the average mind of the citizenry *could*, if worse came to worst, learn the mechanism of the internal combustion engine and so mitigate the holocausts on the roads during holiday weekends. The collective intelligence *might* frame and see enforced decent zoning laws. The fact that these attainments are as yet neglected by the great American public seems no reason for accusing the machines. I am told that a Broadway producer, having read a script about the destruction of Sodom and Gomorrah submitted to him by an aspiring young playwright, mused that he did not see how there could have been so much sin in communities that had no telephones. Here we are in a field where the invention itself does not have to assume full responsibility for human fallibility.

But if in an age of machines and of helpful gadgets our propensity be nourished to live with less and less understanding of all that we ought to comprehend, what happens when our debilitated faculty is told that it has to live under the shadow of nuclear weapons that by their very nature defy the few lingering canons of rationality?

Virtually all reports on the general behavior of Americans add up, so far, to a pattern of further and further regression into the womb of irresponsibility. There is everywhere documented a refusal to accept what I would hopefully term adult status. I shall construct a dialectic too simplified to suit any social scientist, but roughly it appears to run something like this. First, because there is nothing this or that particular individual can do to prevent the bombs from falling, then, if they do fall, the fault is none of his. Although they be launched by manmade missiles or dropped from manmade jets, and although man be exterminated, he remains morally immune, an innocent victim of the machine. Second, if, as several analysts assure us, the threat of mutual obliteration will itself keep the bombs from falling—as it prevented the use of poison gas in the last war—then our citizen can also claim that the fault is none of his. These may be the sheer alternatives with which we are confronted; there would seem to be no third recourse.

Well, that predicament is dire enough. But I see how no one, in the light of the historical development that I have sketchily indicated and in which, as I have endeavored to suggest, we are all involved, can with self-respect complain about the situation in which we find ourselves, since we have all done our utmost, knowingly or inadvertently, to produce it.

Obviously we cannot turn the clock back to the idyllic industrialism of Theodore Parker. What, then, can we say? We may say that without recourse to romantic isolationism we are able to resist, and will resist, the paralyzing effects upon the intellect of the looming nihilism of what was formerly the scientific promise of mechanical bliss. Scientists and humanists are today joined in their appreciation of the urgencies, and of the difficulties, of the consultation. Upon all of us, whoever we be, rests the responsibility of securing a hearing from an audience either dazzled into dumb amazement by the prestige of technology or else lulled into apathy by the apparently soothing but actually insidious triumphs of functional science.

Supposing that my analysis has any validity, then at the end of it we come, by cumbersome indirection, to the problem of the officially designated "humanities" in a civilization conducted amidst machines. I have tried not to put this cause in the center of the picture, for, as I have suggested, it does not belong there. Most of the keening over administrative slighting of the humanities has as little relevance to the mainstream of historical movement as did Thoreau's magnificent tirades from the shore of Walden Pond. Except, of course, that not much of the modern complaint reaches Thoreau's eloquence or wit. Nothing is to be gained by acknowledging in advance a purely ornamental function, or by proclaiming an inutility for which compensation is to be found in "poetry," in order to demand a shelter for the arts within a capitalist order.

The Cassandras of our time have exaggerated the danger when they cry, "Woe! woe! the scientists and the humanists can no longer converse!" Sir Charles Snow is a salutary sort of Cassandra, because he is not hysterical, and furthermore is living proof that the dialogue can be conducted. So a conversation is possible; in the basic sense, the humanist and the scientist are both on the same side of the barricade. It is not required every time a historian and a chemist meet for lunch that each impart to the other the sum and substance of his erudition. It is only required that they respect in each other an achievement of "mind." Baseball is endlessly fascinating, but it need not be the sole noncontroversial diversion when intellect meets intellect.

If such reflections have relevance for conclaves of scholars, they have an even greater importance for our relations to the public, albeit the amorphous, mind. In this direction the scientists, or at least the students of science, have lately been doing the better job. Admit that they have an immense prestige to support them, and that in a paradoxical sense the incommunicableness of their mystery is an incentive for attempting to communicate; they have addressed the public in various degrees of agonized clarity and, to that extent, they have built dikes against the flux of irresponsibility. By contrast the humanities have, I must confess, not functioned so effectively, despite the media offered by FM radios and by paperbacks. Under the large rubric of humanities, in this indictment, I include not only writers on history and literature, but social scientists, political scientists and even, although grudgingly, economists. Despite the protests of many of these that they do communicate with the public, it is in such areas that the analysis of the mind in America has itself been undergoing a fragmentation into theses and monographs. These productions are intellectually respectable, but too often they add up to a tiresome jumble. They become a disease, and the endeavor to check the disease oddly enough turns into an agent of contagion.

When humanists complain that vulgarizers pre-empt the market, they must also admit that they have to blame their cumbersome styles, the dismal catalogues that they substitute for perceptions, and their insensitivity to the living concerns of the populace. They prove themselves as unheeding as are those of whose unheedingness they wail. They too affect an innocence, behind which they conceal their inability to assume responsibility in the world of mechanical stress. Yes, there are subjects everywhere within the "humanities" that cannot be popularized, in which no such effort should be attempted. But where is the line of separation? Only in the mind that can address with respect another mind.

It may be that every exertion toward a community of learning is bound for a long time, for the remainder of our existence, to come to no decisive conclusion. But for us, is success the only goal? Upon those who have the concern, and to match it the energy, rests the self-assumed burden of responsibility. Having accepted the hospitality of the obligation, we cannot shake off the consequence. Yet, is it nothing but a burden? Is it only a dead weight we have sullenly to carry about the streets? Is it merely an ordeal to which we must submit? Not in the least. Like the precious, beautiful, insupportable and wholly irrational blessing of individuality, with all the myriad quandaries of responsibility therein involved, the responsibility for the human mind to preserve its own integrity amid the terrifying operations of the machine is both an exasperation and an ecstasy.